In Orbit!

To Lydia,
   Hope you enjoy This brief
version of my life. PAT and
I appreciate you're Keeping
IN touch with us. All the
best to you and your family

Jack

In Orbit!

The Journeys of an Orbital Surgeon

John S. Kennerdell, M.D.

WORD ASSOCIATION PUBLISHERS
www.wordassociation.com
1.800.827.7903

Printed in the United States of America.

ISBN: 978-1-59571-506-7

Library of Congress Control Number: 2010920665

Designed and published by

Word Association Publishers
205 Fifth Avenue
Tarentum, Pennsylvania 15084

www.wordassociation.com
1.800.827.7903

Contents

Preface

I have assembled information about my life and travels at the suggestion of family, friends and colleagues who are of the opinion that my career and travels are of sufficient interest to be recorded. I am not so sure that is true, but I have developed a unique medical specialty and have, partially as a result of that endeavor, traveled extensively around the world to lecture in this special area of ophthalmology and to evaluate patients in various foreign countries. I will attempt to describe my life's experiences as a medical world traveler. I will try to avoid unnecessary details about my life and technical details about my specialty, unless these are important to the overall story.

Acknowledgments

I want to acknowledge my loyal and loving wife, Pat, who encouraged me to tell the story of my life emphasizing the professional and extensive travel aspects as a series of journeys. She tirelessly reviewed and corrected the manuscript, even after I could no longer look at it.

Also I would like to acknowledge my departmental secretary, Bill Reidel, who helped me to develop the manuscript and engaged our publisher, who is located in Tarentum, my home town, which is very appropriate.

I also want to recognize my many colleagues, fellows, residents, friends, children and grandchildren, all of whom have enriched my life.

I want to thank Michele Luznar who became secretary to the new ophthalmology department at Allegheny General Hospital and then became it's department manager in 1992. She has been invaluable in working with me and the staff to develop the department to the successful position it enjoys today.

In Orbit!

The Early Journey

I was born on July 31, 1935, at home and according to my mother, on
the hottest day of that year. My mother, Myrtle Shirk Kennerdell, was
40 years old and my father, Frederick Harold Kennerdell, was 45 at
the time of my birth. My brother, Edward (Ed) was 17 and my sister
Margaret (Peggy) was 11 years old when I came into the world. They
were more like an aunt and uncle than a brother and sister through my
early years. I was reared essentially as an only child with older parents
of a middle-class stature, which was a very pleasant experience. My
father, a jeweler, optometrist and watchmaker, owned, with his brother,
a small town jewelry store in Tarentum, Pennsylvania, which was quite
successful during the 1920s through the mid-50s before the shopping
mall appeared. Because ours was a family business, everyone contributed
by working from time to time in the jewelry store, which was, in retro-
spect, a solid family experience. We lived in a middle-class small town
suburban home on Freeport Road, built by my father in 1924. The
neighborhood, Natrona Heights, was populated by other middle-class
families whose breadwinners largely worked for the steel or aluminum

industries concentrated along the rivers of Pittsburgh. Tarentum, a town of 30,000, was home to Allegheny Ludlum Steel Company, which eventually developed Titanium Steel. There were many children in our neighborhood, so I developed close early friendships with several boys living within a block or two of my home. These are Jim Grogan, Nelson Hicks, Jim Benford, Joe Nock and Joe Zahorchak, who have all remained lifelong friends.

My mother was Pennsylvania Dutch from Lancaster, a great but strong-willed mother. She completed high school and was working in Lancaster when she met my father, who was in watch-making school. My father, a mild-mannered, but hard-working person was from Tarentum, our hometown. He was adventurous as a young man, but eventually returned to the family jewelry business started by his father. My grandfather, Edward H. Kennerdell, was a very successful small-town businessman and at one time, owned a floral and a dry cleaning business as well as the jewelry store. He was a jeweler and an optician.

A word about our roots, which on my father's side of the family, date back to early 19th century Wigan, a small textile manufacturing town near Liverpool, in the Lancashire District of England. The original United States immigrant was my great- great- uncle, Richard Kennerdell, a textile manufacturer from Wigan who, in about 1832, came to Pittsburgh and then ventured up the Allegheny River to a place called Scrubgrass, north of Kittanning, where he diverted a stream from the Allegheny River through a paddle wheel connected to his woolen mill. He arranged for sheepherders to raise sheep on the grasslands above the river and then processed the wool, which he sent down the river to Pittsburgh on flatbed barges. He was quite successful and built a large house above the river and eventually became the mayor of Scrubgrass, which was renamed Kennerdell and still exists on the Allegheny River as a fishing resort community. The town of Kennerdell thrived during the 1840s, and when oil was discovered in Titusville further up the Allegheny River in 1858, it grew rapidly as a port for sending the oil down the river on flatbed barges to Pittsburgh. Unfortunately, its prominence was short-lived, as the development of the railroad changed the transport of oil from the port to more efficient transport by rail. The town then returned to a smaller size and the house of Richard Kennerdell burned down. However, some of his furniture was saved and is now in the Smithsonian Institute in Washington, D.C. The family split then into two parts, one settling in Kittanning and the other, my grandfather's, in Tarentum. We have a fairly elaborate family tree researched by an aunt Elizabeth Kennerdell, my dad's cousin from the Kittanning branch of the family. She worked very hard on the genealogy of the Kennerdell family. My ancestors include a soldier-of-fortune, a criminal, and other United States immigrants.

In 1936, the year after my birth, we had a severe flood in Tarentum, which invaded my grandparent's home on First Avenue near the Allegheny River as well as the jewelry store in the center of Tarentum. Our house, in Natrona Heights, was filled with guests and apparently I received a lot of attention from those who were temporarily housed with us.

Shortly after my birth, it was discovered that I had an unusual skin disease, ill-understood at the time, which was atopic (neuro) dermatitis. Apparently, my father's mother had a similar ailment. This difficult inherited skin disease affects various parts of the body including the face and neck, and favors the anterior arm at the elbow. It causes relentless itching and this results in crusting and bleeding at times from fingernail injury. Because of the intense itching and discomfort, I was shuffled from dermatologist to dermatologist and treated with various colored ointments and even low-dose radiation therapy to my arms. The disease was worse during the first decade of my life, with gradual decreasing intensity throughout the rest of my life. I believe this condition has influenced my journey, although I was able to overcome it for the most part mentally and physically. It was difficult for my parents as well as myself, as they tried to find a cure—there was none at that time, or as of this writing. It made me self-conscious, but fortunately my friends and colleagues understood the problem and I suffered little from social harassment concerning it.

I grew up in the time when most childhood activities were physical, self- or group-planned and outdoors. We joined together to instigate various games, some self-designed, others organized by us in the form of baseball, football and basketball games which were unsupervised by adults, but provided a great deal of pleasure and opportunity for physical development as children. My baseball team, the Carlisle Street Panthers, lost more than half of our games with the other pick-up teams. We had a great deal of fun and obtained donated uniforms and equipment. As a result of these experiences, I learned that my athletic skills were modest, which disappointed me because I enjoy sports. Partially as a result of that understanding and the limitations that atopic dermatitis set upon me, I developed my skills as a student. Fortunately, in the early grades I found that I easily understood the material presented and had a good memory. My grades in school were consistently high and I was recognized as an excellent student from my early days in public school.

During my early grade school years, I particularly enjoyed history and geography, the latter of which does not seem to be considered as important now as it was at the time of my schooling. I began the first grade when war broke out in Europe and still remember the daily turns of events that occurred during World War II, as emphasized by the cartoons in the Pittsburgh *Post-Gazette* and the comments of my father who, as all Americans, had a keen interest in that conflict. Every day, the radio and the paper discussed the daily progress of the war in Europe and then in the South Pacific. It was an unsettling time for young people such as myself, who were subjected to blackouts and fears of being conquered by either the Germans or Japanese, both portrayed as very cruel and savage people. It was impressive, even to a child, that people, united in a common cause, worked together very well. As kids, we collected newspapers, bottles and cans, which were turned in to central locations to be recycled for the war effort.

Of course, times of turbulence can bring out defects in one's psyche. For instance, we had a kind and talented fourth grade teacher who suddenly thought that we were being observed by spies from the high school, which was 500 yards away across rolling terrain. Fortunately, at the age of 9, we were all old enough to realize that this was not real and we reacted in those days as polite students who did not ridicule her for her suspicions, although we joked about it among ourselves. At the age of 11, I remember the final surrender of the Japanese, which was accompanied by cheering and honking of the horns on Freeport Road, in front of my home in Natrona Heights. The exuberance of the final surrender lasted for several days. It was the beginning of a happy period in my life.

Three summers in the mid 1940s I spent at Calvary Camp on the shores of Lake Erie in Ohio with some of my friends, Jim Benford, Nelson Hicks, and Jim Grogan. Those were fun times with competitive athletics, crafts, games, fireside singing and swimming. One adverse event: upon arrival I was assigned to a cabin with eight double-decker beds. I was assigned a lower bunk, unfortunately, under a bed-wetter. After complaining to the cabin counselor, I wound up with the upper bunk, which was considerably drier.

During, and shortly after the war, my father built a summer home on the west bank of the Allegheny River at Clinton, a small village between Freeport and Kittanning, about 20 miles from our home in Natrona Heights. It was situated in a large lot on the riverbank. A large wooded hill on the opposite side of the river compared to the Palisades on the Hudson River in New York. It was a very picturesque place and the family spent many Sundays there, being restricted by the six-day work week at the jewelry store. This was probably my first short journey at the end of my grade school years. Of course, we went there for various holidays. During my junior high school years, I spent a large portion of my summers there and developed a new set of friends in that community.

The house was built because of the boom in the jewelry business during and after World War II, primarily during the holiday season. Dad purchased a speed boat that was capable of pulling a water skier and we introduced water skiing to that portion of the Allegheny River, teaching many of our reluctant, but then enthusiastic friends, how to water ski. A close friend of mine, Paul Jack, and I were a nuisance on the river as frisky water skiers, passing ropes over people in canoes and dodging diving boards in a fool-hardy manner. I learned to swim early at the YMCA, so I was fearless in the river. It was polluted at that time with varying types of debris floating down the river. Some of my friends were forbidden to join me in river activities, but, like those who grew up in Egypt, I guess I developed an immunity early in life to the ailments thought to be brought by the river and never developed any type of sickness as a result of it.

When I was in primary, then in middle school, my mother took me on the train to Lancaster, Pennsylvania, to visit her parents for a week during the summers. They lived frugally on a side street in a row house in Lancaster, from which we walked downtown to shop and socialize. I enjoyed those trips, especially the train ride—including the horseshoe bend near Altoona. My grandmother died young and, although I met her on the first trip, I don't remember her. My grandfather, John Shirk, for whom I was named, was a five- and ten-cent store clerk and floor manager. He never made much money and was not a favorite of my father, although I was named after him, I was called Jack instead of John from the beginning. I signed all my early school papers as Jack Kennerdell and had to return later to correct the error.

One summer when I was about 10, my dad took me to New York while my mother visited her father in Lancaster. I really enjoyed that trip, including the train ride and the sleeper car. I remember distinctly trips to the Statue of Liberty and the Empire State Building, as well as eating in restaurants that were much fancier than what I had been exposed to in Tarentum and surrounding areas. This was my first experience of traveling to a large impressive city.

I breezed through my years in junior high school with less difficulty with the atopic dermatitis and developed my first interest in girls, normal for the age. It began with mixed parties, then progressed to clandestine necking. At the end of junior high school, with continued excellent grades, I was elected May King, a great surprise to me because I never thought I had such popularity. It thrilled me because I was interested in the attractive May Queen, named June, whose interest in older boys precluded any attention despite my numerous efforts—a great disappointment.

It was about this time in life that my father took me to Pittsburgh with him to buy wholesale jewelry. We went to the Clark Building on Liberty Avenue, which still exists, to visit various wholesalers of watches, diamonds, and jewelry of various types. The experience of helping to select the jewelry in the summer to sell, particularly for the holidays, was fun, but I always opted for the conservative, expensive pieces, which I was told would not sell to the average customer. My dad was right, of course; my mother, who accompanied us at times, had an uncanny knack for picking things that would sell. I began to get an inkling that I was not a businessman, at least in the jewelry business. We always had lunch or dinner at Frenchy's restaurant on Seventh Street, which was a highlight of the trip as they served great seafood and French fries, better than those restaurants in Tarentum. Of course, with the smoke from the steel industry in Pittsburgh at that time, we often returned home with soot on our shirt collars. Industrial smoke now has been eliminated, but my lungs are probably a little black from those early years.

I entered public high school without fear of academic challenges, joined various clubs and proceeded to develop longer and more intimate relationships with women, especially one, Joanne, who was my first love.

However, it was during the end of that year that my parents informed me that they had been in touch with the principal of the high school, who told them that I was not working hard enough, but still obtaining superior grades. Therefore, his advice was that I should be sent to a private school where the academics would be more challenging. I was willing and enthusiastic about that prospect, but needless to say, in the midst of developing an intimate relationship with my first love, and about to obtain my driver's license, which would provide freedom for many activities, I resisted at first. The principal was right, however, that my high school was mostly comprised of students who were not destined to go to college and that there were not sufficient programs to challenge other students to work harder.

I reassessed my position and decided that, since I was not destined to be a high school athlete, which would give me an edge with the girls and that I really was not challenged by the high school curriculum, I would agree to attend a prep school. It was decided that I should attend Kiski Prep in Saltsburg, Pennsylvania, about 45 minutes from my home, which was more convenient and less expensive for my parents. Kiskiminetas Springs School was located on a high bluff above the Kiski River across from the picturesque town of Saltsburg. We used to say that it was built on a bluff, and run on the same principle. This joking expression was learned from the upperclassmen.

The Kiski Journey

It was my first real solo journey, arriving at Kiski in the fall of 1951. The school was dedicated to those who were preparing for college, including athletes who needed an extra year to upgrade their scholastics before joining college athletic programs, particularly in football at competitive schools. Therefore, the student body was of very mixed academic talent, which I found to my advantage. Unfortunately, Kiski at that time was undergoing an experimental program where one subject at a time was taught instead of the usual mixture of different subjects taught throughout the year. For instance, if math was taught for the first eight weeks of the year and you were graded in math, you did not see another math problem until the next year, a real disadvantage in the transition to college. It was easier to focus on one subject at a time and so the academics at Kiski were no more challenging—in fact, maybe less— than they were in the public high school. However, the prep school reputation would allow me to apply to a variety of colleges.

When I arrived at Kiski, having driven my parents and myself to the school, with my newly acquired driver's license, I was assigned to the most remote house converted to a dormitory, named Reese Hall. It was a quarter-mile walk from the house/dormitory to the main campus. My parents departed, having left me with my few belongings and a new roommate, Curly Workman. I was sorry to see them go. I also felt a loss of the independent transportation status that I had with my new driver's license. However, looking at Kiski as a new challenge, I settled in with my new roommate, who was a very nice person. There was one problem, however, in that poor Curly had chronic hiccups. He hiccupped day and night and was not able to find any type of relief. This, of course, made it difficult to sleep and I was relieved to be in class or study hall away from the chronic hiccups. I stuck it out with Curly and learned to sleep even under that type of noise until December, when unfortunately he got so sick that he was transferred to the infirmary and then left Kiski permanently. I do not know what happened to Curly, but I hope that his life improved. He was sick and thin from his chronic hiccups.

I was reassigned to two roommates; one became a lifelong friend, Ivan Dobson. The other was John Sigmund, whose whereabouts are unknown to me. We were a feisty trio and unfortunately, it was at that time I learned how to smoke and drink alcoholic beverages. Both smoking and drinking, especially the latter, were frowned upon at Kiski, so we would use various subterfuges to obtain cigarettes and alcohol—even hard cider at times–to satisfy our perceived desires. I think that all-boy schools have great merit in bringing out individual capabilities and personalities. However, because of the confinement at a critical age, sometimes untoward side effects can occur. With the single subject curriculum, it was very easy for me to complete my work in the daytime study halls, so that at night I was free to think about other ways to find pleasurable activities. I spent a great deal of time thinking about the attractive, bright, aggressive girlfriend that I had left at home, and devised a number of ways to escape on the weekends to see her and to drive my parents' Oldsmobile. I had a knack for describing a variety of sick relatives who did not exist and finally, I talked my parents into letting me drive back and forth in one of their cars. The car had to be left with a professor at the school, but at least I could look at it during the week.

Kiski had a great athletic program that allowed all students who were physically able to participate in various athletics all year. I enjoyed the experience of being on the junior varsity prep school football team, which allowed me to compete in a sport that I liked at my level. We played at small high schools, junior varsities of larger high schools and other prep schools. Particularly enjoyable was beating Mercersburg Academy in my senior year, because a childhood friend, Jim Grogan, was playing on the opposite team. I also participated in baseball as a substitute on the varsity, but in basketball I was too short to make the basketball team, so I became its manager.

Two years at Kiski, however, proved to be most enjoyable and challenging in a variety of ways. I was caught up in the required athletic activities and the close friendships that I made at Kiski, especially in my junior year with David Post, now a life-long friend. I was impressed by the interest that the professors had in each individual and I was very satisfied with the small classes, despite the fact that the single subject curriculum was flawed—and dropped shortly after I left Kiski. Sometime during those two years, I decided that I wanted to be a physician. The decision did not come easily because I was slated to take over the jewelry business operated by my father. My older brother was already an ophthalmologist. My grandfather was an optician, my father and his uncle were optometrists and my grandfather greatly influenced my brother to become a physician, in particular an ophthalmologist.

While at Kiski I joined the glee club, primarily to get out of the school to go to concerts. Those concerts were greatly anticipated because of our bus trips to prep schools for girls. One year we went to Grier Prep School in Tyrone, Pennsylvania, to find that the junior and senior girls were restricted from the party after the performance due to widespread shoplifting among those glee club members. We found ourselves dancing with freshmen and some sophomores, a great disappointment at the time.

In my senior year, Dave Post introduced me to Kay from Indiana, Pennsylvania, an attractive brunette. I took her to the senior prom and was quite smitten by her, but later she blew me off for the football team quarterback. I did see her just prior to her marriage five years later, when she was having second thoughts about her approaching marriage, but we could not rekindle any relationship. She went on to graduate from Syracuse University and married a man she met in college.

My brother, Edward, graduated from medical school in the early 40s and entered the military as a physician. He was stationed in England, then France as part of the invasion and finally was stationed in Munich Germany, following the war, treating patients with dermatologic disorders, especially those related to syphilis. He returned to the United States after the war to study ophthalmology and opened a practice in Tarentum, Pennsylvania, our hometown, in 1951. It was sometime during 1952 that I decided to become a physician and I was discouraged somewhat by my parents in that regard. I was told of the long educational process and the difficulties of medical school. However, as a good student I was not put off by the academic challenge. I decided I did not want to be a jeweler after spending summers and Christmas vacations in the jewelry store waiting on customers and doing numerous jobs around the store, including window trimming, which was assigned to the youthful member of the family who could climb into the windows easiest. I now understand why I was selected for that job at the time.

As a senior at Kiski, I was encouraged to enter an Ivy League School by the faculty and was accepted at Princeton, even with the possibility of a scholarship. David Post decided to go to Colgate University, an all-male school in upstate New York. However, after a year and a half in an all-boys school, I decided that a men's college was not in my best interest, since I had so much interest in parties and girls. Therefore, after much consideration, I chose Bucknell University in Lewisburg, Pennsylvania, a college that was attended by my sister, who obtained a master's degree in psychology there and was living nearby in Muncy, Pennsylvania with her husband, Bill George, a chemical engineer, who had also graduated from Bucknell. I thought that Bucknell, a co-educational school, offered a good possibility of gaining entrance to medical school without the competition of Princeton, and that I could manage good grades in that college and still have a great deal of fun in the process. In addition, I did not think my parents could afford the increased cost to go to Princeton. My parents seemed very satisfied with the choice and I accepted the offer to attend Bucknell University.

I graduated from Kiski as the best all-around student and the most likely to succeed and was offered a job as head counselor in Kiski's summer camp in the hills above the main campus. This was a well-paying job and it was an honor to be asked. However, my brother insisted that if I decided to become a physician, I needed to be introduced to the profession as an orderly in Allegheny Valley Hospital in our hometown of Natrona Heights. Therefore, a disappointed Kiski graduate became an orderly in the hospital. The orderly, of course, is the lowest order of staff directly attending patients in a hospital. The various jobs assigned to an orderly included bedpan management and catheterizations of men required for a variety of reasons. These particular duties were not pleasant to me, but I was able to observe the physicians, some of whom were friends of my brother and my parents and the experience did not discourage my choice of careers. I managed to get through the summer of '57 with a new appreciation of the entire scope of the management of patients in a hospital. I believe I also acquired hemorrhoids that plagued me for several years, from lifting patients from a variety of positions.

During that summer, I dated a variety of girls, having lost my first love to a rival. I was disappointed at the time, but as with most youths, seemed able to adapt and went on to date other girls, some of whom I met during my travels as a member of the Kiski Glee Club, or to whom I was introduced by friends during my time at Kiski. It was also during that summer that I talked my parents into acquiring a white Buick convertible which I was then allowed to take to college, a situation that did not meet with the approval of my brother, because he had not been similarly treated when he went to college. I think the difference was economic and the fact that my parents were older and more indulgent.

The Florida Journey

Speaking of indulgence, it was during spring break of my senior year at Kiski in 1953 that my parents took my sister, a young married mother of two, working on her master's degree at Bucknell, and me, on my first long-distance trip to Fort Lauderdale, Florida. I think this was the start of a lifelong interest in travel. Fort Lauderdale at that time was uncrowded, with beautiful wide beaches and several motels and hotels. After a long automobile trip in the recently-acquired convertible, we arrived at a motel in the heart of Fort Lauderdale. The hotel was across the street from the ocean, with which I immediately fell in love. I do not remember much about that trip except that I got sunburned, despite using protective suntan lotion, because of my very pale skin and having lived my entire first 16 years in Pennsylvania. My parents and my sister were more prudent. I do remember a large hotel on the beach near our motel, which had a unique restaurant that was beside and below a swimming pool so you could see the swimmers through windows in the restaurant. It was interesting to look at things moving under water. I had never even been to an aquarium at that time. Of course, the tropical foliage and the flat landscape, together with the ocean, fascinated me and remained an interest all my life. I also remember the long ride home in the automobile and this may have begun my aversion to long-distance automotive travel, although I have done a considerable amount of it in my life.

Despite my job as an orderly, I enjoyed the wonderful summer of 1953, with my free time at our summer home on the Allegheny River in Clinton. I had the speedboat, and my summer friend, Paul Jack and I skied all over the Allegheny River in the pool below Lock 6. We tried to land on the rocky beach without falling down and sustained several bruised knees and legs. Summers pass all too quickly and soon it was time to prepare myself to enter college.

The Bucknell Journey

I arrived at Bucknell in my white Buick convertible in September 1953 to learn quickly about the changes that were imminent in my life. Upon reviewing my curriculum, I was surprised to learn that I had several difficult classes, as I had registered in a pre-med curriculum. I thought that I could even include advanced math, but upon testing, I found that my math skills, acquired in the fall of 1952, did not translate into knowledge of algebra in the fall of 1953. Therefore, I was put in the basic algebra class my freshman year. It was probably a blessing.

There were 53 pre-med registrants in a school of 3000, which emphasized engineering and business. The pre-medical curriculum was difficult and that, together with the rushing of fraternities in the fall of 1953, made concentration on my studies difficult. I was rushed by several fraternities and finally settled on the Phi Gamma Delta fraternity, for which I have no regrets. I know fraternities are controversial, but to those who are socially oriented, they provide a comfortable home away from home in the college setting. I was initially assigned to a dormitory room with a colleague in pre-med who subsequently flunked out at the end of the first semester. My first semester grades were less than satisfactory, with two Cs in chemistry and math; therefore, I knew that I had to improve my academic efforts if I was ever to have a chance to enter medical school. Having been through the fraternity rush and the rigorous change in academic challenge, I focused on my studies during the second half of freshman year and improved my grades to the honor level. During the spring, however, I had a set back when my father had a heart attack from which he fortunately recovered. He was the sole support of my education and it would have changed my life considerably if he had succumbed to the heart attack. At the end of my freshman year, I spent the summer at home again, working as a lab assistant with the local hospital and continuing to enjoy our summer home on the Allegheny River. My father gradually recovered from his heart attack and went back to work as owner of the jewelry store. I was also absorbed by an early college romance with Nancy, an attractive blonde from Long Island who joined Kappa Delta, our sister sorority; the romance faded over the summer of 1954, much to my regret.

I returned for my sophomore year intent on focusing on academic performance and managed to get through the difficult sophomore curriculum, which consisted of quantitative and qualitative chemical analysis, physics and other difficult subjects. As a sophomore, I was not involved in distractions of the first year, so I was more able to concentrate. Nevertheless, I had a marvelous social life at Bucknell, dating several different girls, but no one in particular. During my sophomore year, however, my group that came through hazing the previous year, which was difficult and somewhat dangerous, decided to insist on a reform of fraternity hazing. After much heated discussion, we settled on a help week to replace hell week. Help week consisted of the tasks that the pledges of the fraternity would have to do to improve the condition of the fraternity house, such as painting and cleaning. This proved to be successful and was continued, as far as I know, after the class of '57 graduated. Of course, since the beginning of the second semester of my first year, I lived in the fraternity in different rooms and with different roommates ever year. During the second year, I roomed with Jim Reimer, a fraternity brother who eventually went on to medical school and became a pathologist. Following the successful completion of my second year with good grades, I decided to take organic chemistry in the summer, which provided me the opportunity to concentrate on that subject alone because it was the most difficult in the pre-med curriculum at Bucknell. Professor Harold Heine was a wonderful man who had a great influence with medical schools and if good grades were obtained in his course and in the biology course, under Hilda Magelhaes, one had an excellent chance of entering medical school. When I finished my sophomore year, we were down from 53 pre-med students to approximately 10. Therefore, I took the easy way out by taking the most difficult course in the summer with Dr. Heine. Fortunately, I completed the organic chemistry course with a high B average, which he considered good enough to recommend me for medical school.

I was social chairman for the fraternity my sophomore and junior years and organized several great parties. However, in the middle of my sophomore year, the school decided to institute prohibition, which resulted in student riots—an unsettling situation, which caused the firing of the Dean of Students who could not control the situation. As social chairman, during prohibition, I set up an elaborate alarm system with pledges stationed at the front door of the fraternity when we had a party with beer in the basement. A foot switch triggered a light in the party room, and beer cups were quickly picked up and replaced with soft drinks, the beer keg and cups were locked in an old coal cellar. I brought the beer keg into the fraternity house in the trunk of my car, a ridiculous risk in view of my ambition to go to medical school. Fortunately, we were never caught and when prohibition ended, my job was easier and safer.

During semester break in my sophomore year, my friends Dick Estus, Al Levesque, and I went to New England in Dick's yellow Dodge convertible to visit Smith College, where I had a girl friend, Sue, who fixed up my friends with dates for one night; we went to the local beer joint where the college crowd gathered. We were impressed by how different the girls looked on Friday night than Friday afternoon when they were in their frumpy class attire. We went on to Winter Carnival at Dartmouth, where we saw the ice statues and enjoyed several fraternity parties. On the way home we stopped at Skidmore College, where we dated some girls arranged by Dick. On the way home we ran into a snowstorm and the windshield wipers stopped on Dick's car. The trip was harrowing, with one of us hanging out the window to brush the snow away. We stopped at Dick's home in Binghamton, New York and had the wipers repaired. Upon returning to Bucknell, Al found out that he had flunked out of school, putting a damper on the end of a fun trip. He later returned and graduated from Bucknell in Business Administration in 1958.

My junior year was decidedly easier as a result of my completing the difficult courses. Some of the electives I took included political science and history, which were interesting, but did not play heavily in the considerations of a medical school review committee. I took a standardized test near the end of my junior year, which was reviewed for entrance to medical school, and became stuck on a math problem, failing to complete the test. Therefore, the results in that particular test were not good in my case. This definitely influenced my medical school application and I was turned down at Harvard. However, because of the excellent recommendation of the Bucknell faculty, I received an early acceptance to Temple Medical School, in September of my senior year, which I accepted, freeing my senior year for more social activities, which I pursued avidly. I was corresponding secretary of the fraternity for the final two years, one of four officers.

Bucknell is a wonderful place to combine social activities with academics. The co-educational student body provided a natural environment for students, most of whom did not choose or need to travel long distances from campus to obtain exposure to the opposite sex. Most of us centered our social lives at Bucknell and actually had marvelous experiences. I strongly believe that co-education is a more natural way of dealing with realities of higher education.

In spring of my senior year, Chuck Deardorff, another pre-med fraternity brother, and I, decided to go to Easter's weekend at the University of Virginia on spring break. We took Chuck's old used car and made it to the University of Virginia on a Friday. We found rooms at a dormitory and dated girls from Hollins College, who were up for the weekend. That was the wildest weekend I have ever experienced. The fraternity parties were continuous and we weren't impressed with our dates, so we ditched them at one fraternity party and proceeded out Rugby Road to another party. Unfortunately, Chuck failed to make the abrupt turn at the end of Rugby Road and crashed through a stone wall. I was thrown out of the passenger seat and rolled down a hill with the stones from the wall. Surprisingly, neither of us was hurt and I proceeded on to the next party where I got help to bail Chuck out of jail. The car was totaled and on Monday we had to hitch-hike back to Bucknell. This was my first and only experience with hitch hiking. The car was sold for junk and Chuck was cleared of any charges in Charlottesville. We luckily recovered from that harrowing experience. The Louis Armstrong concert on Saturday afternoon was the highlight of the trip.

I was active in several extracurricular activities in college including the Glee Club for a short time until they found that my tenor voice was failing. I participated in the student newspaper and other activities, but I spent most of my energies making sure that I completed the pre-medical curriculum successfully and enjoyed the social activities in the fraternity. Some of my fraternity brothers became life-long friends. I worked as a kitchen manager-assistant for meals for two years while at the Phi Gamma Delta house. I graduated with a 2.3 average out of a 3-point system, which was fairly good, but not superb. I thoroughly enjoyed the social activities around graduation and went home to spend the summer as a pathology assistant to Dr. Stephen Miller at Allegheny Valley Hospital, which I found most interesting. I assisted at the evaluation of pathological specimens and at autopsies. I tricked one of my friends, Nelson, into entering the autopsy room, and I must say seeing the corpse on the table had a striking effect on him. This, of course, was done after hours, as that type of activity was frowned upon.

During college, I enjoyed a variety of girlfriends, some of whom were wholesome and cute, but one was more worldly, Jeanne. I cavorted with her toward the end of my college years, which displeased my parents a great deal. Fortunately for me at that time, a permanent relationship did not occur, because I was entering a new journey in life in medical school.

The Temple Journey

After spending the summer as a pathologist assistant, I entered the Temple University Medical School in Philadelphia and again experienced one of the greatest changes in my life. I arrived by train with a colleague from Bucknell, Tom Johnston—one of the survivors of the pre-medical program at Bucknell. We were both enrolled in Temple and proceeded to the school to enter into the first year in the fall of 1957. The medical school was located in the very poor and dangerous section of north Philadelphia on Broad Street. We were warned to be careful of the area at night and despite our white coats, we were not immune to dangers of a lower class neighborhood with many bars and considerable violence.

Tom and I rented an efficiency apartment on the second floor of a house, five streets back from the medical school in north Philadelphia and proceeded to take on the rigors of a medical education. The first year consisted of anatomy, physiology and biochemistry in the fall, which were extremely difficult subjects and required my undivided attention for at least 12 hours a day. The studying was intensive and almost eliminated any other form of activity at that time. In the spring, pharmacology and histology were equally difficult subjects. I do not remember much more than studying during that first year of medical school and both Tom and I finished with good grades.

After the first year of medical school, I went back to my job as a laboratory and pathology assistant at Allegheny Valley Hospital and Tom got married. Therefore, when I returned for the second year of medical school, which was the second most difficult year of my life, I lived in the Alpha Kappa Kappa fraternity house, which I had joined during my freshman year. Fraternities were not as important in medical school as they were in college and yet the Alpha Kappa Kappa house provided a home for me during my sophomore year. I acted as food manager for the fraternity, which provided my board while I was living in the fraternity. The cook, Myrtle (my mother's name), was very good, but she liked to drink cheap wine. Part of my job was to keep her supplied with wine during dinners, especially dinner parties, or risk the reduction in her performance that would certainly follow. The locals at the neighborhood bar got to know me, as I stopped regularly to get a jug of Mogan-David wine for Myrtle to preserve our dinner.

I became president of the fraternity my sophomore year, which astounded the chief of surgery, who was a member and advisor to the same fraternity. At a reunion dinner, he chastised the membership for allowing a sophomore to become president when the job really belonged to senior. I totally agreed with his assessment of that situation and as a result, I left the fraternity at the end of my sophomore year and moved, together with three colleagues that I met during the first two years, Dick McGuire, Dennis Mahoney and Warren Kistler, to a rented small house on Ogontz Avenue, which was north of the medical school by about 20 blocks.

In my junior year, the clinical instruction began, which was much more interesting. We were sent to a variety of different hospitals, so it was necessary to have transportation at one's disposal. My roommates and I all had cars at the time, so we were able to get around the city. The clinical years were easier to manage academically, but still required a great deal of study after long hours in the clinics. Our social life was limited and we often cooked our own food. Warren Kistler was the official cook, and the rest of us assisted at cleaning and manual dishwashing. We dated a variety of girls during that time and squeezed in a little social activity. We were poor and our social drink consisted of mostly inexpensive Schmitz beer, the brewery being near our house. We did have interesting parties at our house, especially a Thanksgiving party, where we tried to cook a goose, which did not provide enough food for everyone. A social life in medical school is not nearly as enjoyable as in college, but we managed to have a good time. I traveled a little bit around Philadelphia, a large but not particularly interesting city— except the western suburbs, which are beautiful. After my sophomore year in medical school, I returned home and worked as a junior intern at Allegheny Valley Hospital and then at the end of the junior year, I had to stay as a newly-appointed intern in my senior year.

At the time, Temple was undergoing an experiment where they deleted the internship and converted the seniors to interns, which required 12 months of working at the hospital to provide coverage for all of the services. It was an intense experience, being thrown into patient management early in my senior year of medical school, without the additional supervision that is provided today in all medical schools. I learned to take care of patients as the primary physician and the emergency room experience was extensive, particularly repairing knife wounds and handling other violent injuries. During that time I also moonlighted at a variety of hospitals, doing histories and physicals for additional money. I also worked in different emergency rooms as a senior medical student without a medical license. That would be unheard of and prohibited today, when emergency rooms are staffed by professional emergency room physicians. At that time, most of the non-teaching city emergency rooms depended on students who were moonlighters to cover the emergency rooms at night. At times, it became very intense with multiple patients with a variety of disorders including severe surgical and medical emergencies. I was paid $15 a night at one hospital in Philadelphia to cover the entire emergency room. At times, I had to send away heart attack victims to other hospitals because of lack of bed space. I quickly resigned that position because of the demanding work and the fact that they would not pay me more for my services. Sleep was almost impossible to come by and I had to return to my duties in medical school the next day. Moonlighting of that type is certainly not a good idea.

Among the few girls I dated in medical school was Beverly, a nursing student at Temple. I liked her very much and planned to keep in touch with her following graduation, but that did not happen. The heavy on-call schedule severely restricted my social life, particularly on the obstetrics service where I delivered over fifty babies and had to fit all the clinic patients' diaphragms, because I was the only non-Catholic student or resident on the service.

I was elected president of the senior class and at the end of the senior year gave the commencement address to the student body, faculty and parents, a proud moment for me. My theme was to give credit to the parents, wives and children who accompanied the medical students through the difficult four years. Some wives and children had to live in rough north Philadelphia, which was difficult. And, of course, the expense of medical school was significant, although at that time it was $900 a semester at Temple, which is a small sum compared to the tuition of medical school today. Graduation in June 1961 was exciting, with my parents and my aunt and uncle (my mother's wealthy brother and his wife) in attendance. My uncle took us to a nightclub in New Jersey and tipped the maitre d' well to seat us near the stage. Beverly was with us and it was a memorable evening to end my formal medical education.

The Internship Journey

During our senior year, Dick McGuire and I had decided with another colleague, David Worthington, to intern in Florida to obtain Florida medical licenses in case we ever wanted to live there in the future. The license in Florida was very difficult to obtain and it was easier to do so if one was a Florida resident. Dennis Mahoney and Warren Kistler decided to go to Denver, Colorado to sample the mountains and to see if they wanted to live there. The reason for these choices, which sounded frivolous, was because we had already had an internship and felt that we were repeating the year. With this in mind, we thought that it would be to our benefit to go to a place where we might like either to obtain a difficult license and experience a tropical climate and/or see another part of the country.

Following medical school graduation, I went home briefly for the last time. In the middle of June, my father traded my car, an old Buick two-door sedan, for a new Corvair station wagon, which I insisted upon because I thought I needed to carry all my belongings with me, including a stereo, golf clubs, etc. It was an unusual car for a single medical school graduate and I received a great many adverse comments about my choice of automobile from my colleagues and the people I eventually met in Florida. Nevertheless, it was inexpensive and practical transportation for those years in transit.

In late June 1961, I headed to Florida with my colleagues. We stopped in Virginia and spent the day playing golf with a fraternity brother, Dick Estus, who was working in outdoor advertising in Richmond, Virginia. We moved on to Charleston, South Carolina, where we spent a night in the city of Charleston and sampled its charm and one of its better restaurants. It was there that I was introduced to baby lobster tails, which are still a favorite of mine. We then stopped in Jacksonville and wound up in a strip joint where we quickly learned that the cost of drinks was beyond our budget. We left promptly and returned to our motel to proceed the next day to Tampa, where we checked in at Tampa General Hospital to begin our internships. As we traveled across the state of Florida, through the heat, I was again impressed by the flatness of the state and the panorama of the big sky. On our way to Tampa, we passed through a medium-sized town called Orlando and were not very impressed. However, at the time we did not realize that it almost was to impact our future.

Upon arrival at Tampa General Hospital we were checked in and toured the facility located on Davis Island on Tampa Bay. The internship included privileges at a nearby private tennis club, which was unusual. We were also housed on Davis Island in apartments owned by the hospital, so that our rent was covered, but we paid for the telephone bills, and we made $80 every two weeks. It seems like a small amount, but at that time, we were able to get by very nicely because our meals as well as our living expenses were totally covered. However, after we were partially indoctrinated, they informed us that instead of being on call every third night, that because of a shortage of filling the quota of intern and residency positions, we would be on call every other night. That was the first and only time I ever almost got involved in a strike. The interns, approximately 12 of us, got together and decided that we had selected Tampa General Hospital for two reasons, one was to complete the necessary year learning more about the management of patients and the other was to sample the lifestyle in Florida. With an every-other-night call, there would be very little exposure to Florida other than the hospital. We decided to inform the hospital that we were going to seek internships at other institutions, if they did not reverse that decision to move us to every other night call throughout the year. One of the places that would have accepted us gladly was Orlando General Hospital and several of us were planning to move to Orlando to pursue our internship, but the hospital, after reconsidering the change, asked the residents in Medicine and Surgery to accept more call and allow us to take call every third night as had been promised.

The internship year at Tampa General Hospital proved to be an interesting and pivotal year for me. I enjoyed the hospital, its staff and my internship colleagues, Dick McGuire, Dave Worthington and Alan Van Sant, a graduate of the University of Pennsylvania. Probably as a result of social lives having been restricted during medical school, the four of us found our future wives during our internship year. We gained a variety of experience in all of the medical specialties and I befriended a young ophthalmologist in Tampa, Rodney Steimetz, who interested me in ophthalmology—although with my brother being an ophthalmologist, I had not planned on pursuing that specialty as a career. All of us pursued licenses to practice in Florida while we were interns, which required a basic science test followed by a very difficult written examination. In my opinion, it helped to have prominent Florida physicians from Tampa recommend us for licensure. We all successfully passed the tests and acquired the medical license, which I have kept active throughout my career.

The clinical caseload in all the specialties was heavy, especially medicine and surgery. The staff was excellent and I saw quite a variety of diseases. In the emergency room I even learned about breaking a voodoo spell from a Shaman who came into the E.R. to break the spell.

Since the internship was essentially a repeat year for me, while obtaining increased experience in all the major specialties and emergency medicine, I began to explore the social life of Tampa to a greater extent. The Florida girls were attractive and fun, but in November I met Mary Ellen Ward, a nurse trained at the University of Virginia who hailed from Elkins, West Virginia and was spending some time in Florida with her friend Sherry Sutton, to experience a different part of the country. Soon we became romantically involved and I dated her for the rest of my internship. During that time, we explored the parks and rivers of western and central Florida. At that time, western Florida was moderately populated and the beaches along the St. Petersburg/Clearwater stretch were beautiful and uncrowded. We enjoyed the beaches, even in the winter when the local people thought that the water was too cold. The winter in Florida that year was delightful, but the summer was hot, humid and polluted with insects. One night, we were driven from a local beach, while attempting a picnic, by insects, and had to return to our air-conditioned quarters to complete our picnic. My friends all dated nurses whom they had met in the hospital and we had a very nice social time on very little money. Our favorite restaurant was the Kapok Tree, set in a unique garden around a beautiful Kapok tree near Clearwater. In February, we all attended Gasparilla day, a huge party, similar to Mardi Gras, featuring various floats. The pirates led by Gasparilla sailed the waters of Tampa Bay during the late 18th century. All of the festival was very exciting and different from anything that any of us from the northern United States had ever experienced.

My parents visited me in Florida during my internship and for the first time in my life, I was able to take them out to dinner. They approved of my new girlfriend and we spent a pleasant week together when I could be off duty. The year flew by and at the end of my internship, I had to decide my next step. I was not convinced of my choice of specialty, so I decided to start my career in internal medicine in Tampa while awaiting my assignment from the military service. I elected to join the Navy, to which I had applied during the latter part of my internship. During the month of July 1962, while beginning an internal medicine residency, I helped Henry J. L. Mariott, M.D., Director of Residency training and a cardiologist, to write a book on electrocardiography. This certainly helped me during the next few years in my career in the military. When I enlisted in the navy in Jacksonville, Florida, I was assured that I would be considered for the flight surgery program, which had been my choice when considering the navy in the first place.

The Military Journey

At the end of July 1962, I received orders from the Navy that I was to report to Camp Pendleton, California to join the Seabee Battalion #11 as battalion surgeon. I was to train at Camp Pendleton with the Marines for a month and to report to Port Hueneme on the coast of California north of Los Angeles. The orders shocked me in that they gave me only a week to leave the internal medicine program and return to Pittsburgh, drop off my car and fly to California for entrance into the Seabees. At that time, during July, Mary Ellen and I decided to become engaged and she elected to return north with me to her home in Elkins, West Virginia while I was in the military service. I drove north with the heat-leaking Corvair in the heart of summer and after reaching home, I returned her to Elkins and went back to Pittsburgh to fly to Los Angeles. Upon arrival in Los Angeles, I took a bus to Oceanside, California and then obtained transportation to Camp Pendleton, where I reported for training with the marines as a Seabee Medical Officer.

It was at Camp Pendleton that I met a Medical Service Corps Officer, similar to a hospital administrator and experienced the beginning of a rocky relationship with administrative types since that time. However, upon the advice of the MSC officer, after having explained my situation of preference for flight surgery, I called Washington and spoke to the chief flight surgeon about my dilemma. I was advised, by the chief of flight surgery who was surprisingly accessible, that if I could complete nine months with MCB 11, he would see that I would get into flight surgery school in Pensacola, Florida in the summer of 1963 and after completion of the six months would only need to spend a year as a flight surgeon to fulfill my obligation. I agreed to the arrangement and was comfortable that my military career would expose me to a number of interesting situations.

At that time, the summer of 1962, I trained with the marines with enthusiasm, rapidly being put through an abbreviated basic training with a quick introduction to weaponry of all types, including hand grenades and automatic rifles. I even fired a 106 recoilless rifle at a tank, but I refused the flame-thrower experience, when offered, because of its high risk. We participated in day and night mock battles and I learned to set up and tear down a field hospital with half the number of corpsmen that I was supposed to have on assignment. During the end of my basic training, I learned that my fiancée was pregnant, so I elected to return home upon discharge from basic training and marry her in Elkins, West Virginia on September 9, 1962. The wedding was quickly arranged, but some of my friends were available for support: Dick McGuire, Nelson Hicks and Jim Grogan. My brother was my best man. The reception was hosted by Jim Hartman, the local florist, at his home, which was beautiful. Following the wedding in Elkins, we took the heat leaking Corvair on a trip across the United States to California.

The beginning of our honeymoon was spent at a lodge on Cheat Lake, a beautiful West Virginia resort. My friends duplicated the key to my Corvair, decorated the car, and moved it to another location in the parking lot. On the morning after the wedding, I was chagrined to find it missing, as it contained all my worldly possessions—but I finally located it at the very far end of the large parking lot and spouted a stream of oaths, which was very inappropriate for a Sunday morning in West Virginia. I undecorated the car, collected my new wife and started our trip west. The first long grueling day was across Ohio to Indiana, where we stayed at a motel near Indianapolis and got the last room, a great relief. During the next two days we shared the most boring part of the trip across the central plains to the mountains of Colorado. I became so bored with the passage through the plains that in Kansas, I stopped to take pictures of cows by the side of the road. However, upon reaching Denver, Colorado, we saw the beautiful mountains and began to appreciate the trip. In Colorado, I visited one of my medical school roommates, Dennis Mahoney and we spent a delightful evening together. That was the last time I saw him. After Denver, we began our trip through the Colorado Mountains, which were exquisite in the early fall and wished we had more time for leisurely exposure to that region. We found the trip through Utah interesting with the combination of desert and spectacular rock formations. We approached Las Vegas after sunset, coming over a hill to see the sky lighted up with neon lights, an extraordinary sight. We stayed at the Sahara Hotel in Las Vegas and were fascinated by the 24-hour life of that neon city. We ate well and gambled a little, but during our stay, I developed a toothache of a serious nature and was anxious to complete the trip, so that I could see Mike Callahan, the battalion dentist who was already stationed at Port Hueneme, to get relief from the pain. Therefore, we left Las Vegas to cross the desert with the heat-leaking Corvair. We had a water bag hanging out the window in case we needed water for the car or ourselves as we crossed the desert. I was in severe pain and had difficulty finishing the trip to Port Hueneme. We arrived on a Sunday morning and I caught Mike before he was off on an outing with some friends and he did a root canal on one of my lower teeth, relieving a purulent pocket and giving me immediate pain relief. Mary Ellen and I stayed at the guest quarters in the naval base at Port Hueneme until we located an apartment off base the next day, which was in the middle of a truck farm with vegetable plants all around us—an unusual setting.

I was indoctrinated into mobile construction battalion (MCB) 11 at Port Hueneme and began the routine of a battalion surgeon working with the seabees. My wife obtained a job as a nurse in the hospital at Oxnard. Our orders were to proceed to Subic Bay, Philippine Islands, to be a part of the naval facility there working to repair the airport, but Typhoon Karen virtually destroyed Guam. Because it is an important naval and airbase, we were reassigned to Guam to repair damage done by the typhoon. Therefore, in November of 1962, leaving a pregnant wife in Port Hueneme, I shipped out with the seabees on a troop ship to cross the Pacific Ocean to Guam. Prior to leaving California, the Battalion was alerted for a possible diversion to Cuba as result of the Bay of Pigs invasion. We were definitely relieved when we found out that we were not going to war in Cuba.

Crossing the Pacific in a troop ship is not the most exciting adventure, but it was interesting. The doctors on the troop ship offered to take care of my seabee battalion, which numbered about 500. As the trip proceeded, I became so bored that I insisted on seeing my own men in sick bay in the morning. Sea sickness was not a problem for the seabees because the troop ship was large and stable, and the weather was good. I had a good relationship with the ship's doctors and at nights we usually broke out some grain alcohol to have a cocktail or two before dinner. This was against navy regulations, so we were lucky to get away with it.

We stopped in Hawaii to refuel for two days, which was a delightful experience. I was able to tour Pearl Harbor, which was very exciting. I also toured Honolulu and most of the island of Oahu. The bars in Honolulu were lively; Waikiki beach was exciting and full of beautiful women. I was fascinated by the surfing that was popular even at that time and particularly enjoyed the trip up through the rain forest to the Pali, a cliff overlooking the northern part of the island where the natives were defeated by King Kamaha-maha, who dominated the Hawaiian islands. Oahu and all the Hawaiian islands are beautiful and full of dramatic scenery. Diamond Head is spectacular and the military cemetery in the crater of the old volcano was very impressive.

We re-boarded the troop ship and spent the most boring part of the journey across the Pacific to Guam. We arrived at Guam about a week later, just after dawn, the view being spectacular with the irregular geography of the island. Guam is truly a beautiful island, but upon arriving at the naval base harbor, we could see the destruction brought by Typhoon Karen. On disembarking in Apra Harbor, we were assigned to barracks while permanent quarters were being developed for us. The infirmary was in a hurricane-proof reinforced concrete building and was undamaged. The seabees were immediately put to work repairing the damage done to the naval facilities and I was assigned to the local dispensary to share the duties with the naval base physician, Norm Takaki, a Japanese-American who is an excellent physician and a delightful person. We shared call at the naval base and at the naval hospital in the central part of the island at Agana, the main city of Guam. Our duty was to take care of the people at the naval base and the Seabees, as well as share responsibilities at the naval hospital. In addition, we were to board and screen all incoming ships and quarantine the sailors until they were inspected for evidence of gonorrhea or syphilis. Guam was the only island in the South Pacific free of syphilis at that time. There was some non-specific urethritis, but we were warned that we were not to allow any of the more serious venereal diseases to enter through sailors returning from leave or ships coming to the island for temporary recreation or duty.

It was certainly interesting to be piped aboard foreign vessels from New Zealand and Australia as the inspecting medical officer for the ships, which were too small to have their own physicians.

On Guam, the Seabee officers, including the dentist, the architect, the chaplain, the engineers, and me, were eventually housed on top of

Nimitz Hill, the site of the previous headquarters of Admiral Nimitz. The Seabees rebuilt part of the old headquarters for us and we had delightful officers' quarters with a bar, restaurant and spectacular views in all directions. The Seabees appropriated all the necessary gear for us; they have a talent for bartering and appropriated useful items for our comfort. I certainly grew to respect the Seabees and their flexibility during my nine months with them.

The U.S. Naval Hospital on Guam was a 350-bed hospital, which was never filled. Since it was understaffed, I had to cover the hospital and the emergency room at night about once every six days. It was a busy time, as emergencies were common. One night, three young children were brought in dead after having been trapped in a discarded freezer. I could only pronounce them dead and talk to the families.

The captain in charge of the hospital was an older orthopedic surgeon who seemed to have lost his clinical competence. As one reaches higher ranks in the Navy, he or she is placed in more administrative positions. I had to meet with him in the morning after a long night on call and he had a huge cup of coffee on his desk but he never offered me a cup. He was only interested in the ship-to-shore calls I received during the night for various reasons, and didn't seem interested in what happened in the emergency room or on the patient floors.

I spent Christmas in the hospital, a lonely quiet place as my wife was in the States and my colleague had his family on the island. I was more interested in being off New Year's, as we had a great party.

One benefit of call was that Norm and I agreed to cover for each other after being on call so I played golf on the magnificent Naval golf courses on the days after I took call.

When we arrived, the foliage was severely damaged or destroyed, as if a war had recently been fought there. However, foliage on Guam recovered quickly, as it does in the tropics. The island assumed its former beauty in about three months. It is rugged country with hills, mountains and jungle in the central part. On weekends, we explored most of the island, including the interior where we saw Japanese tanks and made several trips to Telafofo Falls, a freshwater falls in which one could sail over the falls into a deep pool, a delightful experience in the tropical heat. We invited the nurses to join us on a couple of occasions, and had great picnics near the falls.

After being three months on Guam, another typhoon raked the island, Typhoon Olive, which was not as devastating as Karen. We spent the hours of Typhoon Olive in the reinforced concrete building that housed the dispensary. The winds were about 100 miles per hour and blew the palm tree trunks almost level to the ground in one direction, and then, after passage of the eye, in the opposite direction. During the eye of the typhoon, which was very still with a weird yellow light, four of us took the jeep and went to Erote Point to get a better view of the typhoon at sea. That was dumb, as we could have broken down and gotten caught in the second part, but we were lucky and returned to the dispensary prior to the winds picking up again. The entire experience was interesting and fortunately the damage was light, consisting mainly of damage to poorly- constructed buildings, mostly those of the natives, and many palm fronds down all over the place.

The views from the perimeter road of Guam were spectacular and the waters around Guam were teeming with tropical fish and other undersea life. Snorkeling was a marvelous experience on Guam and one can snorkel from any shore site out to the edge of reef and see fish and coral of various sizes, shapes and descriptions. Guam is where I began my interest in tropical water sports, including scuba diving. I started to take lessons in scuba diving at Guam, but unfortunately did not complete the course prior to my departure. The graduation of the diving course in Guam included a dive in the shark pit, an ocean pool below a steep cliff on Guam where wet garbage was dumped. You could see several different types and sizes of sharks from the top of the cliff on any given day, particularly around the time of garbage disposal.

Mike Callahan and I traveled all over Guam in our jeep. The best restaurant was the officers' club at Anderson Air Force Base, 30 miles from the Naval Base at the opposite end of the island. During my time there, with my group already understaffed, I lost a corpsman to a motorcycle accident He was coming down a hill and failed to make a turn, running into a guard post and suffering a chest injury that was, in my opinion, not managed properly. He subsequently died of sepsis. His buddy, in the back of the bike, only suffered a badly-injured foot. After that experience, we had motorcycles outlawed on Guam for several years, but I am sure they have returned since then.

In the officer's club I met a destroyer escort skipper, a lieutenant commander, who explained his mission was to survey U.S. protectorate Western Caroline Islands on a cruise. Usually, he had a high-level corpsman evaluate the health of the islanders, but he wanted to know if I would accompany him on a cruise as a doctor. I jumped at the chance, got permission from my Seabee commanding officer, and left for a week on a destroyer escort radar ship on the fringe of a South Pacific storm. That ship really rocked and rolled. I only felt well on the bridge looking at the horizon. The trip was exciting in that we simulated a depth-charge run with one of our submarines at night. They would turn on their lights if we got a simulated hit. The island surveys were exciting in that we had to go over the side of the ship on net ladders and get into a zodiac piloted by one of the chief petty officers and off we went over the reefs onto various islands. The sea sickness subsided on the zodiac and was replaced by fear. The natives greeted us warmly and I traded them cigarettes for small wooden statues they had learned to make from Japanese invaders during WWII. The natives came to me with their complaints and I handed out antibiotics and aspirins to many of them. One woman handed me her cancerous breast, which was very advanced in the disease, and I recorded her name to turn in to the hospital at Palau who would send for her to be taken to the hospital. The trip was an unforgettable experience for me, despite the mild sea sickness and the nights spent on the top bunk of our officers' quarters with my nose about one inch from the ceiling. As the second highest-ranking officer, I sat near the captain at dinner and the food was excellent.

I enjoyed the entire Guam experience and it further stimulated my love of travel, especially in the tropics. In some ways, I regretted leaving Guam, but I was anxious to get home to my family. In April 1963, I learned that I had a baby daughter in California named Nancy Louise, who was born healthy. I received the information while playing volleyball at the officers' quarters. At first I did not believe it, but radio transmission confirmed that she had arrived. Therefore, instead of accompanying the troops home aboard ship, the MCB captain allowed me to fly home to California. That was the longest flight that I have ever taken. It was a four-engine prop plane and we landed on Wake Island, then in Hawaii where we had to spend two days due to engine trouble. We flew onto California. During the entire flight, I played gin rummy with the supply officer, Joe Blazina. At the end of the trip, we ended up virtually even as far as the bets were concerned. That reinforced in my mind the law of averages.

Upon arrival in California, of course I was met by my wife, Mary Ellen and my new daughter, Nancy Louise. I was delighted to see them and the reunion was pleasant. However, I knew immediately, on the first night, that my life had drastically changed. When a baby is added to family, the whole situation changes and we were focused more on the child than each other.

Shortly after returning to California, I was transferred to Pensacola, in June 1963. Again, we drove across the country, this time by the southern route, which I found most interesting. We stopped more frequently in the desert states and then tried to cross the plains as quickly as possible, having remembered the boredom they caused on the way out. We were granted short leave, so I returned to Pittsburgh to see my parents, so they could see the new granddaughter. In two days we packed the Corvair station wagon again and drove to Pensacola, Florida to begin my training as a flight surgeon. I think, again, the long drive across the country and down to Florida had saturated my desire for long automobile trips.

The flight surgery training in Pensacola emphasized ophthalmology, otolaryngology, psychiatry, and physiology, as they applied to aviation. The schooling was extremely interesting with excellent teachers and I developed an interest in ophthalmology, although I resisted, because of complete and in-depth exposure to this specialty. I learned to refract and to evaluate eyes medically. Of course, no surgery was involved, as flight surgeons are not qualified to do eye surgery. During flight surgery training, I also learned to fly and soloed a T-37 aircraft; I was the first one to do so in my class. This training was followed by some training in formation flying, which I enjoyed and adapted to very well—but I missed the carrier landing which we were going to experience in the backseat of a plane. The shortage of time and bad weather prevented that experience. However, I did experience a day cruise on the carrier Lexington, watching planes land and take off, which was fascinating.

We enjoyed living in Pensacola, at first on the beach in an old house, but the insects drove us out and we rented a small suburban house to finish the school. It had only a small gas heater in the hall, and was a bit cold and damp in the winter. We socialized with young married couples who had children—again a new way of life.

I did well in flight surgery and at the end of the tour in school, I was given a good choice of duties for the following year. However, I learned that my wife was pregnant with our second child, so I had to forego a trip on a carrier through western Europe, stopping at numerous ports of call, in favor of a post as a flight surgeon at the South Weymouth Naval Air Station south of Boston in New England—my second choice, as I wanted to experience living in New England. Therefore, once again back in the car in December 1963, with young Nancy, we were off to West Virginia and Pennsylvania for brief visits with our families and then on to South Weymouth Naval Air Station. I rented a home in nearby Brockton and commuted daily, soon acquiring a second car, a five-year-old used Volkswagen which I enjoyed very much. During the year at South Weymouth, a weekend warrior naval air base where naval reserve pilots would come in on the weekend and fly the necessary monthly four hours, I accompanied them on many flights over northern New England and often out to Nantucket Island for lunch, which was a unique experience. I was able to fly as a co-pilot in helicopters all over the coast of New England, which was very exciting. I did general physical exams on the naval aviation applicants and took care of the general medical problems of the base personnel and their families, a rather boring medical practice. We transferred all our serious cases to the naval hospital in Boston. During my year, I was able to attend grand rounds at Massachusetts Eye and Ear Infirmary, which further spurred my interest in ophthalmology, so I applied for residency training during that year. Among other programs, I applied to the University of Pittsburgh Eye and Ear Hospital. I wanted to start in January of 1965, and at that time the Eye & Ear residency was taking a third ophthalmology resident, six months off the regular rotation. In most programs, residencies begin in July. After only three years, the Eye and Ear residency resumed starting residents only in July, but I was one of the few who obtained a January residency out of sheer luck. The chairman knew my brother, who was a volunteer at the clinic and asked him if he knew a John Kennerdell. He said that I was his brother, so the chief, Murray McCaslin, accepted me without further evaluation. I did come to the University of Pittsburgh for an interview and met the faculty at that time. The other applications that I had were still pending, but I thought that I did not have much of a chance of obtaining a residency in Miami or at the University of Oregon because of the late application, so I canceled them and accepted a residency at the Eye & Ear Hospital of Pittsburgh. I decided to return home to Pittsburgh, partially so that my parents could appreciate our young children while they were growing through the early years.

During 1964 we traveled throughout New England and Cape Cod as much as possible and I enjoyed the entire experience. New England is a beautiful area of the country and well worth covering in detail. There are quaint little towns and the coastline is spectacular. People in New England were not as friendly as they had been in California or Florida. I found in this country the people are more friendly and quicker to accept strangers the farther west you travel. Nevertheless, we made some friends in New England, mostly people in the service such as ourselves, and had a pleasant time. My parents visited us in New England on one occasion. In August 1964, my son Jeffrey John was born at South Weymouth Hospital, and life became even more hectic with our young family. I served the rest of my time at the Naval Air Station seeing members of the full-time military, weekend warriors, and doing physicals on aviation applicants. I moonlighted at Brockton Hospital during my time there to make extra money and I received flight pay for four hours flying each month which actually saturated my desire for flying and probably is the reason I did not pursue a pilot's license. During my time there, I met Jim Pirie, from Alabama, an A-4 bomber pilot, and his wife Barbara. Jim took my wife to the hospital for delivery as I was on call at the Brockton hospital and subsequently I took his wife to the hospital for delivery as he was on a training flight. We were close friends and subsequently Jim, assigned to Vietnam, became a prisoner of war. He survived to return to the United States. I talked with him by phone on his return and we vowed to meet, but so far it has not happened.

I received an honorable discharge in January 1965 and I elected not to join the active reserve. This was fortunate, in that I was never called back to military service in Vietnam, despite the combination of flight and combat training that I enjoyed with aviation medicine and with the Sea Bees.

The Residency Journey

In the middle of January 1965, we packed the two cars and drove home on a very cold weekend, one child in each car, to move in with my parents for two weeks while I found quarters for the family. I was able to purchase a new home in a suburban Pittsburgh housing development near Monroeville. The new house had three bedrooms, with a den, family room and a single car garage. It was quite unusual for someone who was just beginning a residency program to buy a house. I used my eligibility for an FHA loan with a down payment of $500 for the house, which cost $18,900. We moved in as quickly as possible and began to acquire furniture and other necessities for domestic living. Previously, we had rented furnished houses. The children were small and the neighborhood was safe, with other children with whom they could play. We acquired a Dachshund puppy we named Gutch, my old nickname. He was fun, but when he escaped the house, he became the neighborhood stud. As the kids would let him sneak out the door with them, we had to give him away and he wound up on a farm near Erie.

In early February 1965, I began my residency training at the Eye and Ear Hospital in Pittsburgh. I loved being at the Eye and Ear Hospital, as it had a unique situation of having ophthalmology and otolaryngology, the only specialties in the institution, so we were autonomous. The training at that time was by voluntary faculty, including the chairman, and so the training was more practical than academic. We saw a large number of indigent patients and helped care for the hospitalized patients of the attending staff. I learned mostly by reading and by practical experience, although we had weekly lectures. We were introduced to surgery early as a necessity to take care of the clinic patients, so my residency provided much surgical experience, including trauma. I did over 150 cataract operations as well as a number of other ophthalmic surgeries at the Eye & Ear Hospital.

In 1966, during my second year of residency, I volunteered to learn ultrasonography at the request of the Department Chairman, by attending a course in Southhampton, Long Island, organized by Nat Bronson, a pioneer in ophthalmic ultrasonography. The trip was delightful, paid for by the department, and the course was excellent. I learned A-Scan ultrasound techniques and later B-scan or patterned ultrasound. I have used this diagnostic technique for the eye and orbit during my entire career, and introduced the technique to the Pittsburgh ophthalmic community, where I did all the ophthalmic ultrasound diagnoses for about ten years.

During my residency, I moonlighted at several different institutions, working at emergency rooms for extra money to maintain the family's conservative, but comfortable lifestyle. The Volkswagen gave out, so I bought a new four-door Buick sedan from the father of a former girlfriend in New Kensington. That was my luxury during my residency training; of course, travel was discontinued during that time because of financial reasons. I proceeded through the residency training without difficulty and felt comfortable nearing the end that I was becoming well-trained in general ophthalmology. Because I began early, I finished early and the surgical experience was turned over to the next group of residents. Therefore, I was free during my last six months to set up a fluorescein angiography laboratory and the electroretinography laboratory at the Eye and Ear Hospital.

During that time, the chairman, Dr. Murray McCaslin, informed me that they needed help in Haiti. A few years previously, a Haitian ophthalmologist, Gerard Frederique, had been trained at the Eye and Ear Hospital, and returned to Haiti to work at the Hospital Deschpelle under Larry Mellon, M.D., in the Artibonite Valley of Haiti. Dr. Mellon received his medical training late in life after rejecting a banking career, to become the physician who developed a hospital, largely at his own expense, in a remote region of Haiti where medical care was extremely primitive. His wife, Gwen Mellon, trained in laboratory medicine, accompanied him and actually became the business manager of the hospital for many years.

The Haitian Journey

In the fall of 1967, Dr. McCaslin asked me if I would go to Haiti to take over the ophthalmology position at this remote hospital because Dr. Frederique had to have bilateral inguinal hernia operations. I jumped at the chance to travel again and was fortunate to be able to take my entire family to Haiti for two months to experience a general ophthalmology practice in a rather primitive country. Dr. McCaslin accompanied us to Haiti. We arrived at the airport at night, a somewhat frightening experience except that he had been there in the past. We walked from the plane to the terminal, and the sign on the terminal announced that Haiti was the second greatest democracy in the western hemisphere. This, of course, was far from the truth, as we learned while we were there. At that time, the dictator Papa Doc Duvalier was in charge and his Tonton Macoute, the secret military police, were everywhere. There were checkpoints along all the roads and one was always cautious remarking about the government of Haiti for fear of reprisal.

We drove through Port au Prince late at night with the torches and candles burning, which was very eerie. There were really very few street lights and we were taken to a beautiful hotel backed up against a mountain that was like an oasis in the desert. Inside the hotel, there were ceiling fans and the atmosphere was tropical, but cool. The rooms were extremely comfortable and we spent a day in Port au Prince, an impoverished city. We toured the market place and traveled around the city to get acquainted and then were taken by car to the Artibonite Valley in western Haiti. The road out of Port au Prince was along the coast and was horrible, with huge potholes and other irregularities. When we turned from the coast at Gonaive toward the Artibonite Valley, the road worsened and when we finally arrived at the hospital and its surrounding compound, we were very tired. It was a very hard drive, although it was probably only about 60 miles. The hospital was developed on the grounds of the former United Fruit Company, so there were some very nice tropical homes in the complex, and we were assigned to one of them. It came complete with a maid, cook and a houseboy. This was a luxury to which we certainly were not accustomed. However, there was no hot water or air conditioning. We suffered many hot nights and cold showers.

I began my experience in the ophthalmology office at the hospital. I found out that Gerard Frederique would be departing in a few days for his surgery and would not return until the end of my stay. Therefore, I was assigned a Creole nurse and a French-speaking volunteer dentist's wife. The patients' complaints were interpreted from Creole to French and then into English so that I could understand. I quickly learned a few words of Creole, so that I could examine the patients more directly. Without Dr. Frederique's help, I learned my way around the institution and quickly assumed a very busy practice filled with unusual diseases that I had never seen in the United States, including Weil's disease (a disease of the liver that causes jaundiced eyes), and advanced neglected cancers of the eye and orbit. It was an extremely stimulating and inter- esting practice and I advanced my surgical experience there, some of which was done by the seat of my pants. During my time there, I did several corneal transplants. Fresh corneas were easy to obtain because the Tonton Macoute was eliminating young political dissenters in Port au Prince, so there were many young eyes to be harvested for corneal transplantation. This is opposed to the difficulty that obtaining corneas was, for many years, in the United States. In our limited leisure time, I often played tennis with the other members of the medical staff at a court directly in front of our house. There was a very small, but nice swimming pool near our house, which was less frequently used than one would expect, considering the heat.

Luckily, during my time there a Dr. Herbert Muntz came to visit the hospital named after Albert Schweitzer, whom he succeeded in Africa. He was a Swiss general surgeon, of superior skill and was an excellent musician, as was Dr. Mellon. He actually did more cataracts in Gabon, Africa than I did as a resident of the University of Pittsburgh in a year. He assisted me on three procedures, including a corneal transplant, and was probably the best assistant that I have ever had. I enjoyed his musical presentation in church with Dr. Mellon, with whom he formed a duet.

During my time in Haiti, I was able to teach my children to swim at the local swimming pool and spent a great deal of time with them. They related to the local children very easily, and were well cared for by our servants.

One day, after a trip to Port au Prince, where I had eaten a salad in the Olafsson hotel, I became very sick with an intestinal infection. Because I was scheduled to do three surgical cases including a corneal transplant, Gerard Frederique, who happened to be at the hospital for a short period, insisted that I perform the surgery despite the loss of fluids, from both ends of my body. He brought a liter of saline to the house and administered it to me prior to taking me to the operating room where I was, somehow, able to perform three cases, including the corneal transplant, only to be returned to my house for another liter of IV fluid. I am not sure how I made it through that day, but I never ate anything uncooked in Haiti again. The rule was that one ate nothing that was not cooked or that one could not peel. Boiled water was the only water to drink or something that came with a sealed top such as a Coke; one should witness the bottle being uncapped and then wipe off the top of it carefully with a clean cloth. Fortunately, none of my family became ill during our time in Haiti and we enjoyed the unusual food, including my first experience with goat cooked over an open fire, which I found delicious and still do. We dined with the Mellons on two occasions, one time with other guests who were on the property. These were very gratifying and enjoyable experiences.

During our time there, we were able to travel throughout the country, including the northern port city of Cap Haitien, which was the city where the confrontation with Napoleon's forces occurred. The rebellion finally resulted in the liberation of Haiti by her natives. One of the leaders was Henry Christophe, an unusual and powerful man who built a citadel on a mountain near Cap Haitien to defend the country upon the expected return of French forces. The citadel still exists and is accessed only by a steep climb along the mountain road, usually done with horses. Once one reaches the citadel, it is most impressive with high walls and turrets where guns were mounted to defend the Haitian forces in the event of an attack. It is amazing how this huge fortress was built on top of that mountain. It required an enormous effort of virtually slave labor to assemble this magnificent structure, which is in partial ruin. It certainly is an impressive edifice and seeing it was definitely worth the difficulties required to reach it.

We also were able to enjoy the Caribbean Sea around Haiti on the western side and in a resort near Port au Prince. The water, of course, is full of tropical fish and is very clear. I unsuccessfully attempted spear fishing at that time, which was before I had completed my training in scuba diving.

Port au Prince itself is a dirty, poverty-stricken city, with very kind and simple people. We visited the market in Port au Prince several times, which is a conglomeration of individuals selling all sorts of foods, household staples and Haitian crafts. Most of the crafts were crude and were not valuable, but some were cleverly done and were worth consideration. Of course, the market is hot and one must be careful not to lose one's wallet, but the people are gentle and are not dangerous. Bargaining is expected and one can often get truly good crafts for a very reasonable or low price. The art in Port au Prince, which is mostly found in art galleries—that is, art of any quality—is primitive, full of color and very appealing. We acquired a few pieces of Haitian art at that time and have collected additional pieces since then during Haitian craft and art auctions in Pittsburgh.

We returned home after two months in Haiti with some unusual pathologic specimens, one being a squamous cell carcinoma, the other being buphthalmic eye, which is a large eye as a result of neuro-fibromatosis, which I had to remove. Just before leaving, my children decided to leave all their toys to the children of our cook, house boy and gardener. In addition, I had acquired a very lightweight gray suit during medical school in Philadelphia, which for some reason I took to Haiti thinking I would need to be in a suit on occasion. I decided to leave the suit with the house boy, a very nice patient chap who took good care of us. Prior to our departure I mentioned to one of my Haitian colleagues at the hospital that if he saw a fellow coming down the road in a light gray suit, it was my suit that was left for him as a present. He informed me that he would never see that suit except if he attended that person's funeral, because he would save that suit to be worn at his own funeral. It would go into the coffin with the house boy. I felt a little sad at the future of my suit, which I did like very much and wore for several years, however, I guess if that is how he treasured it, I had to appreciate his point of view.

We returned from Haiti full of our experiences and I had developed increased expertise in surgery that was not available at the University of Pittsburgh Department of Ophthalmology. Our return was uneventful and the children went back into their usual routines. They were attending kindergarten and pre-school at that time.

During the last three months of my residency, which ended January 31, 1968, I set up the ERG lab at the University of Pittsburgh. This was done with the help of Professor Gerhart Werner of the University of Buffalo, an expert in electroretinography. We actually set the equipment up in a lead-lined room to prevent outside electrical interference because these electroretinographic tracings were obtained from the brain after viewing an object and were not very powerful. One had to delicately place the electrodes on the scalp and attach contact lenses to the eye. It was very difficult to obtain good results, but we were able to achieve them in the laboratory with his expertise and instruction. I also set up the fluorescein angiography lab at the University of Pittsburgh, which was destined to become much more of an integral part of ophthalmic diagnosis than electroretinography. Of course an angiogram now has become a vital factor in evaluating retinal disease and is found in most practices that include a retinal service. It is now managed, appropriately, by retinal specialists who are employing its information on many of their patients.

During my residency, I also worked with an ophthalmology group in the southern suburbs of Pittsburgh, the South Hills Eye Associates. I saw their patients on Saturday mornings, which also gave me some additional income during the residency years to take care of my family and the house that we had acquired. Because I was comfortable with that group, I elected to join them on completion of my residency at the end of January 1968 and began a suburban practice of general ophthalmology in Mt. Lebanon with a branch office in Canonsburg, Pennsylvania. I moved my family from Holiday Park near Monroeville to the South Hills, where we rented a townhouse before and after our Haitian experience and then bought a three-bedroom house on Park Ridge Drive in Mt. Lebanon, overlooking the park that contained the tennis complex and was adjacent to the high school. The park setting was pleasant and the children were able to begin school in the Mt. Lebanon school district, which has always been excellent.

The Maine Journey

In the summer of 1968, with agreement of the group I joined, I spent two and a half months in Maine at the Lancaster course at Colby College, studying didactic ophthalmology. We stayed in a cabin on East Pond, near Waterville, Maine where the course was held. The summer on East Pond was pleasant. The children increased their swimming skills in the cold East Pond. I did some bass fishing with limited success. The one time I did catch some bass, the neighbor said that the bass he caught had worms, so my wife threw mine away. I had colleagues living nearby, George Buerger and his family and an older doctor who completed his ophthalmology training later in life, Jack Jordan. We socialized with them often in the evenings and on the weekends.

We traveled to Booth Bay and Bar Harbor, beautiful coastal resorts and fishing ports, on the weekends. I also canoed the Kennebec River, with the canoe moving among floating logs, an unusual and slightly risky experience. Dave Croisdale from the University of Virginia and I sailed in a small sailboat on East Pond, upsetting it several times. Dave, a bachelor outdoorsman, eventually practiced in a small town in Idaho, enjoying the outdoors.

Most of the ophthalmology taught at the Lancaster course I already knew, but there were some things which were certainly helpful in studying for the board examinations, both written and oral, which I took in the fall of 1968 and the spring of 1969, passing the oral boards in June 1969 and thereby becoming a board-certified ophthalmologist.

The Private Practice Journey

Following the very pleasant summer in Maine, I worked with the South Hills Eye Associates and began to develop a practice of my own in their group. The practice was typical suburban ophthalmology with mostly routine patients. We performed cataract surgery and a little bit of extraocular muscle surgery on Fridays. I found during my two years there that, after the board examination challenge was over, I had a significant let down in my interest in ophthalmology, doing routine evaluations for the most part. I had an exciting surgical experience during my residency and in Haiti and I felt that my talents were gradually deteriorating following my board certification. For that reason, despite a generous early partnership, I decided to consider other alternatives. I had a Florida medical license and I was seriously interested in returning to Florida for practice because I enjoyed the geography and the warm weather of that state. However, again considering my alternatives, I thought that I might be interested in academic ophthalmology.

I conveyed this thought to Ken Richardson, the Chairman of Ophthalmology at the Eye & Ear Hospital at that time and it so happened that he was looking for faculty members to be full-time salaried in the tenure stream at the University of Pittsburgh, practicing at the Eye & Ear Hospital. Dick Katzin, a general ophthalmologist, had joined him in practice and he had sent Frank Cignetti, a resident one year behind me, to California for corneal training; he was to return to do cornea and external disease. Ken Richardson had post-graduate training in glaucoma. He considered me as a third choice for starting neuro-ophthalmology at the Eye & Ear Hospital after two others had turned down the position. He arranged for me to have an interview at Johns Hopkins in late 1969 and they accepted me for a fellowship. The Neuro-Ophthalmology Department at that time was run by the great Frank Walsh, a legend in neuro-ophthalmology and Dave Knox, his young partner who has pursued a career in neuro-ophthalmology at Johns Hopkins. However, in my interview, I asked what surgical procedures they had done in the past year, because of my extensive training in surgery at the University of Pittsburgh. Dave Knox answered that he had done some tarsorrhaphies, which is closure of the eyelids to prevent corneal exposure. That is a fairly simple operation and it told me that if I pursued a career in neuro-ophthalmology as it was classically done, I would not be able to do any type of significant surgery in the future.

When I told Ken Richardson that I did not think that I wanted to be a non-surgeon, he suggested that I consider another approach. Apparently he was desperate for somebody to open neuro-ophthalmology at the University of Pittsburgh, because there was no such service before that time. He suggested I consider spending a year with neurology and neuro-surgery at the University of Pittsburgh while doing consultations and seeing some ophthalmic patients to earn my salary at $35,000 a year, half the private practice salary, which would allow me to consider a future in that specialty area. I thought that this would not be a formal fellowship, but would allow me to explore the possibilities of combining neuro-ophthalmology with surgery in the eye and orbit, thus neuro-ophthalmic surgery was born.

I had become experienced in ultrasound during my residency and I was finding lesions in the orbit with the ultrasound that I had set up at the University of Pittsburgh. I did not think it would be possible to develop a career this way, but in January 1970, my father died. This was a dramatic moment in my life, because I was very close to him and I was upset about his passing. I knew my mother would be alone as they had been together for well over 50 years and that it was not a good time to leave the community.

The Academic Journey

I agreed to try the program suggested by Ken Richardson, dividing time with neurology under Henry Higman who was very helpful to me, and with neurosurgery headed by Tony Susan, who was also helpful and enthusiastic about this concept. I saw patients of all sorts during that year at the University of Pittsburgh, mostly a variety of troublesome problems that I tried to sort out. During the first part of 1970, with my father's passing and the difficulties of being introduced into new areas, I was somewhat depressed and nearly decided to reconsider my previous intention to go to Florida, but during the latter part of the year, I began to figure out that I could discuss neurologic and neurosurgical problems with the ophthalmology residents and staff as an authority, and in turn could go to the neurology and neurosurgery meetings and expound on ophthalmology findings in neurologically disturbed patients. This gave me a feeling of importance in the area that crosses between the specialties involved in neuro-science. During that time, with my experience in ultrasound, it occurred to me that I could improve treatment approaches to the orbit, an area that was not well understood prior to the development of ultrasound, CT scanning and then MRI scanning. Fortunately, I entered the field at the threshold of these discoveries and was able to develop an expertise in evaluating neuro-ophthalmic patients as well as patients with orbital and periorbital disease. I went to neuro-ophthalmology meetings at that time, but I had no mentor. I tried to present cases that had orbital surgical implications emphasizing the fact that a neuro-ophthalmologist could engage in surgery in the orbit and in the orbital-cranial junction if accompanied by a neurosurgeon.

One elderly patient I saw, early in my new career in consultation, had a pituitary tumor and a left 6th nerve palsy that caused double vision. For some reason it was postulated that the 6th nerve palsy was due to adrenal insufficiency. I had been studying neuro-anatomy of the visual system at the time and knew that the 6th nerve ran just lateral to the pituitary gland on its way to the lateral rectus muscle in the orbit. I insisted that the 6th nerve palsy was due to lateral extension of a pituitary tumor, which proved to be the case when found at craniotomy. This case increased my confidence as a neuro-ophthalmologist and the 6th nerve recovered after removal of the tumor, with correction of the double vision.

I was fortunate in the early 70s to meet Melvin Alper, a neuro-ophthalmologist in Washington, D.C. who was trained by Frank Walsh at Johns Hopkins, a classic non-surgical neuro-ophthalmologist, who had continued to do ophthalmic surgery and learned how to approach the orbit surgically. I expressed my ideas to him and, fortunately, he introduced me to the people in neuro-ophthalmology, explaining the ideas that I had. Although I was fearful of rejection, the idea of orbital and peri-orbital surgery was accepted by Frank Walsh, David Cogan and Bill Hoyt, the senior and most experienced neuro-ophthalmologists in the country. I developed good relations with them with Mel Alper's help and felt more comfortable in pursuing my crossover career as an orbital surgeon with neuro-ophthalmic background. Eventually, I developed the term neuro-ophthalmic surgeon, which is what I consider myself to be. As mentioned, with the ultrasound I began to find tumors in the orbit in the early 70s and supplemented the ultrasound with standard radiologic techniques and arteriography, which were not very helpful in orbital disease diagnoses.

In 1972, Joseph C. Maroon, a young neurosurgeon, returned from advanced training in microsurgery at the University of Vermont and joined the faculty of neuro-surgery at the University of Pittsburgh under the new chairman, Peter Jannetta. I talked to Dr. Jannetta about my desires to join with a neuro-surgeon in this endeavor and he whole-heartedly agreed, but he was busy developing his own approach to hemifacial spasm and facial pain, theorizing that a small blood vessel was compressing the 7th or the 5th nerve as it exits the brain stem. He was developing a technique to lift the blood vessel from the nerve using a small sponge cushion, which would alleviate the problem in some of these patients.

I asked Joe Maroon if he might be interested in joining me to acquire more surgical experience in the orbital and peri-orbital regions. Fortunately, being new on the faculty, he was most enthusiastic about this idea and with his help and cooperation, we developed a neuro-ophthalmic/neuro-surgical team and approached all deep orbital lesions together. It was coincidental and fortunate, that at the time we began our collaboration, computerized tomography developed and was soon acquired by the University of Pittsburgh, followed by magnetic resonance imaging. With our expertise in ophthalmology and neuro-surgery, combined with these neuro-diagnostic techniques, we were able to find and identify orbital and peri-orbital lesions more efficiently and earlier in the development of many of the lesions. We then developed an approach to management of these lesions including development of the instruments and retractors necessary to get into the orbit from all directions and to develop a team of oncologists, neuro-radiologists, radiation oncologists, otorhinolaryngologists, ophthalmic pathologists and cytologists to join us in a multi-disciplined approach to the orbit and peri-orbital area. This became a strong focus of my academic career and allowed me to develop expertise in this area, with the help of my colleagues. This anatomic area had really not been focused upon in the past. It fixed my future in academic medicine as we presented papers at the various meetings. We created a display on orbital microsurgery that was shown at the Academy of Ophthalmology and were awarded a prize for innovation and substance in 1975. Our display also won a certificate of merit at a scientific exhibit at the annual meeting of the American Medical Association. Both Joe and I had gained expertise with the operating microscope in our own specialties and adopted its use in the orbit with good results.

However, it did not always go well as we developed our expertise. We diagnosed a physician's wife with an orbital tumor–probably a hemangioma. We didn't know, from our rather crude CT scans, the true relationship of the tumor to the optic nerve. We performed a microsurgical lateral orbitotomy and found the tumor to be medial rather than lateral to the optic nerve behind the eye. We rolled the tumor over the optic nerve to successfully remove it, but blinded her in the process– probably by interfering with the blood supply to the nerve during our surgical manipulation. The fact that the orbit was a dangerous place to operate was reinforced and we expanded our efforts to develop more ways to enter and leave the orbit safely. That case also reminded us that the patients on which we have had complications are more firmly placed in our minds than the many successes.

In 1975, I took my first fellow in neuro-ophthalmology and orbital surgery. His name was Sriram Sonty; he was from Hyderabad, India. He was very flexible and an excellent fellow for the beginning of the effort to train people in this area. He spent six months with me, then went to Boston to do six months of pediatric ophthalmology. He eventually received additional training in glaucoma and practiced general ophthalmology, with a special interest in glaucoma in Chicago, Illinois. He has kept in touch and still comes to the fellowship reunion at the yearly Academy of Ophthalmology meetings. He didn't practice neuro-ophthalmic surgery but gave me experience in teaching fellows.

At the same time, Arthur Grove from Harvard had seen our display at the Academy of Ophthalmology on orbital neurosurgery and suggested that we consider forming a group to discuss problems relating to the orbit because there were no colleagues in our respective academic centers who were interested in the orbit. Art Grove had an ophthalmic plastic surgery background and was very interested in orbital diseases. I decided to contact him and suggest that we select a group of people who might be interested in forming an orbital study group. We met with twelve people we had selected at the Academy of Ophthalmology in Las Vegas, Nevada in 1976. The structure of the group was made up of two-fifths neuro-ophthalmologists, two-fifths ophthalmic plastic surgeons and one-fifth ophthalmic pathologists. We decided on the name of the Orbital Society. I agreed to host the first meeting at the University of Pittsburgh, Department of Ophthalmology, at the Eye & Ear Hospital in the spring of 1977. We decided to keep the group small and have people join who were very interested in the orbit. At the first meeting we invited the local team including Joe Maroon of neurosurgery, Ralph Heinz of neuro-radiology, Bruce Johnson of ophthalmic pathology, and Al Deutch of neuro-radiology. We also invited the residents and fellows at the University of Pittsburgh to participate. The meeting was a great success and the Orbital Society was launched. Art Grove became secretary. We did not want any other officers because we wanted to keep this a small congenial group with pointed and frank discussions. This society has been of great interest and satisfaction to me as it is the meeting that I look forward to every year, where I can discuss difficult problems with my colleagues from around the world. It has become an international society with members from various countries in Europe and Australia. The 25th anniversary meeting was held at the University of Iowa in June 2001 and I gave the first theme-oriented presentation of my experience in the management of optic nerve sheath and sphenoid wing meningiomas.

Following the development of the Orbital Society, I went on to train fellows in neuro-ophthalmology and orbital disease. The second fellow was an ophthalmologist from Georgetown, Louis Mark, who trained with me for a year; because of the fact that the field was young he did not pursue a career in this subspeciality, but went on to practice in Florida as a general ophthalmologist. The third fellow was Jorge Kattah, a neurologist whom I interviewed at the Pennsylvania Academy of Ophthalmology meeting. I did not have other candidates at that time and I was reluctant to take a neurologist, but I agreed to do so. He was a delightful fellow and he learned neuro-ophthalmology extremely well including how to use ophthalmic instruments like the indirect ophthalmoscope. However, we did not get past the temporal artery biopsy in the surgical area because he was definitely non-surgically oriented. He developed an important career in neuro-ophthalmology at Georgetown and has gone on to become the chairman of neurology at a branch of the University of Illinois at Peoria, Illinois.

In the latter part of the 1970s, Joe Maroon and I began to address the problems of changing the methods of treating the patients with optic nerve sheath meningiomas and sphenoid wing meningiomas. In addition, we developed the techniques for decompressing the orbits in patients with severe dysthyroid orbitopathy, including a four wall decompression which included removal of part of the orbital roof done by Dr. Maroon and the other three orbital walls removed by me. This was an exciting time of development of our skills with the new diagnostic modalities and we began to publish frequently on the diagnosis and management of orbital disorders. My fourth fellow was Tom Spoor, an aggressive surgeon, who wrote several papers with me on different orbital and neuro-ophthalmic problems. Tom went on to the University of South Carolina and then to Mobile, Alabama and finally to Detroit where he settled at Kresge Eye Institute and has developed a significant career in neuro-ophthalmic surgery. He has published a book on Neuro-ophthalmic surgery and focused mostly on ophthalmic plastic surgery as his career developed. He made several contributions in the field of orbital diseases, including the various aspects of optic nerve sheath decompression for chronic papilledema in a variety of patients. Largely it was employed in obese females who developed chronic high intracranial pressure, which can lead to chronic papilledema and subsequent blindness due to compression of the optic nerves.

After establishing that I was comfortable with an academic career in 1973, my wife and I decided, for some reason, to move further away from the city to obtain a bigger house on a golf course. We moved from Mt. Lebanon to Upper St. Clair on the St. Clair Country Club golf course and I joined St. Clair Country Club as a social member. I enjoyed living on the golf course watching the kids grow up and attend school. At that time, we acquired a dog, a Lhasa Apso named Ruffles, who immediately became a member of the family. From 1973 until 1977, we lived in Upper St. Clair and during that time, the children advanced in school and we got involved in the social affairs of the community, which included regular parties. As a social member of St. Clair Country Club, I could only play golf once a month and I focused my attention on platform tennis, an outdoor winter sport that is a cross between racquet ball and tennis. It is a social sport and I enjoyed it very much, starting to play for the Upper St. Clair B team and traveling around the suburbs of Pittsburgh once a week in the winter to other clubs to compete in platform tennis. I did not pursue golf because the children were young and I wanted to be involved in their activities, which I did as a little league manager and then an assistant manager. I also was an umpire for my daughter's softball league. It was very interesting and enjoyable, although frustrating at times when parents got too involved with the children's activities. Ruffles had an unexpected litter of puppies, mixed breed, of course, which we were able to place with nice families. At that particular time, my wife became involved in real estate to supplement our income, which was reduced as the result of my returning to academics from a lucrative private practice. She worked hard on weekends and I filled in by taking care of the children when I was not working, which was from Saturday noon till Monday morning.

We had an unsettling robbery at gunpoint while living in Upper St. Clair. One night a thin young man with a gun (maybe fake) and a stocking mask entered our bedroom and demanded money. I jumped out of bed, rushing to the closet where I had a shotgun (unloaded of course) when my wife jumped out of bed and announced that she had $150 that she was going to use to take my mother, who was staying with us, to lunch. The robber agreed to take that money and marched us downstairs, where my wife took the money from her purse and threw it at him. He picked it up, marched us into the kitchen, and told us to turn away. Subsequently, just before leaving, he suggested we get a better lock for our sliding glass door. After he left, I ran for the shot gun, loaded it, and gave chase in my bare feet across the golf course, stepping on pine cones that fell from the pine trees behind our house, ending my chase.

The next day the police arrived and asked if I kept drugs in the house since no one had been robbed at gunpoint in Upper St. Clair for a long time. I replied sharply that I only had eye drops. We found out there was a troubled young man living across the golf course who was in special school for delinquents. I went to the school, and of course, couldn't recognize anyone because of the stocking mask. During the robbery, the dog didn't bark, and fortunately, my mother didn't wake up. No apprehension of the culprit ever occurred.

The First European Journey

In 1976, we felt financially secure enough to take a vacation. Mary Ellen had found a good elderly babysitter, Mrs. Matchet, who agreed to stay with the children and see that they got to school, to allow us to take a three-week trip through Europe. This trip whetted my appetite for further travel in the future. We had selected a tour by Globus, a European travel agency, which turned out to be an excellent choice for our first experience. We flew from Pittsburgh to New York and on to London, where we were met by the tour director, an Austrian studying banking. He was multilingual and an excellent tour guide. Later, in France, we were introduced to our bus driver who would take us all through Europe, a Dutchman who wore wooden shoes throughout the trip and was mostly interested in women, although he was a superb driver, getting us in and out of various difficult places all over Europe with ease. I would recommend a comprehensive tour of Europe for the first visit for anyone who is beginning to experience foreign travel.

Of course, this trip was economy class, so we arrived in London to stay at a modest hotel, outside the center of the city, but were exposed to the various parts of London, including Trafalgar square, the British Museum, and the changing of the guard at Buckingham Palace. We toured Windsor castle and had a tour of the Tower of London. We had free time to explore some of the streets of London; we were introduced to the pub life through a pub tour and visited several restaurants. The experience was good for a starter, but it was with a group of about 60, which made it somewhat trying at times. We proceeded from London through the English countryside to Dover, where we took a ferry across the English Channel to Calais. Upon landing at Calais, our driver brought a bus and with that we proceeded to Amsterdam, a delightful city. We were introduced to the canals of Amsterdam, the Reich's museum, and the neat restaurants. There are many interesting facets to Amsterdam and it is very colorful. One of the highlights of the trip was a visit to the Zuider Zee where I sampled herring fresh from the sea for the first time and saw the pretty Dutch houses and shops in the small towns of the land reclaimed from the sea. Another highlight was a trip to the flower market where wholesale flowers were sold at that time in the spring when we were there. It was fascinating to see the huge numbers of flowers being auctioned in this very large building. Again, we stayed at a modest hotel near the airport, which was very uninteresting, but comfortable. The bus proceeded then to Belgium and we stayed in Brussels, a beautiful city where we were able to tour the downtown area. The hotel there was more elegant and we took a side trip to Brugge, a walled city in western Belgium, which was a very busy sea port in the Middle Ages. It is an extremely charming place with beautiful indoor/outdoor restaurants, churches and shops. Surrounded by a moat, the city has many beautiful scenes. It is truly one of the most attractive places that I have seen in Europe. Brussels was a bustling city with charm, especially at night. We proceeded from Brussels to Paris and were introduced to Paris through another modest hotel. We had a complete bus tour of Paris and visited Notre Dame and the Louvre, and had a side trip to Versailles. Paris is charming and quite beautiful. It requires several days to appreciate its charm, but we were only there for two days. We did manage to sample the night life in the Moulin Rouge where we saw the beautiful long-legged French dancers. We also spent part of the day at Montmartre, the art district of Paris, which is not to be missed. Various artists demonstrate their works around a central park. The art was varied and interesting, with many French scenes, and was affordable.

From Paris we went into Germany to Cologne for a brief stop and saw the large cathedral. We proceeded south to take a day river cruise on the Rhine River, with high hills and beautiful castles on both sides. We then went to Heidelberg and toured the castle on the hill above the city with spectacular views. From Heidelberg, we went through the Black Forest to the Rhine Falls near the beginning of the Rhine River.

We went on to Switzerland through Zurich and stayed in Basel, the home of Rolex watches. It is a beautiful city with a lake and a pier projecting onto the lake, where entertainment was provided by musicians with a beautiful long Swiss horn. The hotel was very comfortable and very European with a bidet, my first exposure to that bathroom appliance which was not popular in the United States. I bought a stainless steel Rolex watch on a visit to the factory, which was much appreciated by the guides because I believe they profited from the sale. Apparently, there was some argument over who would get what part of the cut from the sale of the watch. I wore that watch for many years and have recently had it restored by returning it to the factory; it is as good as ever, an excellent time piece that I acquired for $600 dollars at that time. We enjoyed Switzerland immensely, bussing through the Swiss Alps on our way to Salzburg, Austria. We stopped in Lichtenstein, a small country between Switzerland and Austria, which is identified by the cows wearing colorful bells around their necks as they maneuver around the fields. This is a picturesque small country and then we proceeded on to Salzburg, where we stayed at a beautiful hotel outside of the city, but overlooking it. Salzburg is another beautiful city, one of the highlights in Europe and we toured it quickly in one and a half days. We walked around the walls of the city and spent time in the shops inside the city. We had dinner in a restaurant overlooking the city, because our guide had many connections there. The meal was excellent and the view was gorgeous. From Salzburg we proceeded to the Danube River, where we took a cruise down to Vienna in one day. The Danube River is not as spectacular as the Rhine. Upon arriving in Vienna, we stayed at a hotel in the city and had lunch at the Hotel Sochar, which is the originator of the Sacré Torte, a dessert famous in Vienna. We were able to see the Vienna woods and attended a violin concert in the park. One of the interesting side trips in Vienna was a tour to a village outside of the city where we had dinner and tasted the Viennese day wines, which are fresh wines of the current year. They are mostly white wines and are slightly sweet, but do not age well. They are practically non-drinkable in the second year of their life. They were very complimentary of the Austrian food and we enjoyed the experience. From Vienna we went through the mountains of southern Austria into northeastern Italy and passed through the mountains of northeastern Italy, arriving in Venice late at night. We stayed at a hotel outside Venice and were taken into Venice by bus and gondola. It was my first experience in Venice, which I thought was a very interesting and beautiful city with its canals, but rather sad in that it is gradually sinking into the sea and some of the buildings show their age. However, the square in Venice and the city center are very interesting, together with the Bridge of Sighs. After a quick trip through Venice, we proceeded by bus to Florence, again having only a one-day stay. Florence requires more time, but this trip did not allow for that. My wife stayed in Florence for the day and I took a side trip to a walled city, Sienna, where they have colorful horse races once a year represented by horses from different sections of the community. This is a pretty, medieval town and the story of the yearly race is most interesting. We met again in Rome at a modest hotel and had tours of Rome including the ancient Roman ruins of the Colosseum, the pantheon, and the Spanish steps. Rome is a fascinating city and requires a great deal of time to cover it. Our trip was so quick that after a day we were taken south to Naples and toured the ruins of Pompeii, which was destroyed by the Vesuvius volcano and then quickly returned to Rome where we were then put on a plane for our return home. It was a whirlwind trip and I would recommend it as a starter, but that is the last time that I ever considered such an ambitious romp through any continent or country.

The Sewickley Journey

It was about 1977 that we discovered that our children were not suited for the open classroom approach that was being practiced in Upper St. Clair. They were not doing very well in some of their courses and after having them tested in math and english, we found out that they were not up to speed in either of those important subjects. Therefore, we decided to sell our house in Upper St. Clair and move to Sewickley, where the kids entered Sewickley Academy, a private co-educational prep school. My son entered the seventh grade and my daughter the eighth grade. We rented a house in Sewickley Heights owned by a banker who was spending part of the year in London. I decided to build a house in Sewickley Heights and found a lot off Spanish Tract Road on Lee Road, which was owned by a prominent Sewickley native who was very wealthy and whose family had been in Sewickley for many years. In order to buy the five-acre lot, which was wooded, I had to have an interview with the owner of the land. It turned out that he was a naval aviator and since I had been a flight surgeon in the Navy, the interview was very brief and I acquired a five-acre lot in Sewickley

Heights. I found a builder through our real estate agent, Prescott Cole, who arranged for the sale of the lot and an architect who worked with the builder. Our builder was Murray Rust and the architect Don Montgomery. The builder and the architect proposed a modern home of wood with a lot of glass and it turned out extremely well. The house had a deck in back and a beautiful living room and dining room with a large family room-kitchen. It was finished in January of 1978 and we moved in. I enjoyed that house as much as any in which I had ever lived. In 1979, we were selected for a commercial by Hungry Man Frozen Foods, which featured three of the Steelers: L.C. Greenwood, Joe Green and Rocky Blier, to be performed in our kitchen. The company brought in all of their equipment and filmed the scene from our family room into our kitchen. I took my children out of school and invited all the neighbors and we had a marvelous day lunching with the professional football players and enjoying the experience of watching a commercial being filmed. Although much equipment was brought in the house, we only suffered a little damage, which they paid for and included a check for our inconvenience. The children did very well at Sewickley Academy, compared to Upper St. Clair. My daughter got involved with theater productions and held the lead in a show that required her to sing; I was surprised to learn that she did quite well. My son played lacrosse and soccer and developed physically. He was not a great student, but he was exposed to smaller classrooms and his grades were satisfactory. It was in Sewickley that the kids learned to drive through the school driver's program. They did well and I bought a large Jeep Wagoneer we called "the tank" for them to drive. I felt safer with them driving a large vehicle than riding with their friends in smaller cars. My daughter elected to go to Hollin's college which she entered in 1981 and Jeff selected Wake Forest which he entered in 1982. I acquired a Volkswagen for her and gave him my Honda Prelude—each in their sophomore years after successfully completing their freshman years at college.

In 1979 we decided to buy a house in Kiawah Island, South Carolina after visiting the island on a previous occasion. I liked the island with its many attractive aspects including two beautiful golf courses and a wide beach. Through a lottery we acquired a turtle house on stilts about 200 yards from the ocean, an easy walk. We bought it with our friends Phyllis and Tom Bisceglia and enjoyed it on three occasions, but I sold it for a profit following my separation from Mary Ellen in the fall of 1981. Fortunately, the turtle house brought a handsome profit which, together with my 1979 Honda Prelude, was the only thing I took from the marriage.

Digression #1

In March 1980, I spoke at a meeting in the Snow Bird Ski Resort outside of Salt Lake City, Utah. I took Nancy during spring break with me to experience western skiing. I had been to Park City, Utah for a previous meeting and found the skiing exceptional. We skied several times during the afternoons after the meetings; on the last day while in a mogul field in the neighboring resort with my daughter (I shouldn't have been there), I fell and injured my right knee. I was taken from the mountains on a sled head-first downhill, a harrowing experience. The injury was a bad sprain of the medial collateral ligament and I returned home on crutches with Nancy's help. Later that year I re-injured the knee in a paddle tennis game and had to have open knee surgery in late December 1980, a painful experience. Following recovery, I began on an exercise program that I have maintained today, which has strengthened my whole body.

During Christmas vacation in 1983, I took Jeff scuba diving to Bimini Island in the Bahamas. I had qualified as a scuba diver in 1978, following a course at the Sewickley YMCA followed by an open water dive at Cat Island in the Bahamas. Jeff completed a scuba course at Wake Forest, so we made several dives at Bimini, including a drift dive along a beautiful coral wall. We spent an interesting New Year's Eve at a bar in the economy class hotel and returned home with a good experience, which I thought best for Jeff following my marriage separation.

The Life-Changing Journey

In June 1980, I went for an insurance physical and found out that I had elevated blood pressure. As a result, I underwent an intravenous pyelogram that resulted in discovery of a lesion in my left kidney that was interpreted as a tumor. I previously had surgery to remove a calculus in the left kidney in the mid-1970s. This occurred at the time of the orbital society meeting in Bermuda run by my mentor, Mel Alper. However, I was advised that unless I had immediate surgery, I was risking further progression of this small coin-like lesion in the left kidney. I was devastated by the diagnosis and submitted to a left nephrectomy by George Berg, a very competent urologist and friend. The kidney was uneventfully removed and the diagnosis was renal cell carcinoma, although a discussion ensued about whether it was really a benign lesion called an oncocytoma. Nevertheless, I had lost my left kidney and had a brush with cancer, which devastated me that year. Two months later my mother died at age 84, which was also a significant loss because she was a wonderful person and we had been close during the ten years following my father's death. We frequently visited her, so that she could interact with the children. 1980 became a pivotal year as I again considered my future options based on the fact that I thought that my five-year survival was questionable. I talked to the chairman of the department then, Stuart Brown, a corneal specialist who had taken over the department in 1973, two years after the resignation of Ken Richardson, who had elected to leave the department and move to Anchorage, Alaska with his wife and adopted children. I believe that his motive was to be closer to his family and to avoid the stresses of the academic life.

Following the bout with cancer, I asked him to take Tom Slamovits, who had trained at the University of Pittsburgh back with me as a partner after he finished his fellowship with Ron Burde in St. Louis as a more classic neuro-ophthalmologist. Brown did not think that I needed a partner, but I was feeling insecure about my future and I did not want to leave the department vacant. Therefore, Tom Slamovits joined me and we had a partnership in neuro-ophthalmology and continued to train fellows. Tom fit into the department quite well as he had done his residency in Pittsburgh, but we had a different style and approach to the sub-specialty. He was more deliberate and tended much more to detailed discussion of various aspects of the patients' problems, whereas I was always oriented toward efficient, timely diagnosis and decision-making. I am more comfortable with a brisk approach to problems and I do not think that this jeopardized my ability to make diagnoses or to decide on treatment over the years. However, I have a different style from most neuro-ophthalmologists who are much more deliberate, taking as long as an hour with each patient, which I could never tolerate.

Following Tom's arrival, we took two fellows in the same year. I decided to increase to two because of Tom's appearance and because we had two excellent candidates, Patrick Sibony, who was previously trained by Simmons Lessel at Harvard and Howard Krause, who came with an excellent background during his residency in ophthalmology at UCLA. Both of these fellows were superb and certainly helped me during the early years following the bout with cancer. Howard was more surgically oriented than Pat, but each had an interesting year with a lot of academic endeavors being completed during that year. They also related well with Tom Slamovits.

In the spring of 1981, I met Pat Williamson, the ophthalmic office manager for my friends Dick Katzin and Frank Cignetti, at a Pennsylvania Academy of Ophthalmology meeting in Bedford, Pennsylvania and, rather quickly, decided to pursue a life with her. My marriage had never been strong and my wife and I both knew it. However, it was a shock to her when I decided to change partners. It was not done very well and it was one of the darker parts of my life, although I am very happy with the choice of a second mate who has been with me for many years. Pat and I left our spouses and wound up living with Joe Maroon, who had also left his wife. We lived in his house in Point Breeze, which was nearly devoid of furniture, that having been taken by his wife to Chicago where she lived. We slept on the third floor on a remaining bed and we had most of our evening meals together, which was delightful in that we helped each other, being a threesome. Joe had no special person at that time and was dating different women, so we occasionally had a fourth, but we did get through a difficult time with our close friendship. Finally, Pat moved into an apartment in Shadyside and because I was troubled with guilt, I rented a townhouse from Bart Mondino, a member of the Department of Ophthalmology specializing in cornea and external diseases, trained by Stuart Brown, who elected to return to his home town, Los Angeles, taking a position at UCLA. He eventually went on to become the department chairman at UCLA and is an accomplished academician. I kept his apartment for about six months. It was in a rather depressing area, although it had a view over the Monongahela river. I liked the view and when an opportunity came to buy a condominium on Mt. Washington overlooking the city of Pittsburgh and the rivers, I elected to buy it because it had been significantly reduced in price as they were trying to close out the building. It was on the ninth floor and the view from this two-story condominium was magnificent. I moved into the building in December of 1982 and then went to Egypt, where I was invited to speak by the surgeon general of Egyptian Air Force, having previously operated on his wife, who had an optic nerve sheath meningioma which extended intracranially.

The Egyptian Journey

In December 1982, I took my children to Egypt with me because my own trip and that of one guest was paid for by the Egyptian government. I was able to afford the trip with the children, and felt that it might soften the blow of my leaving the household. The trip was very interesting. I had traveled to Egypt previously with my wife, as a guest of my former fellow Mohammed El-Hoshey. Our first trip to Cairo was interesting, but I had lost my luggage at the airport and had to return to the airport to claim it, an uncomfortable experience. On our first trip in 1979, we stayed in a French hotel, the Meridien, on an island in the Nile River and were entertained by my former fellow, Mohammed El-Hoshey and his sister, who is a travel agent. We saw the highlights of Cairo, especially the pyramids, and had a pleasant experience as a guest of my fellow in his home. I lectured at the hospital in Cairo and met the surgeon general whose wife I had seen in the United States.

On that same trip, we also flew to Israel and went to Jerusalem, where I lectured. We were able to tour the city, including the Wailing Wall, and traveled south to Masada, the high cliff fortress defended by the Jews against the Romans in the first century A.D. It was a spectacular site and we bathed in the salty Dead Sea on the way back to Jerusalem, passing through Jericho where we examined the old ruins. We flew to Elat on the Red Sea, where I enjoyed scuba diving with a pretty Dutch woman instructor.

When I was invited back to Egypt with the children, by the surgeon general, we arrived in the middle of the night to be escorted from the plane by the military—bypassing all of the immigration process— taken to a special room where we were given soft drinks, and awaited our luggage. When our passports were cleared, we were taken by military vehicle to our hotel in Cairo, where we were able to sleep for about six hours, after which I had to lecture to the Air Force ophthalmology group that following afternoon. Needless to say, jet lag was a factor at that time. However, following the lecture, my children and I were taken on a much more comprehensive tour of Cairo, with a Colonel in the Egyptian Air Force who was a surgeon. In addition, he was a very good tour guide and showed us the highlights of Cairo including the old city market, the City of the Dead, the great pyramids in detail including a camel ride for the kids. We viewed the pyramids and the sphinx at night during a spectacular light show. The next day I was asked to evaluate a pilot who had one upper lid retracted from mild Graves' eye disease. He was a Colonel in the Air Force and a leader of a flight group. They were about to ground him because of slight lid retraction, because he did not look right. He had no double vision and was perfectly functional. I advised them to let him fly, but they refused. I suggested then that they correct his lid position and they agreed that I should do it. I operated on him in the Air Force hospital in a non air-conditioned operating room, with open windows, a canvas gown and no gloves. My assistant was a contact lens specialist who knew nothing about surgery. I everted the upper eyelid and removed an auxiliary upper lid muscle called Mueller's muscle, which was a rather bloody operation because they did not have a cautery. By using many sponges and much patience I completed the operation and then was taken for lunch to the Air Force Military Club on the Nile river. It was in a beautiful building with a great view of the river. Halfway through the meal, I discovered that although I washed my hands thoroughly following surgery, there was some blood that had dripped down onto my elbow. I quickly went to the men's room and removed the remains of my experience at surgery. That experience virtually cured me of operating in another center without my own equipment and personnel. The Egyptians, however, could not have been more gracious and they asked me to see the pilot the next day. Fortunately, his lid was in excellent position and they agreed to allow him to resume his flight status.

I delivered several lectures in Cairo and then the kids and I were escorted on a beautiful trip to Luxor and the Aswan Dam. Luxor is a magnificent place near the Nile River where the tombs of the pharaohs were dug into the mountains. We were crossing the river to the tombs of Luxor when I saw a Mercedes Benz on the shore. I thought to myself that someone important must be arriving since they had an air-conditioned car ready. It turned out that the Mercedes was for us; my children and I were taken by air-conditioned car to visit the tombs dug into the mountains, including King Tut's tomb in the Valley of the Kings. The experience could not have been more exciting for the children and I was very impressed. We returned to Luxor, stayed at the hotel, visited the ancient Luxor temple, and then proceeded to the Aswan dam, where we stayed in the Cataract hotel overlooking the groups of islands and the river which are called Cataracts, the name being derived from obstruction to flowing water such as was the case of the multiple islands in the Nile river at Aswan. We returned to Cairo and then were taken to the Suez Canal where we lunched in the officer's club, watching boats pass by in the Suez Canal. Again, it was very impressive for the children. We returned to Cairo and then proceeded to Alexandria where we were joined by one of my former fellows' relatives who showed us all of Alexandria, including an ancient archeological site where a famous lighthouse was located. Upon our return to Cairo, we stayed over night and visited the Cairo Museum, which was magnificent, containing the mummies of previous pharaohs and many other ancient Egyptian relics. We returned to the United States with fond memories of our friends and experiences in Egypt. I don't think the children will ever forget it.

The Mt. Washington Journey

I returned to the condominium in Mt. Washington in January of 1983. In February, Pat left her apartment in Shadyside and—after a brief time living with a friend—joined me in Mt. Washington, where we began our life together. During the year of the move, my fellow was Steve Dresner who came from Louisiana University Ophthalmology Department at the request of Henry Van Dyke, a friend and colleague who was a classic neuro-ophthalmologist of high caliber. Steve and Paul Rekhoff, our design engineer, helped me move my few belongings from the townhouse in Greenfield to the condominium in Mt. Washington. Steve had an interesting and productive year. He wrote an article on non-specific orbital inflammation, which has proven to be of long-term interest, frequently referenced. He went on to obtain a second fellowship with Francois Codère in Montreal, Canada and then moved to Los Angeles where he set up practice as an ophthalmic plastic surgeon with neuro-ophthalmic interests. Howard Krause had returned to UCLA following a period with the University of Texas at Dallas because his family and his wife's family are from Los Angeles. Howard was neuro-ophthalmologically oriented; he and Steve both are on the faculty at UCLA. Pat Sibony, who had been with Howard Krause, went to the State University of New York at Stoneybrook, where he eventually became Chairman of the Department of Ophthalmology.

We acquired more furniture and completed the decorating of the condominium, including the kitchen, which I designed. Mt. Washington was a delightful place to live, and we began to experience the advantages of city living, including a number of close restaurants, and the convenience of department store shopping. We attended many of the city's events during the years that we lived in the condominium, including the Three Rivers Regatta several times. We had a couple of Fourth of July and New Year's Eve parties because of the spectacular fireworks display clearly seen from our condo. We never tired of the exquisite view of Pittsburgh from Mt. Washington through our two-story windows.

The Bermuda Journey

In May1982, Pat and I decided to attend the International Neuro-Ophthalmology Conference in Bermuda. Joe Maroon and his first wife, Cindy, accompanied us as he and I were presenting a paper on orbital surgery at the conference. We arrived in Bermuda and were taken to the Pink Princess Hotel in the downtown area of the capital city of Bermuda. The hotel was magnificent and it was the first real trip that Pat and I had taken together. We toured Bermuda thoroughly and enjoyed the conference. We particularly enjoyed the motor scooters that are prominent in Bermuda as cars are very restricted to permanent resident ownership. We went across the bay to the other Pink Princess Hotel on the beach and played tennis in the magnificent weather. I was able to scuba dive on two ship-wrecks, which was a great experience. There are many shipwrecks aground around Bermuda, all available for scuba diving.

We loved our experience in Bermuda, the people, the food and the atmosphere. It is one place to which I wanted to return and repeat the experience. It is very beautiful and weather in the late spring was terrific.

In 1983 - 84, I trained Walter Hartel, recommended by Tom Spoor, who came from the Air Force for neuro-ophthalmology and orbital disease training. Eventually he returned to the Air Force to complete his obligation and then joined a practice in Dayton, Ohio. Walter is a very talented surgeon and diagnostician and I had always been a little disappointed that he did not pursue an academic career, but he is a very successful neuro-ophthalmic surgeon in Dayton, Ohio.

The Acting Chairmanship Journey

To digress, the Eye & Ear Hospital was founded in the late 1940s and developed in the 1950s and 60s, because of the inability of ophthalmologists and otorhinolaryngologists to obtain hospital admissions and surgery time for their patients, being superceded by surgeons who claimed that their patients were more emergent. For that reason, during the time when Ophthalmic and ENT surgery required a hospital admission and a rather lengthy hospital stay, the Eye & Ear Hospital was established and flourished. During the 1970s as I was developing my career, the rapid improvement in Ophthalmic and ENT surgery gradually reduced the hospital census to the point where the Eye & Ear Hospital was threatened for its existence. At that time, many changes were made and floors were altered to accommodate other activities. Administrators were blamed for the loss of admissions and there were changes in the hierarchy of the hospital, to no avail. The days of the Eye & Ear Hospital were inevitably numbered. During the early 70s, as a young assistant professor, I was able to acquire three houses on Lothrop street across from the Eye & Ear Hospital, which I sold, on the recommendation of Ken Richardson, the chairman at the time, with a slight profit to the Eye & Ear Hospital. This enabled them to obtain a foothold in the block between Montefiore and Presbyterian hospitals, where future development would occur. The medical center eventually bought the rest of the houses on that block and as the Eye & Ear Hospital deteriorated, plans were made to build an Eye & Ear Institute on that property.

In 1982, Stuart Brown, partially blamed for the decrease of in-patient care of ophthalmology, was asked to leave the department. He obtained the chairmanship at the University of California at San Diego. That began a dark period in my career as I was named Acting Chairman, a job that I would not wish on my worst enemy. The deterioration of Eye & Ear Hospital continued and I was unable to recruit further full-time staff to improve ophthalmologist census and activities in the operating room. The retinal service comprised of Lou Lobes and Bernie Doft was particularly difficult to manage at that time as they were providing a great deal of income, but were salaried, as were the rest of the full-time faculty. I did manage to distribute the bonuses at the end of the year to members who were clinically productive, easing the situation somewhat, but it was never satisfactory. Sometimes during meetings with administrators and board members when I was Acting Chairman, I thought I should be wearing a gun. I was a candidate for the Chairmanship and I think I hurt my chances by being the Acting Chairman at a difficult time. In the end, the Chairmanship went to Richard Thoft, a corneal specialist from Harvard who was prominent in research. After he arrived in July of 1984, I decided that I had to leave the institution.

It so happened that in 1984, Joe Maroon left the Department of Neuro-surgery to begin his own department at Allegheny General Hospital, encouraging me to join him in that institution, which had become quite prosperous and was promoting the neuro-sciences. I looked into other chairmanships, but decided that I would prefer to start from scratch, so to speak, at Allegheny, which had no Department of Ophthalmology at that time. It had a small division run by Bob Nickeson, comprised of private practitioners who held a clinic for senior residents who rotated from the University of Pittsburgh, mainly supervising their surgery as required. The clinic was practically run by the senior resident who was rotated to Allegheny General with minimum supervision. Therefore, there was no such thing as a significant presence of ophthalmology at Allegheny General.

My last fellow at the Eye & Ear Hospital was Floyd Warren, from New York, a pleasant, hard-working fellow, who returned to New York to practice neuro-ophthalmic surgery with Mark Kupersmith, a neuro-ophthalmologist who sent him to me to train, particularly in the surgical aspects of our programs.

The India Journey

During 1984, my last year as Acting Chairman at Eye & Ear Hospital, I was invited to speak in India by Dr. Nagpal of Amenabad. He stated that if I could provide transportation for myself and my companion, he would see that we were entertained and taken care of in India. I negotiated with him a situation in which I would lecture in Amenabad, but would also lecture in other major cities, hosted by the local ophthalmologists and housed by them in hotels or clubs. To my surprise, he agreed and Pat and I took one of the most interesting trips of our lives. We then began a series of international journeys that we have enjoyed very much. Of course, my portion of the trip was supported by the University of Pittsburgh Department of Ophthalmology; in my unhappy situation as Acting Chairman, I was trying to travel as much as possible.

We flew to New York and in coach seats took the long trip to Bombay, India. We arrived in the middle of the night and were besieged by baggage handlers, a frightening experience. We managed to fight our way to the curb side with some baggage handlers, whom we tipped, and found a taxi that took us through the very dark streets of Bombay on an unsettling ride to the Taj Mahal Palace Hotel near the famous Gateway to India on the Bay. It was a magnificent hotel, like an oasis in the desert. The lobby was beautiful and the pleasant night clerk took us to our room. We were advised not to drink the water, but to brush our teeth only with bottled water and avoid the fresh vegetables and fruits that were uncooked. We heeded his advice carefully and spent a pleasant night at the hotel, relaxing from our arduous trip. The next day, we awoke to a view of the beautiful arch monument, called the Gateway to India, beside our hotel. That day we visited Elephanta Island across the bay from Bombay, which contained the ruins of a Buddhist shrine and was populated by monkeys and people who dressed up in native costumes to be photographed for a price. The island was beautiful, very hot, and the boat ride across and back was spectacular, with views of Bombay. We toured the city the next day and saw the huge market place. The poverty in India is overwhelming and the only things to look for in that country, in my opinion, are ancient artifacts and the magnificent buildings that were developed in the past. The next day we flew east to a small Indian city, Aurangabad, and stayed in a beautiful hotel. There we hired a guide to take us to the Ajanta and Ellora caves, which were built prior to the 10th century A.D. This was a splendid experience, unequaled anywhere else in the world. The Ajanta caves were a series of caves and large carved religious structures along a shelf at the side of a large canyon. The Ellora caves were characterized by a huge religious structure that was carved out of a mountain beginning at the top and working down. The various rooms and statues were impressive as to the enormous amount of work and skill required to develop them. The statues were very erotic, which created a great deal of interest among the tourists. The Hindu religion is somewhat erotic, with sex being considered a very natural part of the religious experience.

We returned to Bombay and then proceeded on to Amenabad, where we arrived in the early evening after a short plane ride. We were taken to a city club, where our host Dr. Nagpal was a member, a one-story structure with a courtyard and very plain, simple rooms. There was a swimming pool in the back, but Pat was concerned about the fact that the shower was allowed to spread all over the bathroom floor, not being contained by a shower stall. There were also some rather large insects in the area around the pool.

For that reason, she insisted that we look at other possibilities and we were taken by a three-wheeled motorcycle around Amenabad to look at other hotels. We looked at one which was quite terrible and then the next one, which looked promising, but when we entered the room, there were huge cockroaches running all over the walls, so we quietly elected to return to Dr. Nagpal's club, where we had a rather pleasant three days. The day following our arrival, I lectured at the auditorium in the university center. It was unique in that there was no ceiling over most of the auditorium and that bird droppings covered the podium and the stage. Milton Boniak of Houston was so distraught by this that he insisted on lecturing first and then left Amenabad to travel to Singapore for the rest of his trip. I thought it was rather amusing and enjoyed the camaraderie of the Indian physicians and their wives. We were taken that night to a dinner in the country, where we found that the entire area was grass or dirt and that we had food that was cooked over an open fire. It was a pleasant area and there was a neat gift shop. This was supposed to be an experience that was typically Indian. Pat and I found it refreshing and amusing, and the vegetarian food was excellent.

An ophthalmic plastic surgeon from Syracuse, Jim Boynton, accompanied us while in Amenabad and he was also delighted with the experience. Following the meeting, Jim, Pat and I were taken by Dr. Nagpal, our host, on a bus to a hill station, which is a resort on top of a high hill overlooking a wide plain about 100 miles east of Amenabad. During the trip, we stopped at the largest dairy farm in India and toured the dairy; we were shown all of the procedures used in processing the milk. We had a fantastic lunch at the owner's house on the property. Of course, that was the last time that Pat would be able to go to the bathroom, so she elected not to drink anything, knowing we had a long ride to the hill station. Indeed, it was a long passage with some stops where the men could get out and relieve themselves along the side of the road, but as the only woman, Pat was trapped. There were animals all over the road and we stopped several times while trains passed in front of us. Finally we began the climb to the hill station, which was truly spectacular going around and around this large isolated hill until we reached the top and found our hotel, which was a pleasant surprise. The rooms were comfortable, so we began to party with the Indian Ophthalmologists. Despite the fact that alcohol was forbidden in Amenabad and most of India, as a local rule, these doctors brought along several bottles of scotch and other liquors, so we had a great cocktail party in the hotel at the hill station. The next day, we toured the hill-top resort, which had magnificent views over the plains of central India, and visited a Jain temple with its unusual religious figurines, magnificent tapestries, and colorful altars. We also took a cruise on a beautiful lake during the evening with music and delightful colored lights surrounding the lake. The next day, we walked around the area and enjoyed the local crafts and various unusual structures. We then returned to Amenabad in the same bus and flew on to Jaipur, the next stop in our journey.

At Jaipur we were hosted by local Ophthalmologists, who arranged for us to travel with a guide to the Pink Palace, a beautiful structure outside Jaipur high on a hill. We arrived by car to the base of the hill, but then proceeded to the top of the hill on the backs of elephants. We had a tour of the magnificent palace and its rooms, with history being described by the local guide, and then rode down the hill on the elephants. In Jaipur, we were able to purchase a silk carpet that was sent by the craft store to the United States; we still treasure it today. I lectured in Jaipur and was hosted at a lunch by the local ophthalmologists. Poor Pat sat through my lectures all over India and, I think, was getting tired of seeing the bloody pictures of the patients on whom we had operated. I use dramatic pictures to keep the attention of the physicians to whom I am lecturing, and this method has worked very well over the years. We then proceeded to Delhi, where we were supposed to catch a plane to Agra, the home of the Taj Mahal. Unfortunately, our plane was delayed in Jaipur and we missed the flight to Agra. We asked for a refund, which we were able to acquire after a long argument, and hired a guide with a car to take us from Delhi to Agra. This proved to be an interesting experience. The driver was a Sikh, with the traditional turban, and an excellent driver who avoided one possible catastrophe after another until we arrived safely in the beautiful city of Agra in a hotel close to the Taj Mahal.

The morning after we arrived, we went to view the Taj Mahal in the early morning light. It was magnificent, probably the most magnificent structure that I have seen. The sunlight danced over the structure lighting it in a beautiful way, including the reflecting pools. We spent at least two hours at the Taj Mahal and then returned to the hotel where we were taken to a luncheon by the local ophthalmologist, which was followed by one of my lectures. The local group was very attentive and Pat and I felt quite welcome. That evening we returned to the hotel and had cocktails with a couple we met; the husband was a reporter in New Delhi for an English newspaper. He and his wife suggested that we all go to see the Taj Mahal at night, which was another absolutely fascinating experience. It appears completely different at night and it is mesmerizing. Certainly it is an edifice that is unequal in beauty, built by a rich man in memory of his wife.

The next day we went to Madras where we were met by one of the members of the Ophthalmology Community and taken to his eye hospital, the front door of which was shaped like an eyeball. This is a truly unique structure and is the design of the ophthalmologist who built the hospital. It is very well-equipped and modern. I lectured at the hospital to the local Ophthalmology group and then we had some time to tour Madras and see the coast of the Bay of Bengal. Unfortunately, we did not have time to tour the tropical area surrounding Madras; we were told it was fascinating, particularly the ancient ruins south of the city.

. We were housed in a very adequate hotel and taken to dinner at a club to which the owner of the Eye Hospital belonged. The food was excellent in the club. Pat and I discovered on our tour of India that the vegetables, prepared in a variety of different ways, were excellent, but that meat and fish were less desirable. We finally figured out that if we practically became vegetarians, we could enjoy the food in India, providing it was well-cooked. The seasonings, especially Saffron, are interesting and tasteful.

After our short visit to Madras, we went New Delhi where we toured the city for two days. We were hosted in New Delhi by the local Ophthalmology Community and I lectured to them followed by an invitation to the spectacular home of a local ophthalmologist. He had a collection of small chests, in which were smaller chests, in which were small dolls. They were exquisite miniature carvings and we enjoyed the experience very much. It was a very private collection and we were able to view it in the confines of the master bedroom with the family members.

New Delhi is the beautiful, crowded capital of India and is home to the Red Fort, which was built after the construction of the Taj Mahal by the same wealthy Indian. It is a spectacular structure with high walls and various interesting parts, including the area where the Rajah held court and pronounced sentences on people who were then punished in a variety of ways. One of the crudest we learned at a ancient fort outside Delhi was that the victim was stomped by an elephant. The fort was also the prison of the builder of the Taj Mahal for a while in the latter part of his life.

The streets of New Delhi were very crowded and poverty was everywhere. One had to focus continually on the magnificent masonry and stone edifices of the ancient age to appreciate the potential of India. We did pass Indira Ghandi's villa, but were unable to stop because of security. She was assassinated shortly after we returned home.

We left India and went north to Nepal because of my interest in seeing the mountainous country and seeing Mount Everest. We flew into Nepal and were taken to a hotel that housed the only gambling casino in southern Asia. The hotel was magnificent, but the gambling casino was extremely crowded and rather small. After a brief visit to observe some of the people crowded around the table, I felt that I would be better off not participating.

We did thoroughly tour the capital and some surrounding towns and found that the ancient edifices of Nepal were wooden, as contrasted with the stone and mason edifices in India. They were magnificently structured, but showed more signs of age. Of course, in Nepal or India, all Hindu temples were forbidden to non-believers, but we were able to see them from the outside and peek into the interior from the doorways.

We happened to arrive in Nepal when they were slaughtering cows as a religious ritual that occurred once a year. Normally, in Nepal as well as India, cows are considered sacred and not harmed. They litter the roads and people give way to them in the streets. It was an unpleasant experience seeing the slaughter of a cow by these people who normally worship them.

In Nepal, from Kathmandu, we were able to fly with the Nepalese Air Force to Mount Everest. We viewed it from the side of Nepal, but could not fly around it because the other side was on Chinese territory. However, the day was clear and the view from the airplane was magnificent. We were even allowed to go up in the cockpit and get a panoramic view of Mount Everest and take whatever photos we wanted. The airplane was an old C-47, the workhorse of the U.S. Air Force during World War II. The Nepalese pilots were good, but very casual. We were glad to return to Kathmandu and get back on the ground.

The following day we toured some smaller towns in the countryside, which also had wooden temples and municipal edifices that were quite beautiful. We bought some artifacts in Nepal, both religious and decorative. One of the them was a dagger, with the sheath decorated by gem stone and metal plaques that eventually fell off after returning to the United States. Apparently it was not very well made. We left Nepal and returned to New Delhi to stay one night in a hotel and rest, prior to beginning the long trip home through Qatar, to London, then on to the United States.

We reflected after our return on the myriad of experiences that we had and that we were lucky to avoid any kind of ill-health while touring India.

The Ontario Journey

In May 1985 while preparing to leave the Department of Ophthalmology, I was invited to participate with Al Putterman in a lecture honoring Wendell Hughes, a famous oculoplastic surgeon from the University of Western Ontario. Al and I arrived in London, Ontario and were housed in a very nice estate owned by the university. We each were assigned to a host, mine being a second-year resident, Garry Condon, who was from Newfoundland. He was a very gracious and personable host and told me that he was interested in a glaucoma fellowship in the United States. At that time, I was planning the Department of Ophthalmology at Allegheny General Hospital and told him that I would be looking for a glaucoma specialist for the department in 1986 or 1987. He said that he would contact me in the future if he could acquire his training and was still interested.

The whole experience in western Ontario was fantastic. The lectures by Al Putterman and I went very well and the audience was very attentive and hospitable. We attended a party at a country club where I met one of the older ophthalmologists, Charley Thompson, who took me under his wing and insisted that I try fly fishing, for which I had previously had lessons in western Pennsylvania. The day following the lecture, Charley took me to a pond where I was able to catch several trout, which he insisted on having cleaned and packed for the trip back to the United States. Actually, somehow, I got through customs with the trout not being inspected by the customs agents, who were more interested in my specialty of neuro-ophthalmic surgery. I returned home with the trout, which surprised Pat (who knew that I was not a particularly good fisherman) and we enjoyed them thoroughly.

Digression #2

Nancy graduated from Hollins College in Virginia in June 1985 and Jeff, from Wake Forest in North Caroline in June 1986. Both graduations were well-done, with good speakers. Nancy then moved to Florida to work in her field of computer science and Jeff, who graduated in Spanish and politics, took a job with *National Geographic* Magazine in Washington, D.C.

The Allegheny Journey

I negotiated with Allegheny General Hospital, with the help of Joe Maroon, and obtained a contract where the new Ophthalmology Program would have Departmental status and would grow to a full-service, academic, research and clinically-oriented department. I developed the Department in the east wing at Allegheny General Hospital during late 1984 and most of 1985, leaving the University on October 31, 1985 to begin my career as Chairman of the Department of Ophthalmology at Allegheny General Hospital. I took with me my current fellow, Jim Garrity, from the Mayo Clinic who was a gregarious, friendly and bright individual who soon knew almost everything about Allegheny General Hospital and Sandra Sabloski, my secretary. We managed to integrate ourselves into the system. In our beginning at Allegheny, they did not even know how to spell ophthalmology and still struggle with that a little bit today. Jim and I were running an 8500-square-foot department with ten examining rooms and about six full-time personnel, including Tony Zanandria, who helped develop the department while I was still at the Eye & Ear Hospital. The beginning was interesting and challenging and I began to recruit additional staff in 1986.

The first subspecialist that I tried to recruit was in glaucoma. I interviewed two or three glaucomatologists and for one reason or another, they chose not to come to Pittsburgh.

I was becoming quite frustrated in 1987. The reason to recruit a glaucomatologist first was that there was the least competition for that sub-specialty in Pittsburgh. Just at that time, I received a phone call from Garry Condon, who told me that he was completing his fellowship and asked whether I was still interested in a glaucomatologist. I immediately encouraged him to come to Pittsburgh for a visit and after intense consideration on his part, he decided to accept my invitation to begin his sub-specialty practice in the Department of Ophthalmology. He was my first recruit and it was fortuitous that we had met previously and I instantly liked him. He was the cornerstone of the growth of the department and thereafter recruiting was easier. My second recruit in Retina was Rob Lewen, who was at the University of North Carolina and tiring of the academic restrictions in income and practice style. His chairman recommended him highly and he then joined us in 1988 as the second sub-specialist. Both men were started on salary in the Department of Ophthalmology. My original plan for the department was to have specialists in glaucoma, retina, and cornea, as well as neuro-ophthalmology and orbital disease.

The neuro-ophthalmology and orbital practice continued to grow at Allegheny and we developed a course on orbital surgery. This was done together with the Department of Neurosurgery and we used fresh frozen heads for practice surgery. The course was restricted and expensive, but very successful for several years. Some of my colleagues in the orbit society attended the course, as well as ophthalmic plastic surgeons, neuro-ophthalmologists and neurosurgeons from around the country.

The Japanese Journey

In 1986, Pat and I traveled to Japan to attend the International Neuro-Ophthalmology Congress. However, we missed our plane in Chicago because of weather restricting us from leaving the Pittsburgh area. We stayed overnight in Chicago at the Drake Hotel, which has a great seafood restaurant, The Cape Cod Room, and then proceeded to Japan, arriving at the Tokyo airport. Because we were late, the organized transportation was gone, so we had to find our way to the train station in downtown Tokyo and proceed to the hotel at a resort several miles away. It was easy to get to the train station after a very expensive taxi ride, but our lack of ability to speak Japanese became a problem in the train station. Fortunately, several Japanese passed by who spoke English and helped direct us to the train. On the train to the resort, we communicated with a family, one of whom spoke some broken English and managed to convey to them that we needed to get to this particular resort. They were on their way to the town where they lived, which was near to the resort and literally took us by hand off the train and to a taxi stand and instructed the taxi driver exactly where to take us. They were very gracious and we were all waving goodbye as we left in a taxi, hoping we were going to arrive at the proper place. The taxi took us directly to the resort and we arrived to find our colleagues, who had already checked in and were enjoying the facility. The hotel was magnificent, as was the resort overlooking Mt. Fuji. I am told that Mount Fuji is only seen infrequently from a distance and yet our entire five days that we were at the resort we were able to see it clearly. We also traveled with the group to Mount Fuji and were able to go halfway up the mountain to an area of shops and restaurants. Some of our friends climbed to the top of Fuji. We walked around Mount Fuji with a guide, but did not climb to the top. It was a fantastic experience; you could see all around the vast plain that surrounded this mountain, which is an old volcano, with no surrounding mountains.

We returned by a bus to the hotel, but our friends who had climbed the mountain were not with the group. We worried about them, but they finally returned that evening, having taken more time then they thought to climb around the top of the mountain and back down and then had to take a taxi back to the resort.

Following the meeting, we were entertained by a Japanese ophthalmology professor and his group of residents, who formed a band and played excellent music. It was a unique experience seeing how these ophthalmologists performed music at such a high level. Apparently, a pre-requisite for getting into his residency program is the ability to play a musical instrument with skill.

After the meeting, Pat and I elected to tour Kyoto, the cultural capital of Japan, which contains the Shogun's palace, the big Buddha and other historic sights including Deer Park. We particularly enjoyed the palace of the shogun with its specifically designed creaky floors, a warning that someone was arriving to do the shogun harm at night. The rooms and tapestries were magnificent. Kyoto is a beautiful city and we enjoyed the experience.

We traveled to Katsakajima, the home of the famous Mikimoto pearl company. The oysters are grown in the bay and seeded with small grains of sand to form the pearl. I bought pearls for Pat and my daughter, Nancy at the company's outlet. We watched the pearl divers in a glass viewing room and visited a religious shrine in the area. We also visited a palace near the ocean built high on a hill, which housed the library of ancient books. It was also magnificent, as was the view from the upper rooms. We departed Katsakajima by bullet train to Tokyo. The fast-moving bullet train was a very interesting experience, the Japanese countryside flying by with its rice paddies and small houses.

In Tokyo, we stayed at the beautiful Hotel Mikado across from the palace of the emperor, but found Tokyo to be expensive and disappointing with its crowds of people. The buildings are modern and remind one of being in New York, except for the appearance of the population. Pat's Mother's Japanese friend hosted us one day, traveling with us all over the city by taxi. We saw some interesting shops and shrines, but in general it was a day of sitting in traffic. Following our departure on the plane from Tokyo, we remarked that we did not intend ever to return to Tokyo, a large disappointment. Even a small lunch, consisting of a salad for Pat and a little bit of sushi and soup for me, cost over $100 at that time. We could not see how people could afford to live there.

The Caribbean Journey

In 1987, Larry Katzin, an ophthalmic plastic surgeon from Miami, organized a meeting in the British Virgin Islands. It was unique in that the invited speakers were all housed on a fleet of sailboats, which sailed from island to island with lectures done on one morning at a block house on St. John's Island. In this unique program, Pat and I sailed with Mel and Jane Alper and John and Gretchen Bullock. We arrived in St. Thomas and stayed overnight at a hotel at the marina, in Charlotte Amalie, where we then boarded a boat captained by a young man from Colorado who had changed his life to become a skipper in the Caribbean. He had his girlfriend aboard as cook. We began our trip on the boat enjoying the camaraderie of our boat-mates, the Alpers and the Bullocks. We met the rest of the group from time to time. We had lectures in a cinder-block building on St. John's. The group then sailed through the British Virgin Islands, another area to which we have returned because we like it so much. The various islands included Tortola and Virgin Gorda, and others as beautiful; the sailing in the Drake Channel was rather safe without large ocean waves. I was able to scuba dive several times during the trip, as the British Virgins has several popular dive sites. I sailed the ketch as much as I desired in excellent weather with a light to medium breeze. We even had water balloon fights with the other boats from time to time during cocktail hour. I particularly enjoyed the easternmost island, called the Bitter End, with its unique bay and its attractive narrow hilly terrain. There were excellent restaurants and a variety of superb views from many directions.

The French River Journeys

Three times I have visited Dave Post on his family island at the mouth of the French River as it leaves Lake Nipissing in northern Ontario, Canada. The island supports a sturdy cabin with running water, propane refrigeration, indoor plumbing, but no electricity. All of the trips were great fun as Dave has made several good friends on nearby islands. Pat and I were welcomed by two of Dave's three wives, Carol and Kay, the latter hosting the last two trips and is a very good cook. The views from the cabin are magnificent in all directions and the water is clear and contains several species of fish, very few of which we were able to catch, even with several efforts. Card and dice games took the place of television, as did great parties with the other members of that neat resort community, especially Larry and Lynn Smith. The unique rustic experience made the long drive to get there worthwhile.

The Italian Journey

In the fall of 1988, I was invited to speak at a cytology conference in Parma, Italy. Pat and I designed a trip through Gerry Heden, our long-time travel agent, to explore northern Italy, passing through Parma to give the lecture.

We began the trip in Milan, where we rented an Italian car and proceeded north to Lake Lugano, a beautiful lake in southern Switzerland. The small town was of medieval design and automobiles were not allowed in the town center. Therefore, we parked the car in a garage and carried our bags to the hotel, where we were shown to our room. The hotel was very small, but quaint and comfortable, in the center of Lugano. We explored the town on foot. Fortunately, a fall wine festival was starting and the streets were filled with people. There were booths selling wine, crafts and food. We enjoyed the festival thoroughly for two days, tasting a number of different wines and foods of the region. It was a spectacular event and we capped it by taking a cruise across Lake Lugano to a hotel where we had lunch and then returned to the town and walked back to our hotel. We left Lugano and traveled past Milan across northern Italy to a vineyard country estate, turned into a hotel restaurant. It was about 30 miles north of Venice and was quite beautiful. We arrived tired, but had an exquisite dinner that evening in the restaurant, which was in the former library. The next day we drove to Venice; we parked the car and went into Venice by boat. We toured Venice, including the municipal center on the square. We crossed the Bridge of Sighs into the prison and toured the waterfront. We took a short gondola ride, which was interesting, but expensive. After our afternoon tour we returned to the car and left the parking lot just as it was becoming dark. As we proceeded north, we learned, to our chagrin, that we did not have headlights—only parking lights. For that reason, we were very compromised traveling in the dark in a strange place. We received constant signals from cars coming toward us that we did not have our headlights on, and it was a harrowing trip. We returned to a small town near the vineyard and tried to ask directions several times, unsuccessfully, finally finding a roadside restaurant where they were able to direct us, fortunately, back to the vineyard. We arrived exhausted and breathed a sigh of relief, vowing to rid ourselves of that automobile as soon as possible. The next morning, we packed the car and left for Parma, which is in central northern Italy. We passed by a large city with an airport and turned the car in to the airport in exchange for a French Renault, which had all its faculties. There was a great argument at the airport about our turning in the car, as they would have preferred for us to have it fixed in Parma, but we were not sure that we could do that and so insisted on a replacement. This proved to be a mistake, as they charged us a great deal for the exchange when we got back to the United States and the American Express Company would not back us even though we were doubly charged for the rental car. For that reason, I dropped my membership in American Express and only used it as a back-up for my optical business.

We arrived in Parma and were hosted by the local cytologist, a marvelous woman who told us that she could have had our car repaired in Parma. The convention was in a large auditorium and it was a one-day conference. I lectured in the morning and at lunch we had a great deal of food and wine, which, unfortunately, caused me to sleep during most of the afternoon conference. It was on cytology, which is not a exciting subject, however, I had been interested cytology at the university and developed orbital cytology for diagnosis of malignant tumors, infections and various types of inflammations.

Following the cytology conference, we went on a tour of the area, including a very elegant lunch at a prosciuto factory where the pigs were processed to make the famous Italian Parma ham. The women working in the processing plant had extremely smooth hands from handling pig fat all their lives. The following day we drove to Pisa, where we saw the leaning tower. Of course, at that time we were not allowed up on the tower because it was in a condition of continuous sideways leaning and they were afraid that tourists would accelerate the tendency for the tower to topple over. It was being restored at that time and braces were in place to keep it standing. There is not much else of interest around Pisa, so we went on to the Italian Riviera, a spectacular area that we enjoyed thoroughly. We first stopped at Santa Margarita Lugare and stayed in a hotel from which Marcone sent the first telegraph message across to a site further down the coast of Italy. The hotel had a spectacular view of the Mediterranean Sea and the village was extremely pleasant. I bought a very nice wineglass at an antique shop there, as I had been collecting antique wineglasses; we had some excellent meals. We walked from Santa Margarita Lugare to Portofino on a path through the forest along the coast, a delightful experience. We walked all over the small picturesque port of Portofino and took pictures. We tasted the small thin-crusted Italian pizza in Portofino and I became a fan of that type of pizza as opposed to the thick-crusted American pizza. We walked back to Santa Margarita Lugare and the next day we went to the southern coast of France, passing through and staying at Monte Carlo, another fascinating experience. We stayed in a hotel directly across from the casino and walked around the city. We toured the casino at mid-day and watched some of the gambling, paying an additional amount to enter the more luxurious rooms where the high stakes were played. We had a drink at the bar, but did not gamble in the casino except for playing a few slot machines. We traveled the roads on the coastal cliffs around Monte Carlo, which had spectacular views of the Mediterranean Sea. We went on to a hotel on the coast near Nice. We stayed there for two nights, and enjoyed the local area prior to returning to the Nice airport, where we turned in the rental car with some difficulty and then returned through Paris to Pittsburgh.

Digression #3

In 1988, the optical shop located in the Ophthalmology Department, run by the hospital, was about to be closed because the hospital did a study that predicted a financial loss. At the time the income was supporting the shop and the optician. I thought it was important to have an optical shop for a full service department and bought it from the hospital for the cost of the inventory. At first, with a very good optician, we made a profit, but with her departure, the next optician was inadequate and we lost money. In 1993, I terminated her and hired Melody Pebley, a superb optician, and the optical shop has been profitable since then, except for the year after Allegheny almost went bankrupt and lost many employees. It serviced our patients, hospital in-patients, and hospital employees and their families, a small but steady business.

In 1987, Michelle Luznar joined the department as my secretary, coming over from the Eye and Ear Hospital, and has gone on to be my right hand person, eventually becoming departmental manager, and has served the department well for many years.

The Irish Journey

In the fall of 1989, Pat and I toured Ireland on our own. She is Irish and I had always wanted to see the "Emerald Isle." We arrived at Shannon Airport in late September and rented a car. This time, based on our previous experience, we thoroughly inspected the car in the parking lot and found that the turn signals were not functioning. We returned to the counter. After confirming our findings, they upgraded us to a Volvo sedan at their expense, which was a great automobile for touring Ireland, the roads being narrow and dangerous. Of course, they drive on the left side of the road. We went from Shannon to Donegal for our first night in Ireland. We stayed at a country house converted into a hotel/restaurant with a three-par golf course behind the house. It was a sensational place with very comfortable high-ceilinged rooms, and the food was fantastic. We toured the town of Donegal, sampling two or three pubs, and the next day, began our trip around the ring of Kerry. This is a peninsula in southwestern Ireland with spectacular views. We started along the southern coast, planning to play golf on the extreme western end of the peninsula, but unfortunately, we were rained out. We stopped at the golf course, which was typical of the seaside golf courses with heavy heather lining the fairways and no trees. We toured the quant fishing village at the western tip of the island. We had lunch in a hotel in the village, then toured the western end of the peninsula and saw the old bell-shaped huts. We drove along the northern part, crossing the island with its many rocky outcrops and many sheep. We returned to Donegal to stay again at the same hotel and then went southeast to Cork. We passed the site of the Blarney Stone on the way to Cork and climbed up the old castle stairs to kiss the Blarney Stone. We were helped by the local Irish people to hang down over the side of the partly-ruined castle into a stone crevice, where we kissed the Blarney Stone while looking 60 feet down at the ground. It was an experience that I could have missed. We found some nice Irish sweaters in a shop near the castle. We went to Cork, a southern Irish town, which we passed through quickly, and stayed at a country estate converted into a hotel and cooking school— Ballymaloe— outside the city. Our room was very comfortable and they too had a small three-hole golf course. We enjoyed our stay there and we had an excellent dinner prepared by the student chefs. We left Cork the next day in the Irish mist and proceeded on to Waterford, where we stopped and toured the Waterford crystal factory. The replicas of their historic cups and other glass figurines that they made for various tournaments and famous people were on display. We went from there to a small walled town and toured that castle in the town, which was interesting. From there, we traveled on to Dublin, where we stayed in a hotel across from a park in the city, a picturesque location. In Dublin we parked the car and used taxis to get around because of the crowded streets. We visited Trinity College and saw the medical school, a very old one. We toured other interesting parts of Dublin, spending some time in the pedestrian shopping areas. The shops and restaurants were busy, lively and fun. We enjoyed our meals in Dublin as we did in all of Ireland, most of them being prepared in the French style rather than in the English style—except for breakfasts, which were excellent and definitely English. While staying in Dublin, we traveled north to see the ancient cave structure built by a tribe of people who populated Ireland prior to the tenth century. The crude rock structure (probably religious) had a hole in the roof that allowed the sun to fill the entire room at the equinox.

From Dublin, we traveled to western Ireland to visit Galway. We stayed in a bright and cheerful country inn near the coast. It was the place where Charles DeGaul stayed when he visited Ireland. In fact, we walked the grounds and sat on a bench overlooking the Atlantic Ocean where he had frequently rested. In western Ireland we crossed peat bogs with their drab appearance—but they are productive in that peat burns slowly and without adverse odors in the fireplaces in the houses and inns of western Ireland. We traveled around Galway, again sampling pubs and various tourist sights, then returned to the hotel near Shannon airport, which was near an old castle that held medieval dinners. We toured the castle, unfortunately not being able to attend the dinner, as we left by plane the next day to return to the United States.

Digression #4

During the middle and late 1980s, the fellows who followed Jim Garrity were Mark Malton in 1986-1987, from the University of Virginia, who has a successful practice in Charlotte, North Carolina. Scott Kortvelesy, one of the residents from the University of Pittsburgh, an excellent surgeon, became a fellow in 1987-88. He practices in Honolulu, Hawaii. When a letter came to my desk that they were looking for somebody with skills in neuro-ophthalmology and orbital surgery, I put it on Scott's desk and told him that if he did not take the job, I would. It was during a period when I was a little depressed at not being able to recruit additional staff, just before Garry Condon decided to join us.

The next fellow, in 1988 to 1989, was Tom Gardner, another Pitt resident who was in the Air Force. During his residency he met his wife, Melissa, who worked at the University of Pittsburgh. Tom was an excellent fellow and after completing his fellowship in 1989, he went to Denver, Colorado to complete his tour of duty and then stayed there to practice neuro-ophthalmology and ophthalmic plastic surgery. In 1989, Mike Kazim, from Columbia University in New York, was sent by Steve Trokel, one of my orbital society colleagues, and became my fellow. He had been previously trained in ophthalmic plastic surgery and was an excellent surgeon. We enjoyed Mike's fellowship and during his time we had a visiting fellow, Dr. Wu from Kwang Chou, southern China, formerly Canton. He was a delightful individual, but his English was broken and he was mainly an observer. He was, however, always cheerful and energetic in learning our specialty. Prior to Wu's arrival, Satoshi Kashi, a Japanese neuro-ophthalmologist trained by Ronald Buide, joined us for six months to learn orbital surgery. He was an excellent fellow and went onto become chairman of the Ophthalmology Department at the Red Cross Hospital near Kyoto.

In the spring of 1990, my daughter, a computer scientist, decided to marry Peter Kocis, an IRS agent whom she met when they both worked for Electronic Data Systems under Ross Perot. We discussed her wedding, which was to be in the fall of 1990, and then discussed my own marital future. Pat and I had not married, but had lived together since 1982. Nancy suggested it might be nice if we married before she did and so on June 9, 1990, with Mike Kazim, Dr. Wu, Joe Maroon and many of our friends attending, we were married at the Lodge at Hidden Valley. The wedding was unique in that we had cocktails prior to the wedding and then the wedding was held on the patio behind the lodge, followed by hors d'oeuvres and a strolling guitarist. We then adjourned to Margie Kress's house for an informal dinner after some of the guests had left. We were married by Federal Judge Alan Bloch, who is jewish, and with my Presbyterian background and Pat being a Catholic, we thought we had three of the major religions covered.

The Hidden Valley Journey

From 1982-1984 when I was going through my tour as acting chairman and deciding to change my life, we frequently visited Hidden Valley with friends, renting condominiums during the ski season. We became interested in Hidden Valley because it is 60 miles from Pittsburgh and quite accessible, with a different climate—usually about 10 degrees cooler in the summer, with lovely western Pennsylvania mountain scenery, highlighted by the Mountain Laurel, which blooms in June. It was originally a winter resort, and although we frequented it many times, we did not decide to buy a place there until 1987, when they opened the first nine holes of the golf course at Hidden Valley. They developed it further with a tennis complex and a recreational building with racquetball courts and exercise area. We bought a townhouse in Alpine Woods, from which we could walk to the ski slopes, also near the golf course. It was a two-story townhouse with two bedrooms, each having its own shower and bath. The downstairs had a living room/ dining room/kitchen combination and was small, but cozy with a stone fireplace. It had a deck in the back, which we upgraded and it was near a very nice pond. We enjoyed the place, joining the golf club. I turned to golf because of the fact that the children had grown up and gone away and that the time was available on the weekends. The golf course is a beautiful mountain type golf course with woods on both sides of the fairways and no fairways coming from the opposite direction. We had many parties and dinners at Alpine Woods and made friends with the people in the area. Some of our other friends from Pittsburgh bought townhouses as well. We had summer parties with croquet on the grounds around the townhouse and even developed a form of golf using croquet mallets and wickets, from which we made a course around the ponds. We had an electric boat race in the pond; everybody bought and ran their own electric boats. Unfortunately, we forgot that these electric boats were on the same frequency so we when we tried to guide them with our remote control devices, they crashed into each other and the race was a disaster. Everybody had a huge laugh and we had a good party. It was comfortable at Hidden Valley because we were protected on the weekends, not having to go out on the roads very often for entertainment. It reminded me of being on the campus of Bucknell University.

The British Journey

In 1990, following our wedding, we decided to attend another international Neuro-Ophthalmology conference which was held in Westminster, south of London. We treated this as sort of a honeymoon, and we flew to London, then headed south to Westminster. I attended some of the conference, but frankly I enjoyed seeing the area and touring Westminster, including its church and its amazing municipal building. We traveled south to Plymouth where we saw the warship, VICTORY, which was captained by Lord Nelson. We ferried out to the Isle of Wight, a beautiful island where the queen of England spent most of her time during the 19th century in a palace that was beautifully restored. We saw the Isle of Wight sailing club and then returned to Westminster.

After the conference, we drove to London, where we turned in the rental car and stayed at a hotel near the railroad station. The next day we took the fast train north along the east coast of England to Scotland. The train trip was picturesque and comfortable; particularly interesting was the view along the rugged east coast of England. We arrived in Edinburgh and stayed in a very nice hotel on the west side of the city. We were able to walk through the city and tour the fortress built high above the river to protect the city in medieval times. The fortress was dramatic and the views from it were spectacular. After a day in Edinburgh, we went north to St. Andrews, which was hosting the British Open Golf Tournament. We could not play there, but we did walk part of the famous course. We had lunch in the village of St. Andrews and then went to the Glenn Eagles golf resort in central Scotland. The Glenn Eagles Hotel and Resort is spectacular and we had a glorious room overlooking the approach to the hotel. We played the Glenn Eagles course the next day and found it to be very hilly with a lot of blind shots. The insects were particularly bad, but our caddy, an elderly Scotsman, was funny and entertained us during our round. That evening the bagpiper came at dusk and played in front of the hotel. That was very touching. The food at the Glenn Eagles hotel was excellent. We went from Glenn Eagles through Glasgow, which we visited briefly—an unattractive city, the capital of Scotland. After a brief tour and lunch, we proceeded on to Turnberry on the west coast of Scotland, where we stayed for a few days and played the golf course twice. The area around Turnberry is rugged and beautiful and we enjoyed staying at that fine hotel with views across the golf course toward the sea. From Turnberry, we drove to England and stopped at York. We stayed in a unique hotel that formerly housed lawyers who were traveling back and forth from Scotland to London. York contains the remains of ancient Roman walls and statues, because it is as far north as the Romans ventured when they were in England. York is a beautiful city and we enjoyed touring it. We traveled south from York then to stay at an estate north of London, which was formerly an active farm. At the time we were there, it had been turned into a beautiful inn with an excellent restaurant. There were sheep in the fields and a lake nearby and we were able to walk around the grounds, which were very beautifully done, especially the gardens. We met some interesting people there, including the current owners. From there we returned to the airport at Heathrow and flew to the United States with good memories of our combined meeting and honeymoon trip. Pat had done a great job of driving on the left side of the road, through roundabouts and cities.

Digression #5

In October 1990, Nancy married Peter Kocis, the IRS agent who was with her in Washington, D.C. The wedding was expensive but fun, held in Arlington, Virginia at an old non-denominational church; the reception was held at a very nice Holiday Inn. Friends and relatives had a great time, with good weather and a great reception. The couple honeymooned in the Caribbean and took up residence in suburban Washington, D.C. where they both worked.

In 1990, Pat Teideken, a graduate of the University of Pittsburgh Ophthalmology Program, became my fellow. Pat Teideken was a good surgeon, but after leaving the fellowship, he joined a group in Massachusetts, which did not work out. He went back to Nashville, Tennessee for a while with his previous ophthalmic plastic surgery fellowship director, then on to Philadelphia for glaucoma fellowship and finally to Lancaster, Pennsylvania where he practices general ophthalmology and glaucoma.

In 1991, I was invited to speak at an International Ophthalmology Conference in Taiwan and was also invited to speak in Kyoto, and we looked forward to seeing that beautiful city for the second time. Also Dr. Wu asked me to speak in Quong Chou (formerly Canton) in China, a country we had not visited.

The Oriental Journey

In 1991, Pat and I took the trip through Japan to Taiwan on to Hong Kong and up to Quong Chou in China. This was extensive and tiring, but a most interesting trip. We flew to Nagasaki and were picked up by Satoshi Kashi and his wife and taken to our favorite Japanese city, Kyoto. We stayed in a traditional Japanese hotel with a futon mattress on the floor. We requested this after seeing one in our previous visit. It was a great experience and then I lectured at the University of Kyoto and was given small traditional Japanese statues dressed in typical clothing. We were hosted by Satoshi Kashi and his family for lunch of sushi, the biggest that I had ever seen and I almost made myself sick eating as much as I could. They also gave Pat and me kimonos at that luncheon. For dinner, Satoshi and his wife took us to a Japanese-French restaurant, serving an unusual combination of exquisite food. It was on a river that runs through Kyoto and we ate outside. The night was cool, but we were diverted by the good saki and the excellent French-Japanese type dishes. We again toured the spectacular Shogun's palace and left Kyoto with fond memories.

We arrived outside Taipei, Taiwan, and on our way from the airport to the city, I was impressed with the number of motorcycles on the roads. We stayed at the Grand Hotel overlooking the capital, Taipei, which was a large elaborately decorated hotel with large rooms and hallways. Rick Anderson, an orbital society colleague and friend, was also a speaker, as was Terry O'Brien, from Johns Hopkins, a young corneal specialist. We were invited by Don Liu, a Taiwanese-American ophthalmic plastic surgeon. The Taiwan ophthalmologists were gracious hosts. After touring the hotel and having an exquisite lunch there, we were able to tour the capital city. It was extremely crowded and traffic was a nightmare. We did see the changing of the guard at the palace, which consisted of very tall, very slim Chinese men who had to pass rigorous physical qualifications to be guardsmen. These young men had waists of about 22 to 24 inches and were very tall. It was an unusual event, particularly because of the physical appearance of the guards in their red uniforms.

We lectured in a large conference center and were hosted at dinner by the Taiwanese. The dinners were interesting in that they used a large Lazy Susan that rotated around the table; we were expected to sample food of several types, including web of duck, pine cone fish, and other exotic dishes that I found interesting, some of them delectable. Pat stuck mostly to rice, as she is not an adventurous eater. The Taiwanese also frequently toasted with a fortified wine that was quite strong and we were expected to stay with them toast after toast. Fortunately, I had enough food that I did not make a fool of myself, but I was pretty well under the weather by the time we got back to the hotel.

Following the conference they hosted us on a train trip along the southern coast into the area referred to as the Grand Canyon of Taiwan. A spectacular gorge, though not nearly as big as the U.S. Grand Canyon, it has some dramatic high cliffs, deep canyons, fast running water and numerous suspension bridges. The trip by bus up through the gorge was very windy. In the park, there was a hotel where we had lunch before returning to a small town near this spectacular geographic sight, from which we flew back to Taipei. That night we were hosted at another banquet, which we had to miss because our plane to Hong Kong was early in the evening. We arrived at the airport only to find out that the plane was delayed by mechanical problems and did not arrive until after midnight. Therefore, we needlessly missed the banquet and sat in the airport for several hours. The airport virtually shut down after 9:00 PM and my wife, Pat, had to argue with the authorities to bring in some McDonald's hamburgers for the people who were waiting, especially the children. We wound up eating greasy McDonald's hamburgers at midnight and finally left Taiwan at 1:00 in the morning, arriving at Hong Kong at 3:00 in the morning, where we were taken by taxi to the Mandarin Hotel. This was another oasis where the night desk clerk understood our plight, having found out that the plane would be late, and escorted us to our room, encouraging us to eat some fruit and drink water, which he provided for us. It was a trying evening, but we slept through the next morning to have lunch in the hotel. We did take the ferry across to the mainland of Hong Kong and toured the area, finding a custom clothing shop where we thought we might be interested in purchasing some clothing. We returned to the hotel and then had dinner at a nearby restaurant, recommended by an old friend, Nelson Hicks, who traveled to Hong Kong frequently. We had a delightful dinner.

The next day we toured Hong Kong, traveling by car up the mountain where we overlooked the entire island and the city, a spectacular sight. We visited religious shrines and homes of very wealthy people before we returned to the hotel. We again took the ferry to the mainland and I arranged to buy some clothing from a tailor for pick-up on our return from China. I bought two suits, a sport coat and pants, which fit well and have held up for many years. We took a boat tour in the afternoon through Hong Kong harbor, an interesting experience because we were passing between the houseboats that were permanent living quarters for some of the people in Hong Kong. We passed by a large floating restaurant, the Red Dragon, which was so big that we decided not to eat there because it looked like a tourist trap.

The next day we boarded the train for Quong Chou in communist China. We arrived at the desolate train station where communist soldiers in padded uniforms were conspicuous. We passed through the tedious immigration line where our passports were carefully evaluated and then proceeded through customs where they inspected our luggage, to the waiting area where our host, Dr. Wu, was waiting with a companion who drove us to an exquisite hotel. The streets were striking in that they were filled with people on bicycles instead of motorcycles. The bicycles were everywhere and again traffic was difficult. The hotel was spectacular, with high ceilings and wonderful bright expensive decorations. The room was western style and very modern. The hotel food was western and quite good. That afternoon I was taken to the hospital with which Dr. Wu was affiliated and I gave a lecture on orbital disease to the local ophthalmologists. It was rather difficult because I had to speak slowly, stopping frequently for translation as virtually none of the doctors spoke English. Of course, we had the mandatory tour of the hospital and then we were taken to dinner.

The next day, after visiting the statue of Sun Yat Sen, a famous Chinese leader, we were taken on a guided tour through Quong Chou out to a small factory where they were making dishwashers for apartments. This was obviously an attempt to guide our tourist interest to their advantage; we had requested to see the countryside and the people, but instead were taken to this small factory. Of course, the people at the factory were gracious and good hosts. We were taken to an exquisite lunch at a hotel in the town where the factory was located. Lunch consisted of many different dishes on Lazy Susans, which, of course, I sampled. In the afternoon, we were brought back to the hotel, with me sleeping most of the way and then were hosted for dinner again that night.

The next day, we were taken to the airport by Dr. Wu and a companion. We found it very difficult to get through the streets which were under repair to finally arrive at the airport in time to catch our plane back to Hong Kong. It was an interesting experience being in communist China. They were trying to demonstrate to us that they were gradually changing their ways, but according to Dr. Wu it would take many, many years. Back in Hong Kong we stayed at the Mandarin and picked up my clothing, most of which was ready. We again walked around the city and had a drink at the famous Peninsula Hotel.

On our return to the airport, we rented the Rolls Royce hotel limousine, which was expensive, but fun, a treat for our anniversary. Our plane then took us back through Tokyo and on through Seattle to home. This was an arduous, but memorable trip, on which Pat and I reflect fondly. It was made so by our being hosted in these different countries. In out-of-the-way places especially in a third world country, it is so pleasant to be hosted by local colleagues, because it alleviates all worries of having to get around by yourself or with a travel group. If a host is not available in a third world country, I would recommend the use of a private tour. It's usually best to go with the smallest tour group one can find.

Digression #6

In 1990, Rob Lewen, having been in private practice in our department for almost a year, convinced Garry and me that we should join him in private practice, forming a corporation and not being salaried any longer. This was possible at Allegheny General because they had a wide variety of financial arrangements with various groups in their departments. They accepted my request to change to private practice. I retained salary for my role as chairman of the department. I also retained the departmental secretaries' salary through the institution, for Michele Andrews, who had joined us in 1987. She eventually became the departmental manager and has stayed with us ever since. The corporation was set up with the three of us being officers, myself as president, Garry as secretary and Rob Lewen as treasurer. The corporation was off to a good start because we were all very busy and we simply shared expenses, which is the scheme that we decided to use if we brought on new members. Rob's and Garry's practices had developed nicely and I was limiting my practice then to neuro-ophthalmology, orbital disease and functional ophthalmic plastic surgery as well as some cataract surgery to obtain sufficient funds for my share of the expenses.

In 1992, we learned that Bob Arffa, who was at the University of Pittsburgh, might be interested in joining us and, after a difficult recruitment, he finally joined us to become the fourth partner in the corporation about a year later. His specialty is cornea and external disease, although he did cataracts and some general ophthalmology as well. With the arrival of Bob Arffa, the department was complete as planned in the beginning, with a specialist in each of the sub-specialties of ophthalmology except pediatric ophthalmology, which I delayed in recruiting because of the weakness of the pediatric department at Allegheny General. In addition, pediatric ophthalmology, although planned in the early stages, did not fit well with the design of our department, especially the waiting room, which could not mix older adults with children. Bob's practice developed well and the department flourished—except that as we grew we ran into more difficulties with personnel and division of space.

In 1991-92, our fellow was Ed Baron, from New York, a delightful individual and hard worker. He was very jovial and the patients liked him. At the completion of his fellowship, he returned to suburban New York City, where he works in a group headed by Rob Lewen's brother. From '92 to '93, we had Russ Edwards, who was on active duty in the Navy and came from San Diego to Pittsburgh for his fellowship. He had previously had a fellowship in neuro-ophthal-mology in the Navy. Russ was an excellent surgeon and a good fellow, being a little older than the average fellow. It was about at that time that we developed the course at the academy, which focused on the evaluation of MRI and CT scans in patients with neuro-ophthalmic problems. The course was successful and Russ Edwards was very helpful in organizing the course, along with previous fellows such as Howard Krauss, Tom Spoor, Tom Gardner, Walter Hartel and others. The course continued for about three years.

In 1993-94, I took two fellows, Carl Rosen who had his residency at New York Eye & Ear Hospital and Todd Goodglick, who trained at UCLA but had an additional year of neuro-ophthalmology with Joel Glaser and Norman Schatz, at Bascom-Palmer Institute in Miami, who asked me to consider him. Although I had not taken two fellows since the early 80s, these two worked out very well and we managed to have enough interesting cases to have both of them develop well in neuro-ophthalmic surgery. They were flexible and had great personalities, Carl going to Alaska to take the place of Ken Richardson, who was responsible for my return to academic ophthalmology. He gave Carl his practice of glaucoma and he has developed his own practice in ocular and orbital trauma. After a five-month delay, Todd acquired Mel Alper's position at the Washington Hospital Center. This was an excellent opportunity, so we had three going-away parties for Todd. Both have thrived in their positions.

During the latter part of the 1980s and the first part of the 1990s, Allegheny General had developed the neuro-sciences with Joe Maroon enlarging the Department of Neurosurgery. There was a strong Department of Neurology and an ENT division, strengthened by the addition of two Otologists in 1993. During my first ten years at Allegheny General, the atmosphere was vibrant. The people were eager to succeed and there was plenty of money available for development, new equipment and research. There apparently was also money to have rather elaborate parties, which I enjoyed at Allegheny, having witnessed the final stages of the Eye & Ear Hospital, which closed its doors in 1987. During my last years at Eye & Ear, there certainly was not a positive attitude or any money for social activities.

In 1992, Anna Miller, a Russian orbital surgeon, came to the U.S., supported by a Jewish agency, to become a research fellow in the department. She was very bright and cooperative, with fair English language skills, but trained only in Russian orbital surgery, not ophthalmology. She was a great research assistant and participated in several department studies. She learned some ophthalmic techniques from my fellows and eventually decided to become an ophthalmologist in the U.S. We obtained an internship and residency for her at St. Francis Hospital and she became one of their best residents. She spent time in the department during her residency and we were proud of her. She is now practicing ophthalmology in the Pittsburgh area. Her orbital surgical skills were not developed because the Russian approach was so different from ours, but we were delighted to work with her. It is gratifying to help educate physicians from other countries.

The Southern Italian Journey

In June 1992, the Orbital Society meeting was held in Capri, off the coast of Italy from Naples, hosted by Julio Bonavolonta, an orbital surgeon in Naples. We flew to Naples and went to Capri on a high speed hydrofoil boat, to be taken up to the exquisite, expensive Quissisana Hotel where the meeting was held. It was a very social meeting. We toured Capri, a beautiful island, home of the blue grotto (overrated), and the ruins of the Roman Emperor Hadrian's Castle where it has been reported that he sexually abused young boys and then threw them off the high cliffs to their deaths. The restaurants were terrific. We enjoyed lunch with Jack Rootman and his son, Russell, at an excellent outdoor restaurant on the way to Hadrian's Castle. Joe Maroon and his wife joined us there, but, unfortunately while there, found out that Joe's son had been killed in a tragic auto accident; he and Lynn had to return immediately to the United States.

From Capri we returned to Naples and took the train to Rome, where we stayed at the Colonna Palace Hotel in the heart of Rome. We toured the ancient Roman sights including the Pantheon, the

Colosseum, the Spanish Steps, the Vatican City and many others. The food was good in the small trattorias in the city. We met with Peter Kocis, Nancy's husband at the time, who was auditing an Italian bank for the IRS. We had a pleasant dinner with him and his colleague at a trattoria near our hotel. We returned to Pittsburgh from Rome.

The Eastern Mediterranean Journey

In 1993, I was invited to speak at the King Kalil Hospital in Saudi Arabia. The invitation was attractive since it was the only way to see Saudi Arabia at that time and they paid for all our expenses, including business class transportation and a very generous honorarium that covered Pat's expenses. Therefore, we traveled business class to Saudi Arabia, arriving at the airport in Riyad to be met by Robert Weatherhead, a New Zealander who specialized in ophthalmic plastic surgery. He and his wife, Sylvia, acted as our hosts during our stay at the King Kalil Hospital. Saudi Arabia is a strikingly different culture than we had ever experienced with its restrictions on women, including their dress, and their ability to drive a car. We assumed that Saudi Arabia was dry and were prepared for no cocktail hour, but they had soon informed us that they had ways of obtaining grain alcohol from an oil company on the east coast and they mixed it in a variety of ways to allow them to continue to enjoy active cocktail hours. One drink was made by soaking the alcohol in Jack Daniels chips. We were housed in a very comfortable apartment and the first night were taken to Rob's house, where we had cocktails and dinner. We were instructed on the rules and regulations inside and outside the hospital complex, and of course, they were more lenient inside the complex, which was largely populated by non-Arabians. The medical administer who had invited me was a colleague in neuro-ophthalmology from UCLA, Bob Hepler, who was living in Saudi Arabia for a three-year term as medical director.

The lecture series was strenuous, with multiple lectures, and was a very intense conference. During that time, Pat was taken to a golf course carved out of the desert with artificial grass mats from which to hit the ball; the whole area was sand and the greens were oiled sand, so that the ball could roll on them. The water hazards were painted sand. She thoroughly enjoyed the experience of playing golf with some of the women on the trip and from the medical complex. She was also taken to the Sook, their very elaborate market, with many types of goods including gold jewelry and precious stones. In the Sook, the women had to wear the Abaya headdress; if they took it off, they were accosted by the religious police. One of the wives did remove her Abaya and was rapped on the arm by one of these zealots, the other girls prevailing on her not to react because of the possible dire circumstances. In the bank one of the women tried to change money and was told that the bank clerks would not discuss it with her, so one of the speakers, Bob Sergott, who was with the women that morning had to negotiate all of their bank transactions. The dinners in the evenings were very pleasant at the hospital complex. We were taken on a tour of Riyad and we had dinner at a restaurant in town. There were several of us at a table and a native Arab and his wife came in. They promptly put a screen between us and their table, so that we could not look at the wife, even though she was veiled–she had to move the veil aside to eat. Some of these religious practices seem archaic and ridiculous. Even many Arabs abruptly change their manners when they get on an airplane to leave the country.

We had a tour of the U.S. embassy and a dinner party there. It was a beautiful complex with splendid facilities and excellent food. In addition, cocktails were served there because we were on American soil.

We enjoyed the weather and all of our hosts at the King Khaled hospital. One night, we were treated to a series of underwater scenes by a scuba diving photographer and I questioned him thoroughly about his techniques because his pictures were superb compared to mine, which were frequently under exposed. We were returned to the airport by Rob Weatherhead at the end of the week and boarded a plane for Athens, Greece, where we took a cruise through the Greek Islands as part of this trip. We stayed in Athens for two days and toured the city, including the Acropolis. Athens is a beautiful city, not very clean, but the small tavernas or bar restaurants have better and less expensive food than the regular restaurants or hotels. Hotel food prices were exorbitant and even the larger restaurants charge way too much for the quality of the food. We traveled to the Port of Pireaus and boarded our tour ship, the Stella Maris, which was of a smaller size with a capacity of only 130. The smaller Greek ship could get into the shallower ports and it suited our time table and went the islands that we wanted to see. The ship was very comfortable, although the weather was cool because it was late April and the first Greek island cruise of that year. We saw several different islands and went to Istanbul, where we stayed overnight, toured the city and went to a night club with a belly dancer. We toured the Topkapi Palace the next day with its great jewel collection, and returned to the cruise. We sailed east through the Dardanelle straights to the Black Sea and returned to the Mediterranean Sea. I enjoyed the northern coast of Turkey, traveling to the ancient city of Ephesus where we toured the city from top to bottom. It was amazing how this ancient city, which was there many years before Christ, had some modern structures. In particular, it had water canals, which flowed down through the city from the mountains above it, and one of these canals through the city had toilets built over it so that the waste material could stream down and away from the city to the Mediterranean Sea, a natural form of human waste disposal.

The island of Rhodes was very interesting, with some well-preserved ancient ruins. Micanos was interesting for its beaches and shopping district.

There also was a very steep island, Santorini, which was part of the top of a volcano. We went up in a cable car to the top, where we had spectacular views and walked through a quaint city. We returned from a very interesting tour of the islands with good weather to Athens, and then returned to the United States. That whole trip was exciting and very different from anything that we had ever done. I think that the Greek Islands are very much worth seeing as part of a cruise. Saudi Arabia is a most interesting place for a visit, providing one is willing to adapt to their archaic religious ways.

The Southwestern Journey

In May 1993, Jeff graduated from the Thunderbird International Business School in Phoenix, Arizona, with a master's degree. Pat and I went to Phoenix after I lectured on orbital surgery at UCLA in Los Angeles. We arrived early and with a rental car drove north to the Grand Canyon through the desert and the forest land in Arizona. The scenery was beautiful, and again, we were impressed with the large Suarro cactus. We stayed at the El Tovar hotel on the southern rim of the canyon, which had a spectacular view. We took several walks and tours around the southern rim of the canyon and were fascinated with the awesome scenery. The highlight of the trip was a spectacular helicopter ride through the canyon. On the return trip to Phoenix we stopped at Sedona, a picturesque town in northern Arizona known for its scenery and arts and crafts centers. We stayed at the Mill Creek Hotel in a valley beside the town. We had a painting of Navaho warriors crossing the desert contracted by a woman who lived on their reservation. The painting was hung in our dining room at Hidden Valley and we really have enjoyed it. Returning to Phoenix, we attended Jeff's graduation, which was also attended by his mother and sister. It was a proud moment as he embarked on a career in international business.

The Roitan Journey

In the spring of 1994, Pat and I joined Garry and Linda Condon on a scuba diving trip to Roitan, an island off the coast of Honduras. We stayed at Anthony's Key Resort, which was highly recommended. I had been scuba diving since 1978 when I was certified. Garry had just taken up the sport and was checked out at Anthony's Key Resort. The place was rustic, but our accommodations were huts built over the water in a small bay, where we could look down and see the tropical fish.

Garry and I took several interesting dives and saw a great variety of undersea life. Near the resort was a dolphin training center; we saw two dolphin shows and were able to dive and swim with the dolphins. The experience was interesting, but the dolphins chased after Linda, making her very uncomfortable. The restaurant was high on a hill overlooking the bay, with great views. The food was ordinary but the bar was active and fun, except for the insects, which were annoying. We traveled by boat to a spectacular beach where we snorkeled and had a great barbecue picnic. We returned from Roitan with great memories of unusual experiences.

The Various Boat Journeys

Over the years I have taken several sail- and power- boat trips with friends and/or significant others. Usually Nelson Hicks was the captain and the rest of us were crew. Our first trip on a rented 30-foot sailboat in the Chesapeake Bay resulted in the navigator (me) getting us stuck on a sandbar while attempting a short cut to our destination, necessitating us to be pulled off by the Coast Guard. My friends never let me forget that mistake. The trip ended well and subsequent trips on the Chesapeake with Nelson and friends were great fun and uneventful as we sampled great meals at several small ports on the bay, including St. Michael's, and large ports—including Baltimore. Later we shared trips on Charleston Bay and along the intracoastal waterway. Since our first trip the captain (Nelson) never asked me again to be navigator. I wound up as a limited-talent deck hand and assistant at cocktail hours.

The Cross-Canada Journey

In June 1994, Pat and I attended an international ophthalmology society meeting in Toronto, Canada, where I lectured at the invitation of John Wright. Toronto is a busy attractive city with many points of interest and good restaurants. We went up in the CNN Tower and enjoyed a great view of Toronto and the surrounding country. We had dinner with Robert Weatherhead from the King Kalel Hospital of Saudi Arabia, in a very good continental restaurant.

From Toronto we traveled west to the Orbital Society meeting, hosted by Jim Orcutt in Seattle, a beautiful city. We went saltwater fishing and I caught a large King Salmon, which the group had for lunch on Saturday after the meeting. The Friday night dinner was on a tour boat that traveled around some of the beautiful islands near Seattle.

From Seattle we went north to Vancouver with Jack and Jenny Rootman, who put us on the trans-Canadian train to Toronto. The train trip was fascinating, with varied beautiful scenery, particularly in the western mountainous area. We stopped at Jasper, Alberta, and shopped in the quaint western town. We met a ship's architect, who designed a sailboat for my friend Nelson Hicks. We had a small state-room with a powder room and upper and lower berths. We shared a shower with other rooms on the car. Pat slept in the upper berth and we both slept well on the train. The days were spent in the observa-tion car and the lounge. We also stopped at Winnipeg, Manitoba, a beautiful city with a copper-roofed hotel. The scenery in Ontario was rugged, with lakes and forests. Finally, we arrived in Toronto and flew home to Pittsburgh.

Myrtle Kennerdell and her third child John (Jack) in late 1935.

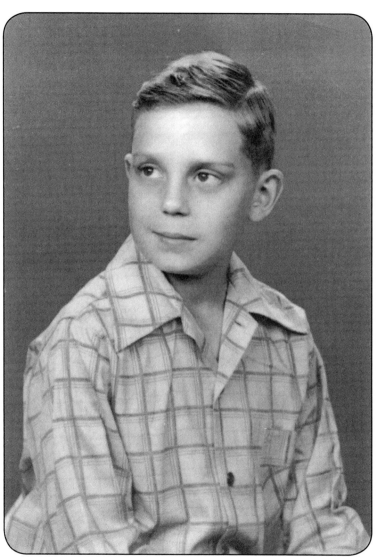

Jack at the age of 11 in 1946.

The Kennerdell family at our summer home in Clinton, PA in 1948.
Top: Jack, Mollye, Edward (brother), Bill George, and Peggy (sister). Middle: Fred and
Myrtle. Front: Judy Kennerdell, Bill George, Jr., and Fred George.

May King and Queen with court in May 1951.

Jack and colleagues at Reese Hall, Kiski Prep,
first home away from home in 1952.

Jack in Cypress Garden Park, Florida with friends on
first long trip from home, 1953.

Phi Gamma Delta, class of 1957 in front of Bucknell Fraternity House.

Medical school, class of 1961. As class president,
I gave the class commencement speech.

Flight surgeon, class of 1963 on the USS Aircraft Carrier, Lexington, just before graduation.

Flight surgeon and daughter Nancy while stationed at South Weymouth, Massachusetts.

Fred, Jeffrey and Jack in Kennerdell, PA in 1966, our only trip there.

Village people looking at an infant cured of tetanus at Hospital DeChapell in 1968. No one recognized the infant in the village that day.

The young Kennerdell family—Jack, Mary-Ellen, Jeffrey, Nancy and Ruffles in 1972.

A young assistant professor of ophthalmology and neurology enthusiastically preparing a lecture in 1974.

A prize winning display at the American Academy of Ophthalmology meeting in 1975; Dr. Maroon is standing on the right. This display prompted the organization of the Orbital Society.

Dinner with the famous Egyptian orbital surgeon, Ali Morfada and his wife at the home of my Egyptian Fellow Mohammed Eli-Hosy in Cairo, 1979. My first international invitation.

The seventh Orbital Society meeting at the Francis Hotel in Bath, England.
John Wright, the host, is front left.

The department of Ophthalmology, Eye & Ear Hospital,
when I was acting chairman in 1983-1984.

The faculty of the All India Ophthalmology meeting hosted by Pran Nagpal, next to me in the front center. My second international speaking engagement which enabled Pat and I to visit several other cities in India.

Three life-long friends, Joe Zahorchak, Dave Post and me enjoying a good laugh at Hidden Valley in 1987.

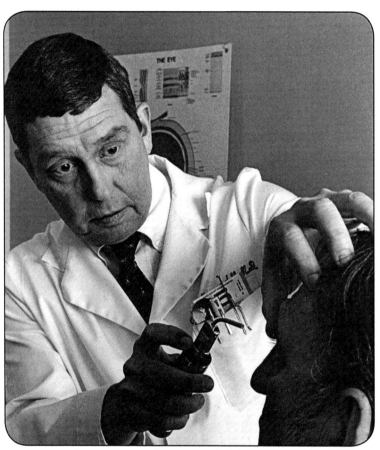

A more mature chairman of Ophthalmology at
Allegheny General Hospital examining a patient in 1988.

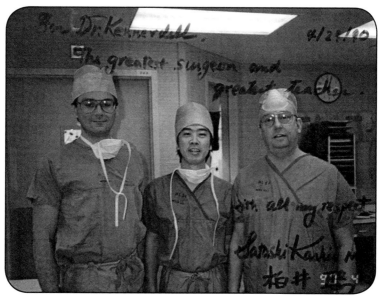

Mike Kazim, Satoshi Kashi and me between surgical cases in April, 1990.

Barbara Maurer (Pat's sister), Pat, Judge Alan Bloch, me, Jeff Kennerdell at our wedding at Hidden Valley on June 9, 1990.

Part of the faculty of the Taiwan Ophthalmological Conference in 1991 visiting the Grand Canyon of Taiwan. The moat is in the center.

The Department of Ophthalmology at Allegheny General Hospital in 1992.

Jack at the King Khalid Eye Hospital in Saudia Arabia during an
ophthalmology meeting in 1993.

Jack at out Grand Canyon in 1993.

A boat drill on a Mediterranean cruise, one of many with Jay and Lou Scheimer and Fred and Mary Ann Wucher in 1995.

Pat and I at a luau after lecturing to the Pacific Ophthalmological Society in Wailea, Maui in 1995.

Dinner with Ken and Ann Richardson and Carl Rosen in Alieska Ski Resort near Anchorage, Alaska.

Jack and Jenny Rootman, close friends and colleagues, at an Orbital Society meeting in Melbourne, Australia in 1997.

Pat and I on a safari in Mala Mala camp in Botswana in 1998 with Wuchers and Scheimers. This was one of the best international trips of all.

Childhood friends get together at Hilton Head Island, South Carolina for New Year's Eve in 1999-2000 at the home of Bob and Naomi McCormick.
Top: Joe Nock, Nelson Hicks, and Jack Kennerdell. Bottom: Jim Benford and Jim Grogan.

Barge cruise with Mel and Jane Alper in Burgundy, France after the Orbital Society meeting in Paris, France.

Christmas with the Condons—Garry, Linda, Liam (our godson) and Maura in 2001. Garry was my first recruit into the Ophthalmology department at Allegheny General Hospital and has since replaced me as chairman of the department upon my retirement in 2007.

Co-authors of *Practical Diagnosis and Management of Orbital Disease*—Joe Maroon, Bill Rothfus, Kim Cockerham and me in 2001.

Bob and Pat Hershock at dinner with us when we all visited the Casa de Campo Resort in the Dominican Republic in 2003.

A "Fellows" meeting and reunion in Pittsburgh, PA in 2004.

Our home at Hidden Valley during spring warm-up and
a snowy winter in 2005.

The family—children and grandchildren in 2008.
Top: Michael, Joe, Pat, and Alan. Middle: Allie, Nancy, Jack, Jeffrey, and Elena.
Bottom: Matthew.

Pat and me at the Great Wall of China in 2008 traveling with Lori and
Gerry Minetti.

Portrait presented to me on my retirement by Allegheny General Hospital and the department of Ophthalmology in June 2007.

The Southeast Asian Journey

In 1993, I was invited to speak at Jakarta, Indonesia. Pat and I flew from Pittsburgh through Amsterdam, then Singapore to Jakarta. We toured Jakarta with our host, but there is not much interesting to see there. We toured the zoo, which was mediocre, but the international symposium was very interesting. We flew from Jakarta to Bali and spent three days in Bali, a spectacular island. We stayed at the Hotel Four Seasons, on the coast. We had an exquisite room with our own private pool and an outdoor shower, which was very, very romantic. The people in Indonesia provided us with a private guide named Archie, who showed us around the island including a trip to the volcano in the middle of the island. We happened to be there during a New Year's festival, and the natives were dressed in their native costumes with baskets of fruit on their heads. It was a spectacular sight. We saw an old palace that was built along the sea; when the high tide comes it is surrounded by water and can only be approached at low tide. We visited one of the national monuments in a park setting with large religious figures of Buddha and other religious relics.

From Bali, we went to Singapore, where we stayed in the Regency Hotel in their famous shopping district—similar to Rodeo Drive in Beverly Hills. Singapore is a magnificent city, which we toured, including its harbor, but it is so sterile because of their strict hygiene rules that it almost seems unreal. We stopped at the Raffles Hotel, where they serve the Singapore sling and had a couple of those one day. We toured the island and saw the monument to those who lost their lives when the Japanese invaded in World War II. We toured a crocodile farm where they raise crocodiles for skins. We bought crocodile skin belts, and during one of the evenings there we met the former Vice Premier of Malaysia, the country adjacent to Singapore. We had an excellent and fun-filled dinner with him, his wife and their entourage. We proceeded from Singapore to Thailand and stayed in Bangkok, which is filled with cars and every other type of vehicle that clogs streets. We stayed at the magnificent Mandarin Oriental Hotel on the Maenam Ping River. In the hotel we were upgraded to a suite, which came with its own floor boy who attended to all our wishes. We were treated to fresh fruit every day and drinks. We toured the area surrounding Bangkok and went out into the country to a religious shrine, then took a river boat cruise from the shrine to the city of Bangkok. We saw many parts of the rich rice-growing country and stopped at another very interesting Buddhist shrine on our way back to Bangkok. At the hotel, during a reception to which we were invited, we met a banker from Australia, Brian Brandon, whom we befriended; we eventually visited him in Melbourne, Australia. We left Bangkok to return to Pittsburgh after a very long and tiring trip, but we enjoyed the whole experience in the Far East—especially the visit to Bali.

The Scandinavian Journey

In the late summer of 1994, we decided to travel with old friends, Fred and Mary Ann Wucher, and his sister and brother-in-law, Jay and Lou Scheimer who lived in southern California. Fred is a pediatrician and his brother-in-law was the producer of the Saturday morning cartoons from which he gained a great deal of fame in the animation world. Since we had enjoyed such a good experience on our cruise to the Greek islands, I decided there were some other areas of the world that demanded a cruise if one wished to see them, one being the Scandinavian countries. Therefore, we arranged a Scandinavian cruise on a larger vessel, The Crown Odyssey, that sailed from England. We all arrived in London and spent the night there, then proceeded to the ship in eastern England on the River Thames. The Crown Odyssey was extremely large and comfortable, housing about 800 people. We left England through the mouth of the River Thames and cruised across the North Sea to enter the Kiel Canal in Germany, which was an interesting experience, and then cruised to Pottsdam in Germany. From northern Germany, we took a train to Berlin for the day and saw the remains of the Berlin wall and Checkpoint Charley. We toured Berlin, seeing the Reichstaq and other monuments of Germany's checkered past. We had lunch at one of the restaurants in one of the old palaces in West Germany and saw the holocaust museum in the center of the city. My wife, Pat, did not particularly like Berlin because of the memories of the war in which her father had participated. We went back by train again, noticing the graffiti all over the walls outside Berlin. While we were in Berlin, we had noted a stark difference between East and West Berlin, the former having many cranes and other construction vehicles trying to replace or restore the drab, unattractive buildings in East Germany. The contrast was striking.

We returned to our ship and that night we sailed to St. Petersburg, Russia, arriving through a long estuary. As we disembarked in the morning, a Russian band was playing to welcome us. St. Petersburg is a spectacularly beautiful city, although, in part, not well-cared for, but the former palaces are well-restored and the large Hermitage museum is very impressive. We toured the museum for half a day, which only was a slight sampling of the many things they have there and then we were taken on a tour around St. Petersburg with its structures that combine European and Middle Eastern influence. Some of the Middle Eastern structures were spectacular, especially the Mosques. We bought some vodka and caviar at a Russian store, which was very inexpensive. There were many people on the street trying to sell trinkets and one could appreciate the poverty that existed in Russia at the time shortly after the end of the Cold War. St. Petersburg is a city that gradually is coming back to its glory and is absolutely worth visiting. We went from St. Petersburg to Helsinki, Finland. Helsinki is a smaller city in a rugged terrain. There is not much to see there, but there are beautiful buildings and a large church in the central part of the city. There is also a church-meeting house carved out of rock in the center of the city, which is very unusual. We had a great lunch in Helsinki and toured the city and the surrounding area. We left Helsinki to go to Stockholm,

Sweden, a much larger capital city with beautiful buildings and parks. The waterways around the city are spectacular and we were able to see the older part of Stockholm, which has been preserved and restored as it was in the 18th and 19th centuries. We strolled the streets and shopped and lunched in the older part of the city. All of us enjoyed visiting Stockholm, but we did not have enough time to explore it thoroughly. We bought some great wine glasses at a factory outlet. They remind us of our Scandinavian trip when we use them at Hidden Valley.

We went from Stockholm to Copenhagen, another very beautiful city and we arrived in time to visit the Tivoli Park at night. Four of us rode the roller coaster in the rain and had dinner in the park. This is the original amusement park and a lot of the rides were maintained as they were designed in the beginning. Copenhagen has a quaint walking district of shops and restaurants. We had lunch in a restaurant that had the best variety of herring that I have ever seen. Three of us liked herring and had a spectacular lunch, but the other three got the chicken salad, a real mistake because they got a very small amount of very mediocre chicken salad, which they did not like, while we were gorging on great herring prepared in four different ways. We toured the rest of Copenhagen, again not being able to explore the city as well as we would have liked. The limitation of these cruises is that one has limited time in each of the cities, but it is a better way of seeing them all than trying to fly from one to the other. We left Copenhagen and went to Oslo, Norway, where we were able to tour the smaller capital; we saw the very unique Vigeland Park, which depicts life's various stages in sculpture, some of them being somewhat lewd, but spectacular in their depictions of people in various stages of life, happy and unhappy. We saw an ancient ship called The Vasa, in its own museum in Oslo, and enjoyed our one-day stay, but we were glad to get back on board the ship because the weather was not so good. We went back to England to depart for home. That began a series of trips with the same group, because we all liked to travel and got along well.

Digression #7

In 1991, Pat and I began to consider a larger home at Hidden Valley. Having lived in a condominium and a townhouse for several years, we thought that we needed a bigger home. Hidden Valley had developed a new area of larger homes called Stonewood and had a model home with an exquisite all-glass kitchen that intrigued us; so after many hours spent roaming the area of Stonewood, I settled on a rock-strewn lot of almost an acre backed by Kooser State Forest, and built a home similar to the model with the large glass-windowed kitchen. It also included a basement, which we made into a game room and a work-out room. The first floor contained the large kitchen and living room/dining room combination, with an excellent view through the woods, to Kooser State Park and across the hills in the winter to the ski slopes at Seven Springs. The sunsets behind the house, viewed from the living room, were spectacular in all seasons. The first floor also included a guest bedroom and bath as well as a study. The second floor consisted of a large master bedroom with a sitting room and a large second guest room, each with its own bath. The house has proven to be wonderful getaway, being only

60 minutes from Allegheny General and only 40 minutes from Pat's office in Monroeville. We have had many great parties and have housed many guests, including family, at our home in Hidden Valley.

In 1992, Dave Post married Kay Howell, and we had their reception, a great party, at the house in Stonewood. They also had a townhouse at Hidden Valley and we have been good friends before and since their wedding.

During the mid 90s we continued to enlarge the department, with the addition of Karen Baker-Lauer, a fellow of Bob Arffa's and Garry Condon's, who joined us as a glaucoma specialist in the summer of 1993 and has continued with the department. In 1994, Thierry Verstraeten, one of the residents who passed through the program from the University of Pittsburgh and eventually went on to become sub-specialized in retina vitreous diseases with an emphasis on macular disease, joined us after having been with the university department for a few years. Both Karen and Thierry were excellent additions to the department and it became a six-member department. We continued to rotate residents from St. Francis—the residents from the University of Pittsburgh, who were formerly rotated through the department, having been withdrawn by the acting chairman, Tom Friberg, who replaced Dick Thoft, the previous chairman, who passed away. Friberg was ordered to withdraw the residents by Vice Chancellor Thomas Detri, a psychiatrist who took over the management of the Eye & Ear Institute. This was a decided blow to the department, but we managed to get a bigger commitment from the St. Francis residents who came through the department to see the indigent patients and benefit from the teaching of our various sub-specialists. The department always emphasized teaching at the fellowship level in glaucoma, cornea and especially neuro-ophthalmology and orbital disease. We entertained medical students rotating with us from the affiliated Medical College of Pennsylvania and Hahnemann University at the request of the institutions. The department continued to grow, and the 8500 square feet which had seemed like such a large space in 1985, became fairly tight with six specialists, three optometrists, and a staff of thirty-two.

In 1994, Kimberly Cockerham came as a fellow in neuro-ophthalmology and orbital disease, having been trained previously as a neuro-ophthalmologist at Walter Reed Hospital in Washington, D.C. The ophthalmology department at Walter Reed was under the direction of Frank Lapiano, an ophthalmic plastic surgeon who asked me to take her as a fellow. She completed her fellowship and returned then to Walter Reed to gain increased experience in ophthalmic plastic surgery, especially trauma and cosmetic surgery. She returned as my partner in neuro-ophthalmology and orbital disease at the Allegheny General Hospital in the summer of 1999. She replaced me as the neuro-ophthalmologist-orbital surgeon of the department and was doing all of the surgery, as I had stopped operating on cataracts in April of 1999 and all surgery in July 2000 because of chronic open-angle glaucoma. It required a series of drops to which I became allergic, followed by filtering surgery on the right eye first at UCLA and the left eye at the University of Utah. The glaucoma became controlled, but requires constant monitoring by Garry Condon, our glaucomatologist.

The Western Journey

In the late fall of 1994, following an Academy of Ophthalmology meeting in San Francisco, a city I always enjoyed, Pat and I rented a Ford Explorer and drove to Yosemite National Park. We stayed in a cabin associated with the Ahwanee Hotel in the middle of the park. It was a lovely cabin and the huge, rustic restaurant was superb. We were impressed with El Capitan, the sheer cliff that highlights the center of the park. We toured the park by car and on foot, and were impressed with the rugged scenery and the large redwood trees. We then drove over the Donner Pass to Lake Tahoe, where we stayed at Harrah's Hotel and gambling casino. Shortly after we crossed the pass over the mountains, it was closed by a snow storm. We drove around the lake and toured Squaw Valley Ski Resort, which is quite beautiful, but skiing hadn't started yet. We gambled a little and then went on to Reno, Nevada, where we stayed downtown at a gambling casino hotel. Reno is much smaller than Las Vegas, with more of a western flair, but we had fun touring the casinos and participating in a fall festival in the city streets with good food and western products for sale. We returned to Pittsburgh with a large painting we bought from Jack Rootman, who brought it from Vancouver to San Francisco.

The Hawaiian Journey

In 1995, a busy year, I was invited to speak twice in Hawaii, the first time by Scott Kortvelesy in Honolulu at the Hawaiian Ophthalmology Society Meeting. Scott had built a beautiful home near the city, high on a hill overlooking the sea and Diamond Head. We toured Oahu after the meeting, saw the Pali, a high cliff on the north side of Oahu with a beautiful view of the island below and the sea. We drove around the island with Scott and Ingrid, seeing some beautiful resorts and the lush rain forest.

Pat and I then flew to Hawaii, the largest of the islands, and stayed at the Kona Beach Resort with individual cottages by the sea, great food, and a terrific luau. We took a sunset cruise on a catamaran and saw several humpback whales. We toured the island from the resort in a rented car, taking in the various sites including the active volcano, Pele, a spectacular sight, and the ranch country. The town of Kona was quaint and we ate in a restaurant overlooking the harbor.

Later in the year, we returned to Maui at the invitation of Jim Orcutt, president of the West Coast Ophthalmology Society. The meeting was at the Maui Intercontinental Hotel. After the meeting we toured the island with a helicopter ride, including the Haleakala volcano and the rainforest. We toured Lahaine, a seaport on the southern coast, and bought two paintings. Then we went on a cruise where I was able to scuba dive and saw some great green turtles. Near the end of our week we took a boat from Lahaine to spend two days at the spectacular Manele Bay Hotel on Lanai, off the coast of Maui—a gorgeous resort with a spectacular golf course. We loved that seaside resort with a special room overlooking the ocean and played the golf course. We had dinner at its sister resort in the center of the island, the Lodge at Koele, which had a mountain atmosphere and great food, including deer tartare made from a small local deer that inhabits the island. We would love to return to Lanai and spend more time in that great atmosphere.

The Mediterranean Journey

In 1995, the Wuchers, Scheimers, and Pat and I took a very interesting cruise beginning in Barcelona, a famous city in eastern Spain, of great beauty and great cuisine. We stayed in the hotel, Musee d'Artes, which was designed for the Olympics previously held in Barcelona. We had a very pleasant stay, dining in excellent restaurants with unusual menus. We cruised to Minorca, a small island off the eastern coast of Spain, which was quite beautiful. They make several different flavored gins which, of course, we purchased and brought home, never to use again. We cruised to Ibiza, another Spanish island, which was frequented by tourists from central Europe in the winter. It was crowded with tourists at the time and it was a very active social island with parties extending well into the early morning. We crossed the island, stopping at the ruins of a very old monastery. We cruised the coast of southwestern France to the port of Sete and then visited the first medical school in Europe nearby at Montpelier. The old medical school was well preserved, with architectural features of southwestern France. We then cruised to Monaco and revisited the famous casino. We then sailed to St. Tropez, a very beautiful Italian island with a very cozy port and a small beautiful town. Unfortunately, it was Sunday when we were there and most of the stores and restaurants were closed, frustrating the ladies. We stopped at another Italian island, Ischia, where we met Julio Bonovolenta from Naples, an Orbital Society colleague, and his wife for lunch and then were taken on a cruise in his boat to see a neighboring island on which he owns a home. We sailed to Sicily, landing on the eastern part of the island in the port of Taormina, which had very steep walls behind it that one had to ascend by either a winding road or a cable car to the top to see the old town, which was marked by narrow streets, historic buildings and quant Italian restaurants. It was a beautiful little town and we enjoyed a day there. We then went on to Venice, where we completed the cruise. Venice is a spectacular place, especially when arriving from the sea. We stayed in the heart of Venice at the beautiful Hotel Danieli and enjoyed the artwork, the glass blowing factory and the excellent Italian restaurants. We bought a beautiful glass sailboat after much deliberation and had it shipped home. It has a lighted pedestal in our living room in the Pittsburgh townhouse. We flew home from Venice, having experienced an unusual and scenic cruise.

Digression #8

In 1996, we hosted the 20th anniversary of the Orbital Society at Hidden Valley in June. Most of the active members and some of the emeritus members attended and we had good presentations. Joe Maroon, my colleague in neuro-surgery, also attended and we had a great deal of fun during that meeting. Unfortunately, the meeting was supposed to be recorded by our photography department, who took pictures only to realize they did not have film in the camera, so we lost some important documentation of the 20th anniversary of the Orbital Society, a real milestone in my life.

The Alaskan Journey

In August 1996, the same group, Wuchers, Scheimers, and Kennerdells, took a trip to Alaska. We flew to Anchorage, Alaska and spent three days with the former chairman of the Department of Ophthalmology at UPMC who had recruited me, Ken Richardson and one of my previous fellows, Carl Rosen. Carl has replaced Ken Richardson in his practice in Anchorage, Alaska. We had a delightful experience with them, staying at the lodge at Alieska, their ski resort, and ascending the ski lift to the top, where there was a restaurant that overlooked the entire mountain. We had a spectacular dinner in that restaurant and then returned to Anchorage to join the rest of the group for a tour of Anchorage. We stayed at the Captain Cook Hotel in the center of Anchorage. We rented a float plane and flew around Mt. McKinley, the highest mountain in North America, on a clear day—a spectacular experience. Then we traveled north by train through Denali National Park, where we saw many wild animals, including moose, elk, bear and fox. We went on to Fairbanks, a smaller northern Alaskan city of limited character, but we took a riverboat trip on the Chena and Tanana Rivers and passed the home of the winner of the Ididorad dog sled race across Alaska, Susan Butcher. We were able to speak with her and see some of her dogs. We then proceeded by bus for a long trip through unnamed mountains, across the Arctic Circle, even experiencing snow at the higher altitudes, to reach Prudhoe Bay. There we saw the oil rigs and put our fingers into the frigid Arctic Ocean. It was my first and only experience of seeing the Arctic Ocean and we saw the origin of the Alaskan pipeline. There was a black bear scare at the hotel, so we were very careful walking about, especially at night. We flew from Prudhoe Bay back to Anchorage and then bussed to the port of Seward where we boarded a large cruise ship, the Crown Princess and toured the inner passage of lower Alaska. This was a spectacular experience where we were able to view calving icebergs and the cities of Sitka, Juneau and Ketchikan. In Sitka, we took the train on a route used by the gold miners up over the coastal mountains east of Sitka. The views were beautiful and on return we took an old-fashioned bus tour of Sitka, highlighted by a trip to the brothel-saloon owned by a famous prostitute during the gold rush. We took a helicopter ride at Juneau and landed on a glacier, where we were shown the famous blue ice. I was able to fulfill a goal of my trip: to acquire a totem pole, in Ketchikan—our last stop. It is about 5 feet high and I had it shipped to my home in Pittsburgh. The totem pole was specially made by the local Indians for sale, as totem poles are usually only made in the very large sizes to be used outdoors for larger institutions or parks. Vancouver, British Columbia, our final stop, is a marvelous city. I am very close to the chairman of the Department of Ophthalmology there, Jack Rootman. I had been to Vancouver on two previous occasions for meetings, during one of which I gave a named lecture for the former chairman at the University of Vancouver. I had toured and skied Vancouver, including the Whistler ski resort. The whole area is quite beautiful and I would live there if I could afford it. The Alaska trip was one of the most spectacular trips that Pat and I have ever taken.

The Australian Journey

In February 1997, we took a very nice trip in conjunction with an Orbital Society meeting in Melbourne Australia. Pat and I flew to New Zealand, where we started the tour in the southern island at the capital of Christchurch. We toured the capital with its beautiful gardens and surrounding area with its spectacular scenery. In Christchurch, we saw the famous eccentric street philosopher called The Wizard. We then crossed New Zealand's mountains, which are spectacular, including Mt. Cook, on a train to the west coast, where a private car took us to the temperate rain forest, where we stayed at the rustic Lake Maeraki Wilderness Lodge. We walked along a rugged beach to view the lonely two-ton elephant seal named Humphrey who resided there. We then completed that long walk on the beach over rocks, finishing with a very precarious climb up a sheer cliff by ropes through a temperate rain forest to return to the small bus that returned us to the resort. Pat found the experience unsettling. We proceeded from there and went down through the western mountains and valleys of southern New Zealand to Queenstown, which is on a lake and is one of the most spectacular settings that I have ever seen. We stayed at the beautiful Melbrook Golf Resort and took a side trip by car to McMurdo Sound, a beautiful fjord where the driver left us and we boarded a boat cruising through the sound with the high cliffs and abundant bird life, to the Tasmanian sea and back. Then we flew back by plane to Queenstown. We then flew from there back to the capital Christchurch and on to Melbourne, Australia.

In Melbourne, we had the Orbital Society meeting in one of the historic rooms of the old medical school. We were treated to a tour of Melbourne, including a lecture on the history of the entire area and that of Australia. Our banker friend, Brian Brandon, whom we had met in Bangkok, took us on a tour of the wine country around Melbourne, which was spectacular. From there we went to Adelaide, where we flew to Kangaroo Island, which we toured. It had recently suffered a fire, so the kangaroo population was in hiding and had been damaged. We saw wallabies and koala bears, but the kangaroos were scarce. The island itself was spectacular, with some great rugged natural scenery including extraordinary rock formations and very high sand dunes along the ocean. We stayed at The Wanderer's Rest, a small country inn with a great view of the ocean and terrific food. We returned to Adelaide and flew on to Cairns in northern Australia, and spent two days in the Kewarra Beach Resort, which was in a lush tropical forest on the coast. We took a gondola from Cairns to the mountains and toured a butterfly farm and returned by train. We flew from there by private plane to Lizard Island, which is a very lush island on the barrier reef with the exquisite Lizard Island Resort. The food and the ambience are superb and the cost of the place reflected it. The scuba diving on the barrier reef was excellent and I had always wanted to dive there. It was the culmination of my scuba diving experience. I have been to many scuba sites in the world, including the Red Sea and several places in the Caribbean. We returned through Cairns to Sidney and spent three days in Sidney touring the city and attended a concert in the great opera house on the bay. One day we rented a thirty-foot sailboat, with a captain, and sailed around the bay past the Sydney opera house, viewing it from the sea—an exciting experience, the wind being a little rough at the mouth of the harbor, which frightened Pat a bit. After a delightful three days of touring Sidney, we returned home to Pittsburgh.

Digression #9

In the department, the fellow who followed Kim Cockerham was Edsel Eng, who had two previous fellowships in neuro-ophthalmology at Will's Eye Hospital and at the Mayo Clinic. He came to learn surgery and eventually went to the Kresge Eye Institute in Detroit as a neuro-ophthalmic surgeon. Later, he returned to western Ontario to join his father in practice. The following year, Brad Schwartz, formerly trained in pediatric ophthalmology and highly recommended to me, joined the fellowship. He was an excellent surgeon and a good clinician, but a bit unruly. Following his fellowship, he eventually joined the department as a pediatric ophthalmologist, but he wound up in Tucson, Arizona doing pediatric ophthalmology and trauma.

The following year, Charlotte Thompson was a fellow who was trained by Simmons Lessell in Boston in neuro-ophthalmology and then spent a year with me after we helped obtain a fellowship in neuro-otology at the University of Pittsburgh for her husband. Upon completion of her fellowship, she had to stay in Pittsburgh and actually practiced in Mt. Lebanon at my original practice, awaiting her husband's completion of his fellowship. He decided to stay for a year, so she spent two years in private practice, which did not satisfy her and finally they both moved to Columbia, South Carolina, where she took an academic position doing neuro-ophthalmology and orbital disease at the University of South Carolina. Later she went on to private practice in Columbia.

The next fellow was Roger Turbin, an energetic person who was previously trained in neuro-ophthalmology by Mark Kupersmith in New York. He developed good surgical skills and following his fellowship, took a position at the Medical & Dental College of New Jersey in Newark, New Jersey, where he is developing a busy neuro-ophthalmic surgical practice. My next fellow was Angela Kim, who was trained as a neuro-ophthalmologist at the University of Michigan by Jonathan Trobe and then came to us to be trained in orbital surgery. She took a position at the division of ophthalmology at Evanston Hospital in Evanston, Illinois, a suburb of Chicago where she practiced neuro-ophthalmic surgery. Subsequently, she moved to Houston to practice at the M.D. Anderson Cancer Center.

The Wyoming Journey

In September 1997, Dick and Sue Estus joined us on a trip to Wyoming. We arrived in the Grand Teton Valley and proceeded to a resort in the National Park, Jenny Lake Lodge, owned by the Greenbriar Resort in West Virginia. The resort was rustic and we lived in adjoining cabins with a great view of the Grand Teton Mountains. The resort food was spectacular. We played golf on two valley courses and one day took a long hike around Jenny Lake, which was beautiful, but a very long way to circumvent the lake. We were exhausted on the return. Halfway through the week, we moved to the Spring Creek Resort high on a hill overlooking the valley near the resort town, Jackson's Hole, which was a delightful western town near a ski resort with good restaurants and shops. There we took an all-day raft trip down the Snake River and saw many animals (moose and elk) and birds (eagles).

From there we took our large RV and drove to Yellowstone Park in Montana, which had been devastated by fire a few years before our visit and had not recovered, much of it being burned out trees. The resort hotel was intact and very impressive. There we saw Old

Faithful, which spouts every two hours. The day was beautiful and we returned to our resort.

At an art auction we bought a photograph of the Grand Tetons and returned to Pittsburgh after a delightful week with our friends.

The New Mexico Journey

In November 1997, after another Academy meeting in San Francisco, Pat and I flew to New Mexico, where we rented a car and drove north through the desert to Santa Fe, an unusually beautiful and quaint city with many shops, craft stores, and art galleries spread all over town. We stayed in town at the Anasazi Hotel, a small but superb hotel named after an Indian tribe who lived there. We walked all over town and bought some nice art objects, including a chain–saw made Suarro cactus which found a place in our foyer at Hidden Valley. We took interesting side trips to see the Indian caves in the bluffs of northern New Mexico and to Los Alamos, the home of the nuclear bomb produced during World War II. Both were very interesting, as was a side trip to the Taos Ski Resort, with very steep, beautiful slopes. The weather was cool but sunny and we enjoyed the trip thoroughly, returning to Pittsburgh from Albuquerque, New Mexico.

The South African Journey

In February 1998, we took one of the finest trips that we have ever taken with the group, the Wuchers and Scheimers, through London to South Africa. We landed in Johannesburg, a troubled city and stayed in the outskirts of Johannesburg in the beautiful Michelangelo Hotel, which had its own group of restaurants and a shopping center, all enclosed for protection from the outside. We toured Pretoria, the capital city, with a guide who had recently been robbed at gunpoint and told us about all of the crime that was occurring in South Africa. Pretoria was very pretty and we visited the place where Nelson Mandela was inaugurated as president, together with the many historic sites in the countryside. We visited a diamond mine, which was an interesting experience in that the building surrounded a huge hole that had been dug to mine the diamonds. There was heavy security on entering and leaving the building. We then returned to Johannesburg, where we took a flight to Zimbabwe. We stayed at the famous Hotel Victoria and toured Victoria Falls, a spectacular sight that I will never forget. It is a huge waterfall, dwarfing Niagara Falls, and it takes almost an entire day to walk along the rim to see it all. Of course, one must be careful of the wild animals that occasionally roam through the area, including lions. We did see a group of monkeys on our tour through the park opposite Victoria Falls. The Victoria Hotel is a spectacular old British structure with a view of the falls from a distance and excellent food and ambience.

We flew from Zimbabwe to Botswana on a private plane and landed at the Mambo Camp, a safari camp set in the flood plane of the Ockavanga Delta of Botswana, which is populated by large groups of the characteristic animals of Africa. We stayed in tents that were elevated on platforms and had private outdoor bath and shower facilities. They were protected by bamboo walls and the tents were very comfortable with wooden floors and twin beds. The dining room was in a separate building and we were accompanied back and forth in the evening by local guides with guns to make sure that we were not accosted by the animals that roamed through camp at will. The first night we were awakened abruptly by a very load roar, which we thought came from a lion that was right in front of the tent, but the next day it was explained to us that the lion was at least a mile away and that the roar of a lion at night is extremely loud and can be heard over long distances. We were glad to be reassured that the lion was not in the immediate vicinity. We did see warthogs roaming through the camp and even elephants that came very close to the camp. We had a marvelous tour of the flood plains in a safari vehicle with an excellent local guide who brought us up very close to all of the wild animals including the lion, cape buffalo, leopard, cheetah, hippopotamus and rhinoceros. We saw all the major animals of the flood plain and large groups of monkeys, impala and many other kinds of African deer including kudos. The animal life was plentiful and we even watched a lion stalk an impala—an interesting experience—as well as observing a lion kill as they were devouring one of their victims, a kudo. We were able to get very close to these animals as long as we stayed in the safari car. One time, while we were stopped watching an elephant, it started to charge us and the driver didn't move the safari car. Apparently, we were not supposed to show fear and the elephant's charge would stop. Fortunately, it did, because I thought maybe we had come to the end of our trip. The elephant had one broken tusk, so they called him "One Tusk"; apparently he was kind of a nasty fellow. We saw him again as we traveled, running along at a distance. At the end of the four days, we were flown back to Botswana airport and then drove back through Zimbabwe to Victoria, where we boarded a plane to Johannesburg, this time staying at a hotel in Pretoria overnight.

From Pretoria we flew east to the second safari in eastern South Africa at Kirkman's Camp where our guide, Alan Jewart, was a native South African who had been born and raised in one of the private game preserves owned by his parents. He was a great guide and took us through the hill country in a safari vehicle for the three days. Again we saw every type of wild animal possible, including the wild dog, which is very rarely seen in South Africa. He would take us out in the morning as they did in Mambo Camp, and in the evening—often staying past dark where we would pursue these animals through the wild grasslands among trees, going through spider webs with large yellow orb spiders in the middle, which frightened the women, but were harmless. The webs were uncomfortable if they struck you in the face and the laughter was mighty as Jay Scheimer kept waving her arms to get rid of the spider webs. At Kirkman's Camp, one night we were eating in what they call a Boma, which is an outdoor dining room with a fire in the center and tables surrounding it. The Boma is surrounded by a bamboo circular high wall. The wall is not very strong, but it is a beautiful setting for dinner. We entered this enclosure through a convoluted passage way, so that animals of size are discouraged from entering that area. However, one night, my wife, Pat, heard a noise outside of the Boma, but the guide said it was the natives doing work. However, the noise got louder and when he listened again, he immediately picked up his gun and headed for the door while telling us all to stay in position. Needless to say, we all followed him outside and were confronted by a huge elephant that was stomping through the woods across the road near the Boma. The elephant saw us and stopped, trumpeted and then backed up and eventually walked away, much to the relief of the guide/hunter, who was supposed to protect us, after we had foolishly exposed ourselves to the danger. The building beside the Boma was strong and I think we could have probably gone inside if there had been more imminent danger.

At Kirkman's Camp, near Kreiger National Park, during an afternoon, when the girls shopped at the neighboring resort camp, Fred, Lou and I were at the swimming pool when we were warned to return to the main house, which we quickly did. We were told that the lions were coming up the road and they like to drink the chlorinated water at the swimming pool, which did not seem to bother them. We were delighted to see the lions, but we were finished swimming for the day. At Kirkman's Camp we were also escorted back to our motel-like rooms in separate buildings with a gun and a flashlight. The experience at the camp was spectacular with, again, all the animal sightings.

We flew back to overnight in Pretoria. The next day at Pretoria, we boarded the Blue Train, a very luxurious train, for an overnight trip to Capetown. The Blue Train was the most exquisite, fancy, luxurious train I have ever been on, with everything included in the trip so that you could obtain food or drink night and day and the meals were sumptuous. The scenery was spectacular on the route and the staterooms were very plush. I really enjoyed that 26-hour trip and only wished I could have been on the train for more then just a day. We arrived in Capetown to find a spectacular city with Table Top Mountain above it. We stayed at the Cape Grace Hotel in an area near the harbor, which was gated and fenced off to prevent unsavory characters from bothering the tourists. It was full of shops and restaurants and we sampled many of each. We took the cable car to the top of Table Top Mountain and toured that area with spectacular views of Capetown and the surrounding ocean. We also drove south by private car to the Cape of Good Hope, viewing the southern tip of Africa, and had lunch at a hotel that overlooked the sea. It was a very pleasant trip and our guide, John Mush, was very informative. While in Capetown, we were treated to a dinner by the tour directors of our South African trip because they had fouled up two pick-ups in Johannesberg. They entertained us at their home, which was in a pretty area in the outskirts of Capetown. They invited friends and we really were treated to a discussion of South Africa's current political situation, including the fact that Mandela was a great organizer of people, but was a very bad businessman, so that the country was not doing well and crime was very prevalent. We toured the wine country of South Africa with our guide, finding it to be a beautiful area with exceptionally good inexpensive wines. We were so enamored by the wines that we had a case of wine sent home and we were fortunate to be able to have it pass through customs and arrive safely. I really enjoyed the wines of South Africa. We then returned from Capetown through Miami to Pittsburgh. That trip was spectacular in every dimension. I would highly recommend that anybody who can afford it, go on a safari in South Africa and Botswana.

The Panama Canal Journey

In February 1999, Pat and I, together with Kim and Glenn Cockerham, decided to cruise through the Panama Canal to Costa Rica. We boarded our ship, the Raddison Diamond, in Ft. Lauderdale and sailed to Key West. I had been to Key West previously at a medical meeting, but I enjoyed the repeat experience of seeing Key West in better weather. We toured the entire city on a trolley including a visit to the southernmost tip of the United States and had an excellent seafood chowder in a local restaurant. We shopped for art, then cruised to Cozumel Island off the eastern coast of Mexico, famous for scuba diving. We shopped and walked around the island in the morning, then took a jeep tour driven by me, after many years of not driving a stick shift, across the island to the opposite shore, which was very rugged. We drove the jeep along the sands of the beach to see some ancient ruins and walked the beach, where we had a nice lunch. We returned by jeep to the ship after dark, a harrowing experience with people on the side of the dark roads as well as numerous bicycles and motorcycles. After we returned the car to the rental area we went to the ship to cruise on to Grand Cayman, an island famous for scuba diving and where Pat and I had spent a week during the Gulf War, when hardly anybody was on the island. (That was a delightful week and we were able to tour the entire island including the turtle farm and various resorts on the island. I dove a couple of times; one of the dives included a dive with the manta rays off the northern coast. This is an exciting experience that I would recommend highly.) On this trip, however, we only had one day, so we stayed in Georgetown, the only town, where we shopped and had lunch in one of the restaurants. Glenn Cockerham went scuba diving and had a good experience that time, but because of the glaucoma, I elected not to dive on that trip. We cruised to Andreas Island off the northern coast of Columbia, which was new to the cruise. This was a very small island and there was not much to see. It did have duty-free shops that were not very good. There was a very old and interesting church on the top of the island. Otherwise, that was not a very good choice of a place to stop. We then entered the Panama Canal, the highlight of our trip, and crossed the canal from east to west. This experience, passing through the locks and viewing the area along the canal, while the history of the canal was being explained, both in the conference room and over the loudspeakers, was fantastic. The Raddison Diamond is a twin-hulled ship and one can stand or sit on the deck above the bow and get a view of both sides of the canal. The entire experience, together with the history of the work through the various cuts they made with great and prolonged effort, was unforgettable. We passed through the western port of Panama City, where we saw Manuel Noriega's famous former home on the canal grounds near the Pacific Ocean. We then went north to the western coast of Costa Rica, where we traveled by bus to a still-active volcano on the way to the capitol of San Jose. San Jose is a dirty city without much to offer; a restaurant on the hill above the city offered great food, together with a spectacular view of the city. We stayed at the beautiful San Jose Marriott Hotel outside the city. The surrounding area is gorgeous, with mountainous coffee farms. We toured the Britt coffee farm, where we were entertained by professional actors who explained with levity the growing and making of coffee. We bought several packages of Britt coffee and shipped them back home. We toured the rain forest near San Jose as well, which is an exceptional experience with cable cars going through the higher part of the rain forest one way and coming back through a lower part of the rain forest, so that you can see it from the top and from the heart of the foliage which is lush and dense. It rained that day in the forest, so we bought ponchos that we used that day and since that time. We returned the next day from San Jose to Pittsburgh. That trip was very enjoyable, being with Kim and Glenn Cockerham, who became partners in the ophthalmology department at Allegheny. I would recommend that trip highly. The only way to tour the Panama Canal is by ship.

The European Journey

That brings us up to about the fall of 1999, when the usual group of three couples decided to tour parts of western Europe, including Luxembourg, followed by a cruise on the Mosel and Rhine rivers of Germany. We flew to Luxembourg, an exquisite old city with its own country, and checked into the Royal Hotel. We toured the city, including the Grand Ducal Palace and the town hall. We found a busy attractive city square where we had dinner. The next day, we traveled north by car with a Dutch couple to spend the day in Bastogne, the town where the WWII Battle of the Bulge took place. The tour guide was a man, Henry Mignon who had been a young boy during the battle, living outside Bastogne. He was hired by Thierry Verstraeten's father, who lives in Luxembourg. The guide was superb and detailed the entire battle with us for a full day. We arrived at a time of a reunion of one of the 101st and 82nd airborne divisions on a hill near Bastogne where they each had their name on a planted tree. We watched them explore the little forest to find their tree and talked to some of them about the battle. We also talked to the mayor of the town of Bastogne, an American who had been elected mayor as a former soldier who had fought at Bastogne. We returned from Bastogne to Luxembourg. The next day we traveled to the Mosel River, where we boarded a beautiful riverboat, the Switzerland II, on which we then cruised through the German wine country along the Mosel, seeing vineyard after vineyard on the slopes of the hills extending up from the river. The scenery was exceptional. We stopped at several small towns, one of which was an ancient Roman town, Trier, with a very stately castle that we toured. We saw several castles in other towns along the way. We rode a cable car across the Mosel to a restaurant high above the river. We then cruised to the Rhine River, heading south. The Rhine River in that part of Germany is spectacular, with high cliffs and many castles of various sizes. We stopped at Boppard, an ancient town on the Rhine, and enjoyed the evening at a festival of food and wine. We went on to the Neckar River and the town of Heidelberg, a famous German town which houses a college and medical school and has a large famous castle on the high hill above the town. I had been through Heidelberg Castle on my previous trip to Europe, but was happy to return to see it again because of the spectacular views of the area. The castle has a very large wine barrel from which they drew wine. We returned to the boat and motored up to the Neckar River to disembark and traveled by bus through beautiful southern Germany to Garmisch, a ski resort in Bavaria. We stayed at the Grand Hotel Sonnebichel and toured the local area including two of the famous castles, Hinderhof and Newschwanstein, of the former crazy King Ludwig II of Germany. We toured Oberammergau, site of the Passion Play. The castle tours were interesting in that the castles were very decorative and beautiful. We then took a bus tour to Munich, which is the capital of Bavaria, and toured the city including its central square with the famous glockenspeil with the revolving figures. We had lunch at the famous Hofbrauhaus in Munich, shopped a bit, and then returned to the hotel in Garmisch. That day, Jay Scheimer became ill with bronchitis and was hospitalized in Garmisch. She was very well cared for, but she had to stay there while the rest of us returned to Munich and then boarded a plane for the United States. The rivers of Europe are very pretty for the most part and interesting. The southern part of Germany is quite beautiful, especially the mountains, as opposed to northern Germany.

Digression #10

In 1998, AHERF (Allegheny Health Educations and Research Foundation), which had developed affiliations in Philadelphia with the Medical College of Pennsylvania and Hahnemann University, had acquired a number of hospitals in Philadelphia during the time of the rapid growth of large institutions. They acquired many medical practices, then found themselves to be extremely financially overextended and were forced to declare bankruptcy. This was a disaster at Allegheny General, with one of the largest medical institutions in the country to have declared bankruptcy. Fortunately, prior to the bankruptcy, the institution was interested in buying the department of ophthalmology and placing everybody on salary again, as we all were in private practice. I had difficulty with the concept and with the institution at that time, as the chief executive officer, an Egyptian named Sharif Abdulhak, seemed to be agitated and inconsistent. With the declaration of bankruptcy, of course he and the chief financial officer and the chief attorney, were fired from the institution. The whole situation was ludicrous in that the board of directors did not oversee these unwise investments and expenditures. At that time, there was a great concern in the department as to the possible failure of the institution and we had to restructure the department personnel, releasing some of the technicians who were paid salaries higher than community standards. We saved my secretary, Michele, to be the department's secretary, paid for by the institution. At that time, the members of the staff decided to hire another group of technicians, one by one, which proved to be difficult and made the department unsettled for a period of almost two years. Fortunately, because we remained private, we were not as affected by the bankruptcy as were the full-timer physicians who lost some of their benefits and almost lost their salaries. We stayed together at that time and gradually restructured the department without the support of the institution, only to regain that support in the fall of 1999. It was during that time when I was having the most difficulty with glaucoma, so it was a very low point in my career. In the fall of 1999, however, we restructured the arrangement with the institution, again obtaining a 15% support for our teaching service and re-establishing my salary as chairman. I also informed them that the department chairmanship should be passed to Garry Condon with the full approval of the other members of the department as opposed to the usual search committee interviewing outside candidates. I have seen too many ophthalmology departments destroyed by the search committee's complete ignorance of the specialty. When they bring in outsiders who sometimes offend everybody in the department, they turn a very good or great department into a poorly performing department with loss of most of its important members.

The Spanish Journey

In the spring of 2000, Pat and I decided to tour southwestern Spain, a long-time desire of mine. We flew to Madrid and stayed at the Hotel Ritz, touring Madrid by private guide, Mauricio Macarron. Madrid is a magnificent city with many fine structures, including an old town with quaint old buildings, squares and tapas bars, bars that feature individual hors d'oeuvres, called tapas. Of course, we sampled several tapas. We toured the Prado Museum with its many sculptures and works of art. The next day, our guide and a driver took us to Toledo, a walled city surrounded by a river east of Madrid, a magnificent location. The guide showed us the old Jewish synagogue, which dates back to the 10th century in the town of Toledo, a town that changed hands through various wars, including the invasion of the Persians. It had many churches and was characterized by very narrow streets through which barely one car could pass. We visited the main church and some interesting shops. We had lunch in a very nice restaurant featuring great Spanish lamb. We returned to Madrid and walked around the city, having dinner at one of the tapas bars near the hotel; we toured a contemporary museum and a very interesting tapestry shop. We traveled by train from Madrid to Seville, a very pleasant experience as the trains are fast, clean and served by polite stewards. We arrived in Seville to stay at the famous hotel Alphonso XIII, then toured Seville's famous cathedral, a huge religious edifice of medieval times that was filled with remnants of the Persian era as well as the Christian era. The Persian influence on southwestern Spain is extensive and the architecture showed its blend of the European conversion of cultures. It is very pleasant to view this unusual type of Persian architecture. We went by train from Seville to Cordoba, where we saw the famous religious center called the Mesquita, a huge Muslim religious complex with great pillars set up in various stages. Later, the Christians placed their church right in the middle of this huge edifice, making it an unique combination of Muslim and Christian religious structures. The guide was excellent, and although the weather was slightly inclement, we were able to see the most important features of Cordoba, returning to the train to arrive in the evening back in Seville. We visited a bullfighting ring on a walking tour. It was not the season for bullfighting, but we saw the area under the ring where the famous matador costumes and the famous bull heads that fought in the ring were kept. It was an interesting experience to see this historic section of famous bullfighters and their victims. We left Seville by car and drove to Jerez, the capital of sherry country, and toured Jerez de la Frontera Sherry Winery and saw the famous white Spanish Andalusian horses. We traveled through southern Spain to Campo del Frontiera, a town on a high cliff overlooking the plains of southern Spain, which was a fortress in ancient times. The view from the top of the cliff was spectacular. We had a wonderful lunch in a hotel overlooking the vast plain from the buttress. We drove through the mountains of southern Spain to the Costa Del Sol. We stayed at the Marbella Beach Club on the coast.

At the club, we met David Douds, a former professional football quarterback with the Canadian Toronto Argonauts. He had a brief football career, but became wealthy as a packaged food producer and acquired a large fortune that he transferred to Ireland, where he lived. In Costa Del Sol, he had bought a house that he was furnishing. He was a delightful individual and we had a fun week with him in the Costa Del Sol. We toured the Costa Del Sol, including the port of Banus, where David spent many a night at an American bar in the harbor called Sinatra's.

We also toured the famous ancient southern town of Ronda in the mountains, another spectacular city built on top of a mountain with walls for protection, overlooking the vast plains and a river that runs through and around the town. We were taken on a tour by an excellent guide who showed us the various ancient edifices, including the old Roman baths and the famous churches. We saw other parts of the aging city by walking its narrow streets. We also toured the Rock of Gibralter, an interesting experience. We were able to take a taxi to the top of the Rock and go through part of the interior, which is honeycombed with miles and miles of tunnels that were military storage areas constructed by the British. Gibralter is still in British hands, much to the dismay of the Spaniards. We spent time in the town with its narrow streets, shops and pubs. It was interesting to be in an English pub off the coast of southern Spain. We walked back across the border into Spain and then drove our rental car back to the hotel. The next day we traveled east along the Costa Del Sol, past the town of Malaga, through the rugged southern mountainous country, to the famous city of Granada, the home of the Alhambra, the famous palace and fort built by the Muslims in the late 10th century. We stayed in the Alhambra Palace Hotel, near the gates of the huge fortress. We toured the fortress with our guide, who spoke excellent English. He showed us each and every feature of this wonderful edifice that was surrendered to Ferdinand and Isabel of Spain at the time of Columbus. The Muslim sultan was an inefficient soldier and virtually gave up as they approached the edifice. His mother was disappointed and called him a coward. Touring Alhambra was a terrific experience. Southwestern Spain is a beautiful area and it takes at least two to three weeks to cover it thoroughly.

The French Journey

In September 2000, the Orbital Society meeting was hosted by Serge Morax in Paris. Patty and I decided to attend the meeting and tour Paris, a city she had never seen. We flew directly from Pittsburgh to Paris and stayed at the Louvre hotel in downtown Paris, near the famous Louvre Museum. We had a private tour of the city and its surroundings, including the gardens and the forest of Paris, the Eiffel tower and the famous Notre Dame. We toured Montmartre and the tomb of Napoleon. We thoroughly covered Paris by day and night and found it to be interesting, with great small bar restaurants, brasseries, which had much better food than the larger restaurants or hotel restaurants which was as true as it was in Spain, Italy and Greece. We toured Versailles Palace with its ornate royal rooms and went to Rheims where we toured the magnificent cathedral, with its internationally recognized exquisite stained glass windows.

We then joined Mel and Jane Alper on a barge trip through Bourgogne (Burgundy). We took a fast train from Paris to Beaune, where we were met by a bus driver who took us through Beaune to the barge. We boarded the Mirabelle, an old working barge, which was re-structured as a floating hotel. The rooms were small, but comfortable, and the food on the barge, produced by a French chef and his helpers, was fantastic. The barge was captained and manned by an English crew, which was a surprise. First we toured the town of Beaune, the wine capital of Burgundy. There we toured an old hospice, the Hotel Dieu, where a rich man had endowed this famous Hospice de Beaune for people who were dying and as they passed through the infirmary with its religious paintings on the wall depicting heaven and hell, they were to be chastised and then able to pass onto heaven. This beautiful, but frightening spectacle was very interesting. We cruised on the barge to various small towns in southern France. At each one, the bus would take us on a tour every day to a different place, including an old Roman walled city and a castle that had been occupied by royalty in the past. We visited a famous chocolate factory—Bernard Dufoux—in a small town and learned how French chocolate is made without preservatives. The whole barge trip experience was fantastic, with a fun group. One could bike or walk along the canal as the barge traveled very slowly through many, many locks until we reached the end of our trip.

The excellent side tours were highlighted by a hot-air balloon trip. We were picked up early in the morning by the balloonists; it was a perfect day with mild breezes. We were taken to an open field where they inflated two different balloons with baskets. The first held 10 people, and there were 13 of us, so three of us, including Pat and I, and one of the boys who worked with the barge, boarded the smaller balloon, which we found a great deal of fun because it was not as crowded. We flew over parts of Bourgogne and saw the vineyards and the various farms and small towns with people waving to us and cattle running in the opposite directions, the balloons frightening them. The balloon pilots were spectacular, the older one with the larger balloon having had more experience; we were told later that the younger one, ours, was on his first year. Had we known that, we might have been a little more anxious. Our first landing was a little rough, through the tops of the trees where we landed in a field, only to find out that the chase cars could not get into the field to collect the balloons. We had to take off again to another field and by that time, the mid-day breezes were coming up, so when we finally landed in the next field, at some distance from our colleagues in the large balloon, we again came through the tops of the trees and had a rather rough landing where the basket fell over and spilled us partially out on the ground. To me, it was quite exciting; it was a little bit frightening to Pat. After we got everyone together, the balloons on the field, we were treated to champagne and the balloonists gave us berets with the balloon's name on the back.

We happily returned to the barge and explained our trip to Jane and Mel, who had decided not to join us. It was a great experience. The rest of the barge cruise was enjoyable, with superb meals; the food and wine were of exquisite quality, very well presented and very filling. We left the barge with regret, but having had an extremely pleasurable experience we will never forget. We took the train back to Paris and stayed overnight at a very nice hotel prior to departing for Pittsburgh.

Digression #11

In the fall of 2000, the departmental group had learned that Bob Arffa was telling our colleagues in Pittsburgh that he was very dissatisfied with his role in the department, as he had been thwarted in some of his management plans for the corporation. The rest of the group—including me—felt that the management should be done in a different way. The group met and decided to ask him to leave. He was given six months notice and told that he could leave voluntarily, which he elected to do on June 1, 2001. He decided to take a position with the University of Pittsburgh.

In December 2000, following Christmas, Nancy and Jeff flew to Pittsburgh to share a second Christmas with us, bringing Jeff's two children, Alan and Elena. Nancy was divorced and Jeff in the process of a divorce, so his wife did not come with them. Jeff had married a Mexican girl who was Alan and Elena's mother. Nancy and Jeff lived in Dallas, Texas for several years, as did their mother. We visited Dallas three times and found it a rapidly growing city with many good restaurants. We exchanged Christmas gifts at Hidden Valley and had a pleasant week together, with the kids taking skiboarding lessons.

The South American Journey

In January of 2001, Pat and I took an organized tour to the Galapagos Islands and to the Inca region of the Andes in Peru. We flew to Guayaquil, Equador from Miami and stayed in the hotel Colon, a lovely and modern hotel recently built in Guayaquil, the largest sea port in the west coast of South America, with a very busy harbor. Otherwise, it is a large and busy city without much to see. We took a tour on our return from Galapagos to see the river walk which they have developed along the wide river that descends from the Andes into the Pacific ocean. We saw tame land iguanas in the central town square.

We boarded a plane for the 300-mile trip to the Galapagos Islands, landing in Baltra to first view the rugged arid terrain of the Galapagos with desert cactus and other arid plants growing there. These islands are the place where Charles Darwin formed his theory of survival of the fittest, the prevalent evolutionary theory of today. The islands are home to a unique group of animals that are not seen in other places in the world. They were supposed to have arrived by clinging to rafts of trees and other debris that flowed into the Pacific Ocean from swollen South and Central American rivers. Other animals are theorized to have arrived there by sea currents coming from the south. The animals consist of a group of unusual birds called Boobies, both blue-footed and red-footed, the latter being able to cling to branches because the red feet will curl over a branch whereas the blue-footed Boobies are forced to be on the ground or on rocks, because they cannot fold their webbed feet. Both feet are webbed in design to allow them to dive into the ocean and eat small fish. A type of frigate bird that cannot fish or hunt has thrived there by stealing food from the Boobies as they are returning to the nest to feed their young. The frigates are able to steal enough food by attacking the back of the Booby; when it turns and opens its mouth, they grab the fish from its mouth. The Booby has learned to eat the fish while still in the water before returning from its dive to thwart the frigate bird, although it must carry food back for the young. The bird population includes a number of different finches that were extensively studied by Darwin and are the heart of his theory. The marine animals include a variety of sea lions that are supposed to have come from southern California and a variety of marine iguanas that are plentiful on the island. There are a few land iguanas that were prevalent on the islands, but were captured or killed by settlers or whalers who had visited there. Marine iguanas are not very edible and have no natural enemies, feeding on algae as they crawl and swim into the shallow water. The sea iguanas are everywhere and one must be careful not to step on them as one is crossing the lava rocks. All of the animals on the Galapagos are friendly, as they have no natural predators.

Our ship, called the M.S. Polaris, was an old freighter from Norway. It was refitted to be a tourist ship and has very adequate rooms with private baths. Every room has a large window to view the outside. We were very comfortable and the food was extremely good throughout the week. We were taken to many of the islands, each having its own habitat of different types of animals and plants. The beaches had a large variety of surface types including black beaches made of volcanic ash, powder-like beaches of fine sand, and beaches that are primarily small broken-up sea shells. One of the beaches has green turtle nests and we were fortunate enough to see some of the green turtles. The scuba diving was average because the water was not as clear as it is in the Caribbean or in the Australian Great Barrier Reef. The water is cool and filled with algae that provides food for the marine iguanas and some of the other animals, but causes reduced visibility. We saw several active and extinct volcanoes and crawled around on the lava rocks on many of the islands. On the island of Floreana, we saw an old naval post office, a box where letters were left by the whalers to be taken home by other ships and then mailed or taken from the port to the letters' addresses. We saw a group of tropical penguins that are only seen in the Galapagos. The whole experience was fantastic and the naturalist guides were terrific. The highlight of the trip was seeing the great land tortoises, which are huge and virtually became extinct because they were harvested by the whalers for meat. They could last for long periods without food and were taken on ships to allow them to have fresh meat after several months at sea. On the Galapagos Islands, they were finally saved and bred. The land tortoises we saw were passing through a farm on the way from the high country to the beaches of the island of Santa Cruz. These magnificent creatures move very slowly and are not afraid of tourists. We were able to get very close to them. We saw some of them that were in a habitat at the research center, protected and fed because they had been taken as private pets, the oldest of whom was Lonesome George. They were returned to the island for breeding purposes, but could not be allowed to fend for themselves in the wild after being in captivity for so long.

We returned from the Galapagos to Guayaquil, full of our experiences, and then boarded a plane to Lima, Peru, where we stayed overnight at the Swiss Hotel, a modern luxury hotel with a good dining room. We toured the city of Lima and went to a museum of ancient Peruvian artifacts. The next day we flew to Cusco in Peru, which is at 11,000 feet in the heart of Inca country. It is the largest city in the Inca region where it was the former headquarters of the Incas. The Incas were a fantastic civilization that only lasted for about a century and a half back in the 10th - 11th centuries A.D. The Incas probably came from the jungle and created these magnificent large stone fortresses and buildings in the mountains at the high altitude. They were thought to be small people as they are today and very much adapted to the altitude. We proceeded from Cusco through Inca country to a hotel in the heart of the valley in the Andes, called the Posado Del Inca. The hotel was our base from which we took several trips to Inca villages where they had markets selling crafts of various types and to a working farm in the mountains, with a magnificent farm house, where we were treated to an exquisite lunch in the mountains of the central Andes.

We were also taken to an Inca burial ground on the top of a hill and we were shown the tombs that were in the side of a very high cliff. The steep ground could not be used by the Incas so they used it for burial sites. Of course, these were raided by the Spanish for the gold and other precious objects that were placed in the tombs with the deceased. During that excursion, we saw a group of Incas bringing large bundles of eucalyptus leaves over the hill down to an area where they were being loaded on a truck. This was the UN's attempt to provide income for the Incas to gather the eucalyptus leaves, which were used for medicines and other things. The Incas received only a couple of dollars for these very large bundles of eucalyptus branches and leaves which are very heavy, carried on the shoulders of these small, but wiry and strong people. We took a train to the heart of the Inca country. The Incas built this magnificent village on top of the mountain, called Macchu Picchu. The village at the base of the mountain contains the very tropically oriented Pueblo Hotel, with rooms scattered over the hillside. It is situated along a raging stream, a beautiful setting. The hotel was very comfortable and the food was good. We toured Macchu Picchu in two days, being taken up by a bus to begin our walk through the ancient village. The walls were built with magnificent large stones and the village is on top of the mountain surrounded by other tall, green mountains that look like cones. We were shown the various buildings housing the rich, the poor, and the religious clergy of the pagan religions that were practiced by rituals, including the worship of the sun. We were then shown the ancient town square where the sacrifices were made. The sun dial above the town square was at the top of Macchu Picchu and it was somewhat difficult climbing over the large stones and stairways to see it. We had some people on the 25-person trip who were quite elderly and it was amazing that they could make it around the top of that mountain. We left the area of Macchu Picchu by train on the way back to Cusco. The train wound through the mountains and the valleys of the Incas and then several steep areas so that we had to switch back in order to negotiate the steep terrain. This was especially true as we descended into Cusco. There were several switchbacks that were made to allow us to get down into the heart of the city. The next day we toured Cusco, including an Inca building with its various unique construction characteristics and the church designed by the Spanish that was rebuilt in an Inca structure. The town of Cusco is not very attractive, but it does have some interesting shopping squares where only tourists are allowed and not street vendors. We bought several artifacts and returned to our Hotel Montasterio, formerly a monastery, which had delightful rooms that formerly housed monks and had a great restaurant and bar. In Cusco, we met one of my fraternity brothers who was on another group tour of the same region, Phil Cerveny and his wife Gwen. We had cocktails with him one night, but we were unable to have further meetings because their trip's schedule did not coincide with ours. We certainly enjoyed our whole entire experience in the Galapagos and in the Andes in the region of the Incas and will always have fond memories of that area. Again, this is a highly recommended trip, which is very different from anything else that we have ever done.

Digression #12

In April 2001, I gave the Susan Alper Memorial lecture at Washington Hospital Center. I was invited by Melvin Alper, Susan's father, who was my mentor and a long-time colleague and friend. Susan died young in an auto accident. I lectured on the management of optic nerve sheath and sphenoid wing meningiomas. Pat and I stayed at the Cosmos Club, a Washington club for accomplished academicians. It was very formal, but the food was great, especially at a luncheon given for us. I received a beautiful engraved glass tray as a gift for the memorial lecture. We visited an art museum and walked around the area near the club, which was beautiful with the spring flowers in bloom.

Our next trip was to Bucknell University in Lewisburg, Pennsylvania, where on June 2, 2001 I received the award for outstanding achievement in a chosen profession. We were with our friends, Pat and Bob Hershock, who proposed me for the award. I received an engraved silver bowl of the Revere type, after giving a brief account of my career to the alumni. It was quite an honor and I was gratified to receive it.

In early June, I went alone to Kansas City to give the Gerald Hyde memorial lecture on the same subject of optic nerve sheath and sphenoid wing meningiomas. The people in Kansas City were great hosts and Neil Miller and I had a good experience participating in their symposium. I stayed over Saturday night at the Renaissance Hotel, a small hotel near the plaza in Kansas City, to attend the resident graduation party, where I won another Revere silver bowl for delivering the memorial lecture.

In mid June we also traveled to Iowa City to attend the Orbital Society meeting. I gave the first Kennerdell half hour lecture. The society is twenty-five years old. Usually there are just fifteen-minute presentations. I lectured on the management of optic nerve sheath and sphenoid wing meningiomas.

At Iowa City, our hosts Jeff Nerad, and his wife Pam, hosted us at two dinners, one in a small restaurant and the second on a farm where they featured "slow food." This is a response to fast food. All the ingredients are home grown and the food is made from basic ingredients. On the farm, which was featured on the TV program "Sunday Morning" on CBS, we had a great dinner. They had their own pizza ovens where very unusual pizzas were made. The experience was unique.

The California Journey

In later June 2001, we traveled to California with my fraternity brothers and their wives. We first went to Carmel, where we stayed at Quail Creek Resort. From there we toured Carmel and Monterey, stopping at its unique seaquarium and driving past Pebble Beach Golf Club on the 10-mile scenic drive. The golf was great and the restaurants selected by Bob Hershock were excellent.

We then proceeded by car to the Sonoma Wine Country, where we stayed at the Kenwood Resort and Spa. It was a beautiful place, with gourmet breakfast included. I even had a massage, a rare event for me. We visited several wineries, which were small and very attractive. We bought several cases of wine from these unique boutique wineries. On our last day we went to the Napa Valley and stopped at two more wineries where again, I purchased wine. We returned to San Francisco for a day at a modern hotel with a great restaurant, then returned to Pittsburgh the next day.

Digression #13

Our book, entitled *The Practical Management Of Orbital Disease*, was finally published in June 2001. I had written the book over a four-year period with many revisions. Kim Cockerham joined the department in 1998. She volunteered to review the book and add additional information in my chapters as well as adding a chapter on pediatric orbital tumors. She also provided the illustrations and the references for the book and became the second author. Joe Maroon, who was the third author, wrote the chapters on the neurosurgical approach to the orbit; Bill Rothfus, the fourth author, reviewed and added the explanations of the CT and MRI images that were in the book. The 184-page book was produced by Butterworth-Heineman publishers and sold for $60 in softcover; it was designed for residents and fellows in ophthalmology. It is very readable and the illustrations are simple figures. It gave me a real sense of accomplishment to have published the essence of my academic career in the twilight of that career.

The summer of 2001 was spent working and enlarging the department. Weekends were spent in Hidden Valley. It was a pleasant and quiet summer. I continue to struggle with the game of golf and we increased the department members with the joining of Glenn Cockerham and Rattehalli Sudesh and Sudha Sudesh into our practice. Rattehalli Sudesh was our recent fellow who joined us in neuro-ophthalmology, ophthalmic plastic surgery and orbital disease; his wife Sudha Sudesh is very well-trained in corneal disease and joined Glenn Cockerham on the corneal service.

On September 6th, Pat and I went to New York to participate in a course organized by Mike Kazim, our 1989-90 fellow who is very successful at Columbia University, practicing ophthalmic plastic surgery and orbital surgery. He organized the course on the current status of management of thyroid disease and I lectured on the four wall orbital decompression. We stayed at the Pennsylvania Hotel, directly across from Madison Square Garden, which is a noisy, crowded hotel and of not the quality that I have been used to in New York. Overall it was satisfactory for the purposes of our visit. I attended the two-day meeting at Columbia-Presbyterian and it was very interesting. We had an international faculty and audience. We saw an interesting play on Broadway and ate at an interesting Italian restaurant on Saturday night in a private room organized by Mike Kazim. We left New York on September 9th and returned to Pittsburgh. On Tuesday, September 11th, while seeing a friend of mine as a patient, Connie Zahorchak, I learned of the tragedy that occurred in New York and subsequently Washington, D.C., instigated by terrorism. At that point, the whole world changed; those in our department as well as all other American and world citizens were shocked and dismayed by this event. We all vowed that we would support whatever efforts the country made in tracking and eliminating terrorists and would not be frightened by their actions.

The Newfoundland Journey

In late September, Garry Condon's mother, Virginia, who had been ill with a glioblastoma of the brain, died in Calgary, Alberta Canada. She was returned to St. John's Newfoundland and Pat and I went to St John's to attend the funeral. St. John's Newfoundland is a very pretty small port on the easternmost part of North America and formerly was a very busy fishing port, but with the over-fishing of the cod fish, it has been reduced to a non-working harbor. A few cruise ships, but no large tankers or cargo ships enter the harbor because of its narrow channel entrance. It is a beautiful harbor and the surrounding town is magnificent. We stayed at the Hotel Newfoundland and toured the entire area, including telegraph hill and the eastern most point of North America, Cape Spear. The funeral was well attended. Virginia was a wonderful woman with many friends. We spent the evening after the funeral with the Condon family and then returned to Pittsburgh.

The New Orleans Journey

In early November, Pat and I attended the American Academy of Ophthalmology Meeting in New Orleans. I have attended the Academy Meetings regularly since 1965 and I have not mentioned them in the memoirs because they were short trips to various cities. This time, however, after September 11th, the Academy was not as well attended as usual. It is usually quite large, with 40,000 people attending including ophthalmologists and all the paramedical personnel. This one was held in the huge convention center in New Orleans, which is the home of Pat's sister and brother-in-law, Barbara and Bill Maurer. We have always enjoyed New Orleans, particularly the food and to some degree the French Quarter, particularly O'Brien's, where two older women play dueling pianos. We had a reunion of the fellows in Brennan's restaurant, which turned out to be a great success with many of the fellows attending the reunion. We also had a successful meeting of the Orbital Society at the Windsor Court, with interesting patient presentations. The whole Academy experience is so huge and so diluted, that I think perhaps this will be our last Academy meeting. I do not seem to get the thrill out of the large meetings as I did in the past. I prefer the smaller meetings that are more tuned to my interests, such as the Orbital Society Meeting, the North American Neuro-Ophthalmology Meeting, or the Frank Walsh Society meetings, which we frequently attend.

Digression #14

Toward the end of the year, we managed to re-arrange Glenn Cockerham's contract with Jim Mondzelewski, so he was primarily working for us in the department heading up the corneal service. The Sudeshes, however, decided to join their family in the Silicone Valley of California, and left the department in March 2002.

Christmas 2001 was spent at Hidden Valley, just Pat and I. Our daughter arrived for a few days before Christmas and then spent Christmas with her grandmother, Louise DiBacco, an 84-year-old woman in Elkins, West Virginia, who had developed lymphoma and was unable to take chemotherapy. Nancy and her cousin Carolyn spent Christmas with Louise, which was a very fine gesture on their part. Christmas was quiet for us, although we attended parties with friends at Hidden Valley.

The St. Croix Journey

In early February 2002, Pat and I joined Pat and Bob Hershock for a trip to St. Croix, to the Carombola Golf Resort. The trip on US Air, which we upgraded to first class, was eventful; a passenger had a stroke, which required us to land in Bermuda while they removed him to a hospital. The layover in Bermuda was not too uncomfortable, particularly since we were in the first class section. We arrived late in St. Croix, where we rented a van and drove to the Carombola Resort in the dark. The roads in St. Croix are two lanes and not well lighted, so we became lost, but finally found our way through the gate and into our condominium, which was near the tee of the second hole of the golf course with a very nice view of the golf course. It was on the second floor and our porch overlooked the tee and across the fairway to the mountains. We played golf for five of the seven days and toured the island for two days. The golf was excellent, the Carombola golf course being the oldest and the only full-length golf course on St. Croix, which is not as well-developed as the other islands. We went into Christianstadt, the main city, at night and ate at several restaurants, particularly Kendrick's, which was excellent. We visited local restaurants near our resort, which were right on the coast with the waves lapping virtually at one's feet and had two great dinners at a place called Off the Wall. We toured the island, including Frederickstadt at the western end of the island in the rainy area. Frederickstadt is a very small town that hosts cruise ships, none of which were there when we visited the town. On our return through the rain forest we stopped at a bar where pigs were trained to drink beer. There were three pigs drinking non-alcoholic beer and we bought cans of beer at $2 apiece and fed them to the pigs—a riotous experience. The pigs were fairly large and we had to put the whole can in their mouths without opening it; they would punch through with their teeth and then pull their heads back and the beer would drain down through their throats, then they would drop the cans in the yard. There was a memorial to the original pig who drank real beer and died of cirrhosis of the liver. We also toured the eastern end of the island and went to the easternmost point of the United States, Udall's point, named for Secretary of State Stuart Udall, who had the land designated as a park. The eastern portion of St. Croix is desert-like, with cactus and other plants that are seen in dry areas. We visited a resort on the eastern end of the island called the Buccaneer, which is the nicest resort on St. Croix. Buck Island off the coast was an excellent snorkeling area, but when we were there the water was a little rough and none of the other people enjoyed snorkeling, so we were unable to sample the undersea life at Buck's Island.

I was not impressed with St. Croix as a resort destination, but we certainly had a wonderful time with our friends and the golf was fun.

The Arizona Journey

In late February 2002, we went to Scottsdale, Arizona with the Wuchers and stayed with them in their time-share in Scottsdale, a condominium with two bedrooms and separate bath facilities and kitchens. This was a very nice resort with a beautiful swimming pool, relatively close to the tourist sites in Scottsdale. We visited Frank Lloyd Wright's Taliesan West, the architectural school that is still functioning. It was the unique flat-roof design of Frank Lloyd Wright, which nestles into the desert and has many of his characteristic architectural designs. We also went to a tennis tournament for women at a tennis complex near the condominium.

We visited Bob and Caroline Fitzsimmons. Bob was my fraternity brother in the class of 1958 at Bucknell and joined our previous summer's journey to California. Bob is a golfer and retired as an executive from a furniture company. He and Caroline live in a very nice house in North Scottsdale near the golf course. We had dinner with them at the Four Seasons Resort, which had a spectacular view over the valley.

Lou and Jay Sheimer joined us on this trip and we did some reminiscing about our previous trips together. We ate at several good restaurants and visited an art show in Scottsdale that featured some large sculptures by David Hiles, a former pediatric ophthalmologist from Pittsburgh. We took a Hummer ride into the desert over steep terrain and were taught how to survive in the desert as well as the remarkable features of the Hummer. We saw a Gila Monster Lizard—not often seen in daylight.

We enjoyed the trip very much. Pat and I have always liked the desert and plan to return one day.

The Vancouver Journey

In March, I was invited to speak at an international orbital symposium in Vancouver, British Columbia, by Jack Rootman. Pat and I traveled to Vancouver and I participated in the orbital society meeting and the orbital symposium that covered a period of four long days of orbital disease and surgery.

The meetings were both excellent and we stayed at the Sutton Place Hotel in central Vancouver, a very well-appointed and well-run hotel.

We then traveled with Jenny and Jack Rootman after the meeting to tour Vancouver Island, where we stayed at the Sooke Harbor House, an exclusive and highly rated resort on the western side of Vancouver Island. The view from our quaint suite was spectacular across the water to other islands with their beautiful rugged shorelines. Unfortunately, the weather was poor with snow, which is rare for Vancouver at anytime, particularly in the spring. The flowers were attempting to come out of the ground, but were curtailed by the cold weather.

We had two exquisite five-course dinners in the restaurant. The wine that we selected with the meals was excellent.

We also enjoyed a trip further west on the island and had lunch at another small restaurant overlooking the sea, which served nice seafood bouillabaisse. We stopped on the way back in a woodworking shop where a man has made a living out of taking old wood with interesting shapes from dead trees that have been knocked down, and making it into a variety of bowls, chairs and cups of all sizes. We bought a bowl for the coffee table made from a very interesting piece of wood.

Despite the weather, we enjoyed being with Jack and Jenny for three days and returned from Vancouver Island across the Sound by ferry and stayed overnight at Jack's house, having dinner at Tokyo Joe's Restaurant, which is reported to have the best sushi on the West Coast. The dinner, selected by Jack, consisted of sushi, sashimi, and other Japanese foods that Pat could enjoy. I thought that the Japanese dinner was the best dinner that I had the entire week.

Digression # 15

On our return from Vancouver, I resumed working in the department with my patients and assisted Kim Cockerham in surgery on some of the more difficult orbital cases, which are referred in from all over the country. We then spent an uneventful late spring and in June attended the 45th reunion of our 1957 class at Bucknell with several fraternity brothers. We had a marvelous time with the group and the meeting was memorable in that regard.

In the early summer our bird feeders at Hidden Valley were damaged severely by a bear, as were the neighbor's. I called the game commission and they sent an officer with a large barrel trap to catch the bear. Doughnuts were used as bait and after several failures we finally caught a young female bear weighing about 170-180 pounds who was taken to show at a youth camp, then moved east to Bedford County where she was set free. We thought we had the problem solved but a large black bear showed up just after I had lunch and I photographed him eating the bird seed. I tried to get the game commission to come back, without success, so he is still at large.

In July and August, we stayed in western Pennsylvania because Pat had one of her technicians take a leave of absence due to a pregnancy and we spent our weekends at Hidden Valley enjoying a very hot summer, playing golf from time to time there. We have developed several new friends at Hidden Valley since most of our previous friends had left the resort. At Hidden Valley, we had the air conditioning on for two weekends, which was very rare because of the fact that it is on average 10 degrees cooler in the mountains than it is in Pittsburgh during all seasons (which provides us with snow in the winter as well as a cooling effect in the summer).

On August 18th, my daughter Nancy delivered a 7-pound baby boy named Michael Joseph Lawrence, three weeks before her due date. The baby and the mother have done well after the birth and she now will be finding that her life has changed dramatically at 39. Her new husband, whom she married on June 29, 2000 in a very pleasant backyard ceremony at her home, is Joe Lawrence. We attended the wedding in Dallas and were very impressed with the backyard wedding with a non-denominational female minister helping them perform the marriage. Some of her friends were there, including her cousin Carolyn and her brother Jeff, who were both in the wedding. She looked quite nice in a white gown, though extremely pregnant at seven months. I escorted her down the aisle. Everything went extremely well and they were happily married and were enjoying their newborn son.

In August, Jeffrey brought his daughter Elena and her brother Alan to Pittsburgh for a visit. We felt that this was a better solution than going to the shore, which we had planned to do, because of the fact that Nancy was pregnant and unable to attend. The children were taken to a baseball game, the Science Center, two amusements parks and had a very exciting week. Pat and I enjoyed it as well. They spent two days with their grandmother, Louise DiBacco, in West Virginia prior to returning to Dallas. Jeff said that they had an excellent time and wanted to return. Alan was 11 and Elena was 7 years old and they were growing up rapidly.

We learned in the Department of Ophthalmology in September 2002 that the St. Francis Hospital was going to be sold to UPMC because they were bankrupt. The residency program at St. Francis, which had rotated residents to our department, was now taken over by UPMC and the future was vague. Initially they decided to rotate the residents to a clinic in the region where St. Francis had been and continue the rotations with us. However, they changed their minds and after meeting with Kim Cockerham, our residency director, decided to close the clinic in Lawrenceville. They decided to continue rotating the two third-year residents and one second-year resident with us but to keep the first-year resident at UPMC for his initial training. They also agreed to loan us St. Francis equipment to place in a room in the Cancer Center, so that the senior residents would have access to clinical space, which is at a premium in the Department of Ophthalmology since we have seven ophthalmologists and three optometrists needing space. We continued to monitor the situation carefully because of UPMC's history of withdrawing residents from us. They rotated the residents with us as long as they needed our help in their education. Therefore, we increased our fellowship program to accommodate the need for clinic coverage and night coverage in the hospital and to meet our educational objectives.

The Northeastern Journey

In late September, together with Fred and Mary Anne Wucher, Pat and I traveled to Montreal and boarded the Royal Princess Cruise Ship for a cruise from Montreal through the mouth of the St. Lawrence River, ending in New York City. We arrived in Montreal in a steady rain and were transferred to the ship; we familiarized ourselves with this beautiful cruise ship with several restaurants, a large main dining room, several bars and nightclubs, and a gambling center. Their exercise center was very well-equipped and, of course, there were a number of outdoor pools, but the weather was cool and they were not used.

The day following our arrival, we toured the old city of Montreal. Because we all had been to Montreal previously, we did not take the grand tour of Montreal, but stayed in the quaint old city of Montreal near the dock where the ship was located. We saw several of the old shops and Pat bought a very nice scarf; we had a drink at a restaurant that overlooked the harbor. We then returned to the ship in the afternoon and relaxed prior to our departure for Quebec.

That evening, we had our first dinner in the main dining room and enjoyed the service very much. The ship was equipped with metal detectors at the boarding area and we were issued identification cards encased in plastic, which had to be presented each time we boarded or departed the ship.

The second day, we arrived in Quebec early in the morning and took the grand tour of Quebec by bus. We were taken to Bridal Veil Falls, then Mount Morency Falls east of the city, which is higher than Niagara Falls, but not as wide. It was quite beautiful to see and I climbed a path to the top and walked over a bridge above the waterfalls, which had a spectacular view of the falls and the water passage to the St. Lawrence River. We were then taken to a large basilica east of Quebec that had a reputation for healing of patients with chronic disease, particularly orthopedic or neurologic problems. On one side of the interior of the basilica, they displayed a number of crutches that had been thrown away by patients supposedly cured by the hands-on treatment and prayers of the priests. The basilica had several exquisite stained glass windows. We were then taken to lunch at a road house near the basilica. They were very well-organized to feed a large group. The lunch was average, the salmon being tolerable, but the chicken was cold and this tourist restaurant was not very appealing. We then proceeded to Quebec City, the only walled city in North America. The city is very quaint and has a lot of character inside the city. We also were taken to the western plateau adjacent to the city where the Battle of Quebec took place, and it was described to us in some detail. We left the bus in Quebec and entered the Hotel Chateau Frontenac, which had a great view of the St. Lawrence River and the old city below the wall. We toured that part of Quebec at the end of our tour and then returned to the ship. The city was very beautiful and one could easily spend a long weekend there having a more leisurely experience.

The next day, the ship sailed east on the St. Lawrence River and entered a fjord, the only one in North America, and we went north to where it was fed by the Saginaw river. The sides of the fjord were high granite walls with forests on top, which were supposed to be in fall colors, but because of the hot summer, the coloring was delayed and they were basically still green. The tour up the Saginaw River was supposed to be accompanied by whale watching, but no whales appeared. We went all the way up the Saginaw to the end, where we turned around in a small lake and then returned to the St. Lawrence River, where we sailed through the mouth of the St. Lawrence around northern Nova Scotia to Halifax, Nova Scotia. This required two full days at sea, which were delightful in that I was able to work out in the mornings. The weather was fairly good, but somewhat foggy on the second day and so we enjoyed the games played on the ship and the camaraderie of our friends, together with the three exquisite meals a day—certainly more food than we needed, but very enjoyable.

The fifth day, we arrived in Halifax in the morning and were taken from the ship for a tour of the city and the surrounding area. Halifax was interesting because of its historic architecture; it has a citadel built on top of the city to protect it, and it has never seen any type of military activity. It is made of stone and covered with sod, so it was very well-situated to view the harbor and the grounds west from the hill. It would have been difficult to assault that citadel in the days before modern weaponry. After we toured the citadel and the city itself, where all the major buildings were pointed out, as well as a beautiful park, we toured the southern coast to Peggy's Cove, an extremely clean fishing village with a lot of character and many picturesque scenes of fishing boats. It sits on a series of granite boulders that were laid by the great glacier and it has a beautiful lighthouse at the end of the harbor. It was very close to the crash site of the Swiss Air disaster that resulted in a loss of all crew and passengers three years prior to our visit. When that crash occurred, the fisherman from Peggy's Cove voluntarily went out to see if they could pick up any survivors. Unfortunately, there were none, but they brought back some bodies and debris to Peggy's Cove. They had ceremonies there for the victims of that airline disaster and a monument has been erected. An artist lived in Peggy's Cove for a long time and was also a very good sculptor. He sculpted a very large granite rock in the northern end of the village, depicting the fishermen of Peggy's Cove and Peggy herself. His ashes were placed in a box that was inserted into that granite rock. We took several photographs of the city and of the picturesque fishing village. On the way back to Halifax we had a large two-lobster lunch in the Lobster Ranch Restaurant, where we received instruction on how to dismantle whole lobsters. We walked around Halifax for a short time prior to re-boarding for our journey to St. John, New Brunswick, an ordinary city with very little character. It does have an interesting large tidal change because the water runs up river at high tide and out at low tide; there is a set of falls near the city beside a large paper factory which reverses according to the high and low tide. We were able to see it rushing out in low tide and then later in the day on a return to St. John we saw it rushing inward. It is a very unique situation, called the reversing falls. Because St. John is not a very picturesque city, we were advised to take the bus tour to St. Andrew's, a very quaint resort town north of St. John on the coast. It took an hour to arrive there, but we had plenty of time to walk up and down the single shopping street and we visited a restaurant overlooking the harbor recommended by Garry Condon, who had recently been there as a lecturer. He stayed at the Algonquin Hotel, a very large old resort hotel with a golf course that overlooks the sea. It is a beautiful and elegant old hotel and we enjoyed afternoon tea there. The town of St. Andrew's is quaint and we walked to a small hotel with six rooms and an exquisite dining room. If we ever return to St. Andrew's, I think we would like to stay at that hotel in the town and enjoy the cuisine. The weather in Halifax and St. John was magnificent, with clear skies and cool temperatures. We returned on the bus directly to the ship and departed that evening for Bar Harbor, Maine.

Bar Harbor is in the United States so we went through customs and disembarked there to get the grand tour of Bar Harbor, including Cadillac Mountain, which has breathtaking views overlooking Bar Harbor and the town. The day was extremely clear and so we could see great distances. We toured the national park there and then spent time in the town of Bar Harbor, shopping and relaxing in a restaurant. Bar Harbor is extremely popular in the summer, when the population swells considerably, but in the winter it is a much smaller population and the craft shops and other stores are closed for the most part. The water was extremely cold as it is in all the maritime provinces, so swimming is not an option even in the summer. The views from the various parts of the national park above Bar Harbor are sensational. We enjoyed Maine lobsters at a lunch in the hotel on the island. We also toured a small town where the former Secretary of State, Caspar Weinberger lived.

That evening we left Bar Harbor and headed for Boston, where we disembarked and took the grand tour of Boston including the Old North Church and Copley Square, then had lunch in the Old Oyster House, which served very good clam chowder and halibut. Following lunch, we toured Lexington and Concord where the initial battles of the Revolutionary War took place and found the tour most interesting, especially with the dialogue provided by the guides. We wished we had spent more time in Lexington and Concord with a more leisurely review of the history.

We left Boston Harbor for Newport, Rhode Island, where we disembarked and took the tour of the Vanderbilts' homes, the most famous one being called the Breakers, an imitation of Versailles in France. It is on the Atlantic coast with a fantastic view and reflects the opulence of the latter part of the 19th and early part of the 20th century, which cannot be duplicated today. The other house, called Marble House, is another magnificent Vanderbilt mansion. The Marble House was slightly smaller than the Breakers, but even more expensively decorated.

We then returned to Newport and spent the afternoon in the quaint town, with many tourist shops and restaurants. The most interesting one was the White Horse Tavern, the oldest tavern in the United States, dating back to the 17th century. It is small and dark, with worn wood floors, but dressed up with dark tables with white tablecloths. It was quite pretty and the food is supposed to be good, but very expensive. Because it was the afternoon, we only stopped for a drink. We had a snack in a harbor house overlooking the harbor, which was also quite nice. We then boarded the ship where we had our farewell dinner that night and then proceeded to New York, arriving in the very early morning to pass by the lighted Statue of Liberty and Manhattan where the ship passengers and crew observed a moment of silence for the 9/11 destruction of the Twin Towers and those who died there. We docked in New York and then traveled by bus to the airport to return to Pittsburgh. The whole trip was characterized by very good weather when we were off the ship on various tours.

The Dominican Journey

In February 2003 we joined Bob and Pat Hershock and Phil and Gwen Cerveny on a trip to the Dominican Republic to a destination resort called the Casa De Campo on the southeast coast. The Dominican Republic is a poor country and without much interest except these spectacular destination resorts that have been developed. We flew to the capital of the Dominican Republic, Santo Domingo, and were taken by van to the resort, where we checked in and were taken to our comfortable three-bedroom house on a golf course. The package included a maid and a butler with breakfast cooked in the house. The rest of the meals were taken at a variety of seven restaurants in the compound, which included seafood, continental, Italian and Mexican. Our itinerary included three days a week of golf and on the alternate days we went to the beach or toured the resort. The beach was magnificent. All food and drinks were included in the package, so we enjoyed pina coladas at the beach and drinks at other bars and restaurants. They have developed a new marina on the resort and restaurants that are not included in the package, but one of them an Italian restaurant Pepperoni, was excellent, although expensive. The resort has also developed a duplicate of a 17th century village in Spain on the top of a high cliff overlooking a river and the ocean. This village was very quaint, with multiple shops and cobblestone streets. It houses three restaurants and a beautiful church that hosts many weddings. The view from the top of the cliff is spectacular. We frequently traveled to the village at night in a van arranged by the resort. We played the Teeth of the Dog golf course, which has spectacular ocean holes. We took a tour of major homes in the resort set up by a charity and then took a beautiful sunset cruise on the Caribbean Sea; the seas were a little rough, so our stomachs were queasy on that trip. The following night we took a trip up the river under the village and back, which was quite smooth; the scenery along the river was typically tropical. The entire two weeks were very relaxing and very enjoyable with our friends. We did not venture outside the resort because there was nothing to see in the Dominican Republic. The resort has many activities, including horseback riding and polo training if one is so inclined. We left the resort with regret, having had a wonderful time; we thought that this is one place to which we might consider returning in the future.

Digression #16

In March 2003, the glaucoma service was very busy and recruitment of another glaucomatologist might be necessary for the future. The neuro-ophthalmology and orbital service continued to grow and the retina service had been very busy and was contemplating a third person. Glenn Cockerham, heading the cornea external disease service had become increasingly busy in that area. We engaged three fellows for the year because of the loss of the residents on June 15th. Allegheny General, as well as other hospitals, had difficult financial times because of lower reimbursements from several insurers including Blue Shield, Gateway and Medicaid.

The Southern Journey

In latter March, we attended the wedding of the son of our friends Nelson and JoAnn Hicks, in Charleston, South Carolina. The entire Hicks family, most of whom I had not seen for years, attended the wedding, which was beautifully done in a small old church in Charleston, a very quaint city frequented by tourists. The rehearsal dinner and the wedding reception were very enjoyable and the food was superb. We enjoyed our weekend in Charleston and then I joined my fraternity brothers in Myrtle Beach for a week of golf, as we had been doing for five years. The week of golf was fun because of the company involved. I only played every other day, spending the off days with Al Levesque, who does not play golf. In late May of 2003, we attended a reunion of seven fraternity brothers and their wives at the Kings Mill resort in Virginia, near Williamsburg. This is a great resort for reunions or parties because the condominiums are located in one group of buildings where you can have adjoining condominiums with two or three bedrooms so we could all congregate together. The golf was fun and the food at the resort was excellent.

We toured Williamsburg, a quaint old revolutionary town; it is very interesting to see the shops and historical materials that are always of interest.

The Ottawa Journey

On June 12, 2003, we flew to Ottawa, the capitol of Canada, a beautiful city with spectacular government buildings. Our five-star hotel, the Lanier, was attractive with a green tin roof. The Orbital Society meeting was well organized by David Jordan, the member from Ottawa. We had a very nice dinner at his house on Thursday evening. On Friday, the meeting was intense.

We had a spectacular dinner at the art museum Friday night, and Saturday night we had a very nice dinner at a French restaurant in the countryside, where I had an excellent caribou steak. Saturday, we toured the National Art Museum. Sunday, we took a canal trip through Ottawa with Jack Rootman on the only sunny day of the weekend. The views from the canal were very interesting as all of the capital structures were pointed out along the way. We flew back to Pittsburgh with fond memories of Ottawa and satisfied with a very successful meeting, convinced that the future prospects of the Orbital Society were excellent.

The Bald Head Island Journey

In late June, Pat and I drove to Southport, North Carolina, about 20 miles south of Wilmington, North Carolina, near Cape Fear, to rent a three-bedroom house on Bald Head Island. A ferry left from a dock in Southport owned by Bald Head Island Resort and very efficiently took us and the Posts, who joined us at the loading dock, to the marina on Bald Head Island. There we were deposited with our luggage and taken by a golf cart using a baggage trailer to a beautiful house called Blue Heron, on the wide eastern beach on Bald Head Island. The house was in a complex of similar Cape Cod-style houses with direct access to the beach via a boardwalk. We were behind some sand dunes and the boardwalk crossed the sand dunes to a wide beach, which was sparsely populated. We enjoyed settling into the house, one bedroom of which was in the crofter, a completely separate suite above a small garage that housed two golf carts that were our transportation on the island. There are no cars on this island except for utility vehicles. We explored the island and found a restaurant called the River Pilot, which was very nice for a casual lunch or dinner, and then found the market in the central portion of the island, which was well-stocked with food and wine. It was surprisingly attractive and the quality of the merchandise was excellent and not too expensive. The first night we had dinner at the golf club, at a buffet that included a wide variety of excellent seafood. The next day, we played golf on Bald Head Island golf course, which was very well-laid out and fun to play. There was a lot of water on the course and, of course, if one got off the fairways into the brush the ball was not retrievable. We had some high scores and lost balls the first two times we played with Kay and Dave. On the off days, we stayed on the beach and enjoyed the ambience of the house. We were joined on Wednesday by Nelson and JoAnn Hicks, who brought their boat, VICTORY, up from Charleston and docked it in the marina on Bald Head Island. The next day Naomi and Bob McCormick, from Hilton Head Island, stayed with us in Bald Head through the 4th of July. We had a marvelous time with them, again enjoying the beach and a parade on the 4th of July comprised of golf carts cleverly decorated. The parade was on the main road of the island. On the evening of the 4th of July, we saw a few distant fireworks but actually had our own party. On Saturday after our friends left on Nelson's boat, we were joined that evening by our daughter and son-in-law, Nancy and Joe and their new baby, Michael. It was a real pleasure to see the new grandson and they came to the house with Joe's daughter by a previous marriage, a 13-year-old girl who livened up the week with her teenage antics. She enjoyed the beach but would not go in the water for fear of sharks. One shark was sighted off the island according to a neighbor, who made the mistake of mentioning it to my wife. Neither of the girls would enter the water, which was very safe and shallow for a long distance offshore. The undertow was mild and not dangerous. I enjoyed swimming in the ocean every day and walking the beach in the early mornings. It had been years since we had a beach vacation and this was just spectacular. The second week I played golf once with Joe. During the week, the baby was taken to the beach several times and seemed to enjoy it; he was very pleasant all during the week, which passed very quickly. We played several games, then Nancy's cousin Susan and her husband showed up for a day and we had fun with them. We played a game called Sequence, which we had learned from my fraternity brothers. Before we knew it we were back on the ferry headed for the mainland and to the long drive home. We reflected on the trip that it was a great vacation spot for families or close friends. It probably was not a great place for a group that liked to go out to dinner every night, because of the limited restaurants available on the island. The island does enjoy a reputation for having weddings in an open pavilion near the marina. The pavilion is very modern and quite attractive. The marina is small and filled with very expensive boats. There is a very old lighthouse on the island that has been restored. The island also has a nature trail and several programs for teenage children, involving sports and nature hikes. I think that this particular island is a very nice retreat for a summer vacation, providing the weather is good, which it was in our case.

Digression #17

In July, Chris Haggerty began his fellowship in neuro-ophthalmology and orbital disease, together with two other fellows in cornea and glaucoma. Chris was referred to us by one of our former fellows, Charlotte Thompson from Columbia, South Carolina, where he trained. He did not have a previous fellowship, so he was starting directly from his residency, which made his training a little more difficult. Kim started him in surgery and he worked with both of us in the clinic. He had a very good attitude and was eager to learn. We have been very busy with a high surgical volume.

The Mt. Gretna Journey

In August, Pat and I went to Mt. Gretna, a small mountain resort near Lancaster, Pennsylvania where our friends Pat and Bob Hershock own a home that was previously owned by her father. This mountain resort is quaint, with large old houses with many bedrooms but only a single bathroom plus a powder room. It has a large covered porch and was built on a nice lot; most of the houses are close together. The town features a number of arts and craft festivals and has a large artificial lake for swimming. There was a huge art festival the week that we were there, which we participated in for two days. There were over 300 exhibits. There was a spectacular storm that hung over the area on Saturday so we spent most of the day playing games on the beautiful huge porch. We went to several excellent restaurants and enjoyed the ambience of Mt. Gretna. It is interesting that I had been to Mt. Gretna at the end of my freshman year in college in 1954. I stayed at an old hotel owned by parents of a Bucknell girl who invited us for the weekend. I was told by Pat Hershock that she remembered the hotel, as she had spent the summers there with her grandparents.

The hotel was destroyed by fire several years ago and was not restored because it was too expensive.

We also visited an interesting old iron forge where cannon balls were made for the Civil War. The Forge restaurant was excellent.

Digression #18

In early September, Kim Cockerham arranged a fellowship reunion to include a course on surgical rehabilitation of patients with thyroid eye disease. Many of the fellows returned for the course and reunion. It was most interesting to see them all and to appreciate the skills that they have developed. They demonstrated new techniques of orbital decompression and orbital fat removal for patients with severe thyroid eye disease. We had dinner at Kim's house on Thursday night and a party at our townhouse on Saturday afternoon. We had a great time renewing old acquaintances and talking about the years since they were fellows. Twelve fellows returned and they all presented challenging and interesting cases on Saturday morning for discussion. The fellowship training for me has been one of the highlights of my career, and it is gratifying to see how well the fellows have done in this field that I developed in neuro-ophthalmology and orbital surgery.

Unfortunately, at the same time, Kim Cockerham informed me that she and her husband were leaving the department and moving to

California to practice near her home. Apparently, her mother had developed fibromyalgia and Glenn never liked the northern winters, being from the South. I was disappointed to see her go, for the department and myself.

The Iron Curtain Journey

In late September 2003, together with the Wuchers, we went on a European adventure to Austria and then to several former iron curtain countries. This is a trip that I had always wanted to take, and we were finally able to arrange it. These countries, formerly behind the iron curtain, had difficulty developing tourism, but now have reached a point where travel is safe and moderately convenient.

We flew from Pittsburgh to Vienna, where we stayed at the Renaissance Hotel. This hotel was not in the center of the city, but we could travel to the city center easily by subway, which is very efficient in Austria. The first night, we had dinner at a neighborhood restaurant, Eberhardt, that was quite good. Everywhere in Austria the service is deliberate and slow and so we were advised to be patient with their waiters, who do not respond to aggressive behavior.

The next day we toured Vienna. We went to the Opera House and were shown various hotels that were famous because of their former occupants, one of whom was Adolf Hitler. We especially appreciated the Socher Hotel, the home of the Socher Torte, a chocolate dessert that is famous around the world. We had lunch at the Socher Hotel and sampled one of their dessert treats. There is a pleasant walking shopping street beside the hotel, and we toured that one day, and took a guided tour of the oldest Catholic church in Austria. The following day, we saw the Austrian circus area with a huge ferris wheel that provided marvelous views of Vienna. We also toured the Belvadere Castle, which was owned by a general who helped defeat the Asian invaders in the 19th century. The Belvadere Castle had beautiful grounds, but we were not allowed to go inside. Then we toured the magnificent Sonnenberg Palace, which reminded us of the palace in Versailles, France. The tour included some of the meeting rooms and bedrooms of the famous Hapsburg family. We actually had lunch in the palace, which was surprisingly delightful.

The morning of the fifth day, we were taken to the airport and boarded a plane for Bucharest, Romania, the first formerly iron curtain country we visited. Our guide, who met us in Austria, was Romanian, as was the other guide on the tour. These guides followed us throughout the tour, and we were divided into four groups with four different buses. We were the red group, which turned out to be the most congenial group. On our arrival in Bucharest, we toured the city and were shown the decrepit buildings that were built by the communists to house the people. These were ugly non-descript buildings, which housed apartments of about 900 square feet each, containing a living room, dining room, kitchen unit, small bedroom and tiny bathroom. There was no air conditioning, and the outside of the building was very drab. On our tour we were impressed by the continued poverty and lack of modernization of the communist structures. Finally, we arrived in this boulevard designed after the Champs Elysees in Paris, only wider and longer, by George Caucescu, the communist dictator who wanted the street to be wider than the one in Paris. He erected an arch, similar to the Arche de Triomphe in Paris, to highlight this beautiful wide boulevard. However, on both sides of the boulevard were the ugly buildings erected by the communists. At the head of the street, however, is the second largest building in the world to the Pentagon in the United States, built by him for his state office building, and his apartment complex that was in the center of the building behind some huge pillars; the view from that balcony looks straight down this wide boulevard that he designed. There are several buildings around the so-called people's government building, which were to house various sections of the government, including many of the communist cronies. They were huge and mostly empty without any people in them. The government chose to use a smaller building in the city for its current headquarters. Caucescu was executed in a people's revolt in 1988 prior to the total fall of communism.

One large building, however, was recently taken over by the Marriott Hotel and was turned into a very elegant hotel with many rooms, some of which, including ours, were a significant distance from the lobby. One clearly had to be in good shape to cover the distance required from the elevator to the room. The rooms were magnificent, being large and well-furnished. The Marriott must have spent an enormous amount of money in this building and they hope to recover it with tourism, which is slowly increasing in Romania.

In the evening after we arrived in Romania, we were taken to a large fairground-like dinner pavilion that had live American and Romanian music, the latter of which was more enjoyable. There were several tourist groups assembled in this large open area, with meals served by Romanian waiters. We sampled some of the Romanian food, which was edible, but not memorable.

The next day, after a complete tour of Bucharest, including some of the parks and the major important office buildings and hotels, we were taken by bus to the Danube River, where we boarded our cruise vessel that was originally supposed to take us to the Black Sea and then back on up to Budapest, Hungary. However, the Danube River was very low because of the summer drought, and instead we returned to Bucharest, after a night on the well-appointed riverboat that had excellent food and service, to the railroad station where we boarded a private train to take us to the Romanian coast of the Black Sea. We entered a town called Constanta, a former Roman town that was now used for seaside recreation for Romanians. Part of the town was very poorly appointed, but there was one rather private area that was exclusive for tourists with money. We visited a moderately comfortable hotel there, and set out to the beach after lunch to put our toes in the Black Sea. The beach trip was fun and then we toured some Roman ruins and an old Russian orthodox church that was exquisitely decorated and not damaged during World War II. We returned by train, which was very comfortable and then by bus to the Apagio, our river boat.

The next morning we took a short cruise to a town called Russe, in Bulgaria, which was very old and also had previous Roman occupation. There we were met by a schoolteacher guide who took us through the town, explaining some of the changes that occurred during communism and after the communist era. We passed a beautiful church and went into the country to arrive at a mountain village, a former castle that overlooked a beautiful gorge in the mountains in Bulgaria. There we toured the ramparts of the castle and were met by two actors who were dressed up as the king and queen of the castle. On the hill near the castle was a huge home that was formerly occupied by the communist official who oversaw that particular area. From the castle in the town on the mountain, we were taken to another part of the town that had a walking street with many interesting stores selling souvenirs and native crafts. We strolled down the street, slowly sampling some Bulgarian bread that was given to us by people dressed up in native costumes. We bought some wine of a local type and a painting of the Bulgarian houses on a steep hill. We were taken from that town to individual homes for lunch, a highlight of the trip. This Bulgarian lunch was hosted by a cardiologist who lived in this small village in the country. His home was very well-appointed and practical. He even managed to create his own chapel outside of his home, which he showed us after an exquisite lunch he hosted with his wife. These home-hosted lunches were marvelous opportunities to get to know the natives and something about their families and how they survived communism. We talked at length with Dr. George and walked through his apple orchard, sampling some of his very sweet apples After the wonderful lunch, we returned by bus through Russe to the ship where we had afternoon cocktails and then dinner while the ship was moving up stream toward Serbia.

In Bulgaria we sensed that the communist regime was not quite as severe as it was in Romania and the people fared somewhat better, although there was still evidence of the ugly structures erected by the communists for housing the people, much resented by the Bulgarians, related by the tour guide. She was very fluent in English and very open in her assessment of the situation in Bulgaria. We left Bulgaria by the riverboat at night and arrived in Belgrade, Serbia the next day at about noon. After lunch, we all left the riverboat in a group to tour Belgrade and the surrounding area. In Belgrade, we were able to see the government buildings destroyed by selective bombing during the Bosnian war, which have not been repaired; their future is undetermined because of lack of funding. Belgrade is a very depressing city with a lot of gray buildings and crowded streets. In the evening, we were taken to a local restaurant on a very dark side street; the restaurant was well-decorated and brightly lit with music playing. Typical Serbian food was served, and it was quite good with the local wines. The next morning, we left Belgrade by bus because the riverboat could not proceed up the river because the Serbs refused to open a pontoon bridge that replaced a bridge destroyed by the allies during the Bosnian war. Our bus tour included a view of the pontoon bridge and at midday a delightful lunch in a country restaurant in Serbia. We then traveled by bus to the second riverboat, the Rhapsody, which was docked in western Serbia. We arrived in late afternoon after passing through the Serbian countryside, which was largely agricultural and rather pretty. Our Serbian guide throughout the night and day described how difficult the communist era was in Serbia and blamed Malosivich and his cronies for most of their problems. She stated that it was unfortunate that there was such bitter rivalry between the various peoples of former Yugoslavia. She was particularly distressed that she had formerly gone to the Croatian coast for vacations and was no longer able to do so because of the anger of the Croatians. If they learned she was Serbian, they would have damaged her car and tried to injure her. The whole problem of this peninsula, which is racked by religious and ethnic problems, is going to remain in disorder for a long time. Serbia will probably not improve dramatically for generations.

We had an excellent dinner on the riverboat and then sailed up the Danube River, arriving at the so-called Iron Gates in early morning. This is a section of the river that is very narrow and has high cliffs on both sides. The first thing we saw was a small monastery hanging on the right-hand cliff with various structures and caves where previous armies had hidden from their enemies. The narrows is a very turbulent deep part of the river and requires special pilots to take the riverboats through this passage. After about an hour the high walls disappeared and the river opened up into a wider segment. At the exit of the narrows upstream, there was a bridge from Romania to Serbia that had never been completed, so it ended in the middle of the river. It was a pathetic sight, without any possibility of being finished in the near future. The rest of the boat trip up the Danube was uneventful. The riverbank was not very attractive, without any interesting buildings for the most part. As we entered the city of Budapest on the Danube, the view became spectacular. The city of Budapest is divided into two parts, Buda on the south bank and Pest on the north bank. We passed between the two and several of the palaces and government buildings were described to us as we moved along. We docked in the western side of Budapest and then proceeded by bus to our hotel, which was in the center of the city on a walking street near the Danube river. The setting of the hotel was picturesque while the hotel, a Nova hotel, was ordinary. There were several restaurants within walking distance which we sampled, and the food was excellent—continental with a Hungarian flavor. While in

Budapest, we toured the entire city by bus and found it to be strikingly beautiful. We were taken across the river to the Buda part, which contained the old palace on top of a high hill overlooking the Pest part of the city. We bought some souvenirs and had lunch in the city near our hotel. The next day we went to a jewelry center in the outskirts of Budapest, which had an excellent display of high quality jewelry. Some of the travelers bought some very nice pieces to take home. We were taken that same day on a trip through the country to a small town called Holloko, which is populated by native Hungarians who have restricted themselves to that area of the country. They have a unique native dress and live a very simple life in the small town. Some of them danced and sang for us and then we had a special lunch in the home of one of the local residents. The host was a woman whose husband was a bus driver and she was very animated and dynamic in describing her home and showing us the things that she had collected. The house was very well-organized and the lunch was superb with native Hungarian dishes and local wines. The guide who arranged all of our activities was also very fluent in English and was very open about the difference between the communists and the post-communist era in Hungary. They fared better than those in Serbia, Bulgaria and Romania but still have a long way to catch up with the rest of the world. One interesting side trip from Hungary was to Kalosca where they raised horses that were used by former warriors on horseback; they could perform multiple tricks including lying down on command and hiding their riders from the view of their enemies. They also demonstrated some riding tricks with their superb horsemen, who were interesting to see. One fascinating display was a man standing on the back of two horses as they galloped around the arena.

The following day, we left in the rain on buses to pass through Slovakia on the way to the Czech Republic. Slovakia is poor and largely agricultural, with a very small capital. We arrived at noon at a village where we again enjoyed a home-hosted lunch. This time the Slovakian guide was moderately fluent in English and she had joined us at our particular house, where we again had a very animated, gracious, gregarious hostess whose husband was in the military. It is interesting that the guide's husband was in the Slovakian military as well. They described life in Slovakia, which had improved from communism, but they were still very poor. The lunch again was exquisite with very good Slovakian food and local wines. The house was warm and well-appointed but simple. Following this wonderful lunch, we waived goodbye to our host and proceeded through the rain to the Czech Republic; as we entered Prague, the rain stopped.

We arrived in Prague, Czechoslovakia to the hotel Don Giovanni, again slightly away from the center of the city but adjacent to a subway stop that allowed us to use the excellent Czech Republic subways. The city of Prague had many old historic buildings that were not destroyed in World War II. In addition, there were several ugly communist structures for housing the people. However, we were able to tour the center of the city by walking and found the Charles Bridge over the local river, which had flooded in the previous summer and now was under drought conditions. There were many crafts and souvenirs available on the bridge. On both sides of the bridge the city of Prague was extremely interesting. The central square had an unusual clock in the city office building, which we watched strike twelve noon. We had lunch in a very nice local restaurant and then toured the city in the afternoon. The day after arriving, we went on a bus tour of the grand palace on a high hill overlooking Prague and were taken to this very, very large former palace fortress with a large orthodox Catholic church in the center. The church itself was spectacular both inside and out, and the various buildings and the walls of this structure were gorgeous. The view across the river into the heart of Prague was spectacular. That afternoon, we found our way across the river and ate at a restaurant on the bank of the river. The food was excellent and moderately priced. I had grilled octopus, which was the best that I think I have ever had in my life. After a leisurely lunch, Fred and I took an interesting tour of the Torture Museum. The girls preferred to continue to shop. We also toured the very interesting jewelry museum earlier that morning.

The next day we again came to the city and toured some of the other parts, studying the well-preserved buildings and arches. That afternoon we went to have lunch at a local restaurant along the river in a different section of the city, where the ancient part and architectural museum were located. The art and sculptures dated back into the time of Christ and were very unusual. Most of them were of religious themes. We had a very difficult time finding the restaurant at lunch, but when we did it proved to be another excellent restaurant, moderately priced with exquisite food and wine.

We spent the last night in Prague in the hotel because we were all tired, and had dinner in the hotel restaurant—probably the least interesting meal that we had on the entire trip. The next morning we were up early to be taken by bus to the airport, where we returned from Prague to Pittsburgh.

That was a very exciting trip, but one where one's flexibility was tested. I would really highly recommend it to anybody in good health who is flexible in nature and interested in recent European history.

Digression #19

Returning to the department, we searched for replacements for Kim and Glenn Cockerham. We encountered a Pitt residency graduate, Reshma Paranjpe, who was taking a cornea-external disease fellowship at the University of Minnesota and was very interested in coming back to Pittsburgh. We offered her a position as a cornea external disease expert in our group. We also entertained Carl Rosen, one of my previous fellows, who was interested in coming back. However, after visiting us with his wife and child, he decided that he could not make the transition because he was very well-established in Alaska and his wife was concerned about the move. We had previously discussed the position with Randall Beatty, an oculoplastic surgeon at the University of Pittsburgh who was trained partially through Allegheny General prior to taking a fellowship with Jerry Harris in Milwaukee. He had spent some time in the US Air Force and returned to the University of Pittsburgh with an excellent reputation in oculoplastic and reconstructive surgery with an interest in trauma. In mid-March 2004 he took the position that Kim vacated. The addition of his expertise to the group will secure the surgical aspect of the neuro-ophthalmology orbital service, but it does . not solve the neuro-ophthalmology part. I continued to practice neuro-ophthalmology and considered alternatives for that in the future.

Christmas 2003 was spent with the Condon family, including Cyril, Garry's father. We had a marvelous time and left early the next morning for Hilton Head Island to have a second New Year's Eve reunion with Posts, Hicks, and McCormicks, friends that I knew as a child and in my early adult years.

The Costa Rica Journey

We went to Costa Rica at the end of January 2004 with my college fraternity brothers and their wives, the Cervenys and the Hershocks. We flew to Costa Rica and met the Hershocks, who had rented a van to take us to the Los Sueños resort in western Costa Rica on the Pacific Ocean. We rented a very large three-bedroom, three bath condominium overlooking the bay and an island offshore. The view was spectacular. The condominiums were connected to the Marriott resort. There were several beautiful swimming pools and many restaurants nearby. We could see the marina from our balcony.

We played golf on an excellent golf course, the La Iguana that meandered through the rain forest and one day the three men went deep sea fishing, where we caught four sailfish. The one I caught weighed approximately 110 pounds and was certainly a challenge to bring in. They were all released, as was mandatory in Costa Rican waters at this time.

Three of us traveled to the national park south of Jaco, the town that was near our resort. To reach the national park we traveled south on a marginal road crossing several dilapidated one-lane bridges. In general, the roads have improved since we had visited Costa Rica in 1998. The national park was interesting and we had a guide named Manuel who had a Zeiss telescope and could spot birds, bats and monkeys in the trees, that we never would have seen without his help. We toured the entire park, which bordered on the Pacific with beautiful bays and wonderful rain forests. We had lunch at the restaurant near the national park overlooking the ocean and returned by car to the resort. We had dinner at several different restaurants, all of which were open and tropical. The food was excellent and the company was terrific. We played hard during the day and went to bed early. We left with regret that we had not decided to spend more time in Costa Rica.

The Florida Journey

In the last week of March 2004, Pat and I traveled to the combination of the Frank Walsh and the North American Neuro-Ophthalmology Society meeting in Orlando, Florida at the Sea World Renaissance Hotel. We rented a car at the airport and drove to the Renaissance Hotel, which was spectacular with an open center. The elevators had windows that looked into the center courtyard. The meetings began on Sunday and lasted three and one-half days. Both meetings were well-attended and excellent in quality. Several of my fellows participated as speakers in the meetings, including Mike Kazim, Howard Krause, Kim Cockerham and Roger Turbin. On Tuesday night they held a dinner for Pat and me, with at least twelve of our fellows in attendance. The dinner was great fun, the fellows ordering a magnum of red wine to celebrate the reunion.

On Wednesday of the meeting, Pat and I played hooky and drove over to Hammock Beach Golf Resort on the Atlantic Ocean between St. Augustine and Daytona Beach. I found Cinnamon Beach, an area in Hammock Beach, in a golf magazine and was attracted by the fact that the beach had cinnamon-colored sand and I liked the name of the resort. I was curious to see what was available there, and Pat and I toured the resort with Bob Deak, one of the real estate agents. The resort was brand-new and the last three condominium buildings were for sale, so we made a reservation to view those condominiums on the sixth to the ninth of May 2004, to decide if we wanted to select one of the condominiums that overlooks one of the golf courses and beyond to the ocean. The golf course is attractive in that 7 of the 18 holes are on the ocean. When we toured the resort we found everything to be new and all the buildings were designed to be hurricane-proof and did not require shutters. The glass in the windows was built to withstand 150 miles-per-hour winds, so hurricane insurance was not required. We were very attracted by this resort and its location and, unfortunately, did not have enough time to cover it totally at that time.

On Thursday afternoon after the meeting, we drove to the central east coast of Florida to see Connie and Joseph Zahorchak. Joe had retired to Florida three years previously. They have a nice home on one floor with a lanai and a pool that included a Jacuzzi, which he uses to help him with mild arthritis. We played golf with them on a PGA east course twice. The two different golf courses were quite challenging. We then drove to West Palm Beach and flew home.

On May 6, Pat and I returned to Palm Coast of Florida to attend the Lottery weekend party and reception to consider buying one of the condominiums on the ocean at Cinnamon Beach. We stayed at the Casa Monica Hotel in St. Augustine, and toured the historic city in a horse-drawn carriage, courtesy of the host, Cinnamon Beach Resort. We were able to obtain passes to play the golf course, which was spectacular and wide open. It was comfortable to play.

We had an exquisite dinner at the Casa Monica Hotel that night and the next day we returned to Cinnamon Beach and toured the resort once again, meeting with Bob Deak and his wife Tracy to discuss the options of the weekend. Our reservation was very late and so our meeting to select a condominium would be late on Sunday, which was not positioned for buying something that we had selected. Therefore, we talked of other options and looked at condominiums that had a view from the back of the units across the lake to a distant view of the ocean. There were many lots in that view which would have future houses that have not been constructed yet. However, none of the houses would be partially obstructing the view from that direction. We talked about that at great length as we returned to the Casa Monica, but decided we only wanted an ocean front property.

The next day, Saturday, we returned to the selection process and walked Cinnamon Beach, which is quite lovely. The sand is truly cinnamon colored. We also toured the Palm Coast town briefly. It really is a large shopping center area with surrounding communities. We drove up Route 95 to visit the World Golf Village, which houses the Golf Hall of Fame. We had lunch at Sam Snead's tavern and toured the village, which contained many restaurants and shops. It is a very attractive place, but it is west of highway 95 and not on the ocean. We felt that we had no interest in it other than possibly playing the course on another weekend. We returned to the Casa Monica, where the resort hosted a great dinner at the Flagler Museum across from the hotel. The museum contained many relics of the previous eras of St. Augustine and the buffet dinner contained everything that one could possibly desire, including sushi rolls and small lobster tails. We met several interesting people over the weekend, including real estate investors as well as a young physician and his wife who were buying property for investment. We learned a great deal about the nature of the resort and the investment potential.

On May 25, we suddenly decided to buy a second floor condominium in Building 600, directly facing the ocean at Cinnamon Beach. We sent the down payment for this condominium, which is pre-construction, but was passed through a previous owner who never took occupancy. The closing was in November, 2004. We thought of it as an investment property.

The Jersey Shore Journey

In mid-June, Pat and I, with Mary Ann and Fred Wucher, took a nostalgic trip to the Jersey shore, staying in Ocean City at a home that was owned by a friend of Mary Ann Wucher. The house was two blocks from the beach near 14th Street. In the past, at the end of spring semester at Bucknell, we had gone down to the ocean and stayed with Bob Beck, whose mother owned a two-story house near the beach in Ocean City. I had not been back to Ocean City since that time. Pat had never been there, so we decided to go on this trip. It was interesting in the fact that Ocean City has certainly not changed in some ways and in other ways it has become a very expensive place with the cost of housing skyrocketing and all of the older homes being rebuilt. The town is still dry, dominated by Methodists, and there is not even the possibility of bringing wine into a restaurant for dinner. We toured the boardwalk, which was longer than it had been previously, but at 14th Street Bob Harbaugh, a fraternity brother, had had his own restaurant for many years. His father owned it when we were in college and he worked there. Now he owns the entire block and has a beautiful condominium over the restaurant called Bob's. We were able to contact him and we were invited for cocktails at his condominium and he told us the story of his many years in Ocean City. His family has maintained that restaurant since the early 1950s.

We drove to Atlantic City for the day and that has changed dramatically with the casinos that have come to that city. It certainly has good and bad features. We were in a spectacular new casino called Bogata, east of the main portion of Atlantic City, but the hotel part is even screened off from the casino people unless you have a reservation or a key to the hotel. The boardwalk in Atlantic City is as busy as ever and the casinos are all along it. They have some new beach bars and the beach has been extended from previous erosion. We had lunch at a place called Lefty's in Atlantic City. The silverware is placed as if everybody were left-handed. It was a delightful experience, but we were glad to leave Atlantic City. We also toured the coast down to Cape May and spent a day in Cape May, a quaint old town on the shore. We stopped at Stone Harbor where I took my young family on a summer vacation many years ago; it has remained a clean and popular place, with good restaurants and a pleasant atmosphere.

The whole week spent in Ocean City was pleasant and nostalgic, but the Jersey Shore is crowded, and I do not think I would care to return. It is amazing that now you have to buy a tag in order to get on the beach. If you are on the beach without a tag, you must purchase one at that time or be kicked off the beach. I prefer places that are not as regulated and crowded. The boardwalk is also restricted as far as bikes are concerned to the morning, at which time they are moving up and down the boardwalk swiftly. In the afternoon, only pedestrians can use the boardwalk. We returned with fond memories of a pleasant week with good weather and good friends.

Digression #20

In July, Nick Schmidt, a graduate of the Syracuse ophthalmology program, having worked with Bob Noland who is a general ophthalmologist in Pittsburgh, joined us as a fellow in neuro-ophthalmology and orbital disease under Randy Beatty and myself.

In August, Reshma Paranjpe joined us as a full-time specialist in cornea and external disease. She is rapidly building her practice and hopes to start a fellowship within two or three years.

In October 2004, Tariq Bhatti joined the department as a fellow in neuro-ophthalmology and orbital surgery. He has had previous training in neuro-ophthalmology under Nancy Newman in Atlanta and was a neuro-ophthalmologist at the University of Florida in Gainsville. He came to learn primarily orbital diagnosis and surgery. He returned to the University of Florida to expand his role as a surgeon. He was very experienced and pleasant to work with.

In early December 2004, we traveled to Florida through Orlando, where we rented a car and drove to Cinnamon Beach, where we moved into the condominium, which had been furnished by a furniture company connected with property management. We inspected the property, which was satisfactory and the view was excellent. The furniture was well-chosen, and we added porch furniture as well as some pictures that were sold to us by a lady in a van who brought the art right to the condominium. It was an interesting experience in quickly furnishing a new condominium, which then was placed in the rental pool for rent beginning in January 2005. During the trip, we visited some interesting restaurants and spent an evening in St. Augustine, where they had very extravagant Christmas decorations in place. We also experienced a drive on one of the few remaining beaches between St. Augustine and Daytona on which you can drive a car. The beach is wide with firmly packed sand and we had lunch in a restaurant overlooking that part of the beach. The return home was uneventful.

We passed Christmas at Hidden Valley; my son, Jeff, and his two children arrived for the week between Christmas and the New Year.

The week started off with the kids being enrolled in snow boarding classes and after an hour, Alan fell and broke his right wrist, which ended his snow boarding experience suddenly. Elena completed the week in snow board school and learned how to handle the snow board well for her tender age of 9. New Year's Eve was quiet with all of us drinking non-alcoholic champagne at midnight at home. On January 6, 2005, Nancy had a baby boy, her second, named Matthew John. She and the baby did well and we celebrated the good news.

The South American Journey

In mid-January 2005, the Wuchers and Sheimers joined us for a trip to South America. We began our journey flying to Santiago, Chile; following arrival, we had a tour of the city of Santiago, a beautiful, clean, picturesque city with an interesting history. The unique central square included several interesting historic sites. We stayed at the Hotel Plaza DelBosque in an area slightly out of the center of the city. The hotel was surrounded by a large number of excellent restaurants, of which we sampled two. It was interesting that we watched the playoff game of the Steelers and the Jets at Hooter's, the only place that carried the football game. In Chile, as in the rest of South America, American football is of little interest. They favor their football, which is known to us as soccer. No one in Hooter's was interested in the game except the four of us. Our towel waving and cheering did not impress them.

The following day, Pat and I took a private tour to the Santa Rita Winery in the Meipo Valley of Chile. The tour was by a private car through picturesque mountains and valleys, with the Andes Mountains in the background. The Santa Rita Winery is one of the most beautiful that I have ever seen, with an exquisite garden and an interesting vineyard with a broad selection of white and red wines. The lunch consisted of the best salmon carpaccio I have ever tasted. The rest of the meal was excellent and accompanied by white and red wine. Of course, I slept most of the way home in the car, but did enjoy the experience of being out in the wine valley near Santiago.

The next day, we traveled by car to the Port of Valparaiso, passing through the Casablanca Wine District where white wine is grown, into a beach resort called Vina del Mar. We toured the magnificent beach area and had lunch in a hotel overlooking the ocean, which had average food and wine, but a terrific view. We then proceeded with our guides to the Celebrity ship, INFINITY; we boarded and found our way to our stateroom for the journey around Cape Horn. The ship was quite large, with two thousand passengers and our stateroom was adequate with a large port hole but no balcony. The ship had many bars and restaurants as well as a casino, which we attended infrequently. The food was adequate to good and it improved as the cruise proceeded. As we sailed out of Valparaiso, we began to notice the large swells of the South Pacific Ocean, which increased as we headed south toward Cape Horn. Our first port of call was Puerto Montt and its sister city Puerto Veras. We arrived at Puerto Montt and had to enter the harbor on a launch because of the large size of the ship and the shallowness of the harbor. We proceeded by bus through Puerto Montt, an old city settled by Germans and some Spanish. The structures in the port were of wood frames and of various colors. As we headed toward Puerto Veras, the land was rolling with cattle and sheep, the main industry, and then we found ourselves in Puerto Veras, a small city on the edge of Lake Llanquihue, the second largest lake in South America, at the base of the Osorno Volcano. The town was small and we visited several retail stores with the usual artifacts. Then we proceeded along the lake to a combination boating and sports club. The view from the clubhouse was exquisite with two of the volcanoes clearly visible in the distance on that day, which was fortunate because the view is usually obscured. There we tasted some Chilean wines and were entertained by a dance troupe. We also had a selection of German sausages, which were interesting. The experience at the club was a lot of fun and at the end, we bought some wine, one of which was called Ovejas Negras (black sheep), which I brought home to keep as a souvenir. We then returned to the ship and that evening sailed on to Cape Horn, entering the Magellan Straits where the waves were quite high and the ship rocked to some degree—but with stabilizers on the sides of the ship, it was not enough to induce seasickness in most of the passengers. We passed by a beautiful glacier where we stopped and took several pictures and then passed through the Beagle Straits to our next port of call, Punta Arenas (sandy point). This small port is in part of a region that is described as Patagonia. The city of Punta Arenas is small, and again we had to arrive by launch. We then boarded a bus for a trip outside the city through the large barren country occupied by large ranches called Estancias, on which single cowboys called gauchos would herd cattle and bring in strays. Our trip took us through this barren country to a place on the shore that harbored burrowing penguins. After a long walk on a board sidewalk, we reached the habitat of these penguins, which were very friendly and unafraid of people. They have no natural predators and they frolicked freely in front of our cameras both on the beach and in their burrows. After watching them for several minutes, we returned to the bus for the long trip back to Punta Arenas, having had a pleasant and unique experience. We then re-boarded the ship and proceeded on through the Straits of Magellan to arrive at a small city, which was referred to as the gateway to Antarctica, called Ushiai. Again, we approached the city by launch and traveled by bus to a railway station, which featured a train ride that was described as the train ride at the end of the world. The train was formerly used by inmates of the prison located in that area for hardened criminals who proceeded by train out into the countryside where they cut down trees to acquire the wood to build the town of

Ushiai. The train ride was interesting and yet somewhat sad. The area that was used to fell trees was relatively barren except for the stumps of the trees that had remained following their removal. At the end of the train ride, we stopped at another station and then proceeded by bus down to a shore line where we visited a lighthouse and viewed the Magellan Straits from the shore near Ushiai.

In Ushiai, we had lunch at a beautiful restaurant near the docks. Following lunch, we shopped at some souvenir stores on the dock. Pat and Mary Ann acquired tea pots called Mate; a strong tea is placed in the pot with water and then the tea is sucked through a straw with some difficulty. These Mates are used in homes as a sign of sharing a friendly drink with people who are close family or friends and are not used in any way as an entertainment in restaurants or bars. It was an interesting experience seeing these unusual pots and then we found them everywhere in Argentina after the initial experience. We returned to the ship and that evening we departed on our further route through the Straits of Magellan and south to circle Cape Horn, a large rock that marks the extreme tip of South America. On top of the rock is a building occupied by a Chilean couple who keep watch on their territory in that area. This large rock island is usually shrouded by fog, but to our good fortune it was not on the morning of our arrival and we were able to completely encircle Cape Horn with our pilot guide taking us through the channel. Cape Horn is named for the town of Horrn in Amsterdam, which was the home of the Dutch explorer who found Cape Horn as an alternative to going through the Magellan Straits, which were heavily taxed by the Portuguese for some years following their discovery of other ships trying to gain passage to the Pacific. To avoid the tax, many of the ships sailed further south around Cape Horn.

From Cape Horn, we sailed to the Falkland Islands, the site of the war between Argentina and Britain in the 1980s for control of the long-owned British Islands. The Falkland Islands are relatively isolated, but are in a location that was used heavily as a jumping off point to

Antarctica and are used for a re-supply of ships going back and forth for whaling. They are also surrounded by very fertile fishing ground that supplies the Falkland Islands with a sizable income, as the fishing rights are sold to other countries. The Falkland Islands are barren and we entered the island on a launch and arrived to meet our guide and to be taken by bus through Port Stanley, the capital of the Falklands, passing a large whale bone statue and a memorial stone pillar to the Falklands War, memorializing those who lost their lives on the British side in that war. The war lasted 72 days and there were many casualties on the Argentinean side and less on the the side of the British, who eventually were the victors. The island is primarily populated by British people, who either were born there or have come there from England. Our guide was one of the latter and was very jovial and showed us what is there—which is very little. We saw the governor's house and a small zoo that housed small deer and some large whale skulls, as well as some smaller animals. We then traveled across the heights of Port Stanley to view some derelict ships that were abandoned in the extreme inner portion of the unused part of the harbor. Then we saw some peat bogs where peat is taken by some of the population in the fall for winter heating in the peat stoves, which are similar to those found in Ireland. Our last stop was at a mine field that still has active mines in a barren plain above Port Stanley. I photographed the sign that warned of the mines. They are not removed because of the dangers of removal and the fact that the island is barren and very few people are unaware of the mine fields. We returned then to Port Stanley and shopped for souvenirs which we then followed by a very interesting lunch at a pub, the Globe, near the crowded harbor; the food and the ambience were very English. We then returned to the ship and that afternoon we sailed across the southern Atlantic Ocean to Porto Madryn, an isolated port in Patagonia. We were able to dock at the pier in Porto Madryn and walk into the city, where we boarded buses for a tour of the countryside, which was extremely barren with large Estancias, to a cliff on the ocean that overlooked the home of several sea lions, which we photographed. I tried a new binocular camera that I acquired for Christmas and got some interesting magnified pictures of the sea lions. From there, we went across the desert country to a small town in the interior that was populated by a Belgian religious sect.

We had lunch in a large clubhouse or a meeting house and were entertained by the students of the music school there, who sang several songs in their native language. It was a very interesting experience, but the food was not good. We then took on the long journey back to the town and were tired, so we did not walk into that particular town but went back to the ship. That evening, we sailed up the coast of Argentina to Montevideo, Uruguay. The next day we took a bus tour of Montevideo and the surrounding area. Montevideo is a very pretty city and relatively safe because many police are patrolling the streets. It is not as clean as Santiago, but the people are friendly and the historic buildings are very interesting. We traveled east to an exclusive beach resort with charming properties and excellent views of the ocean near Montevideo. There we took several pictures at a park on the borders of the Platte River as it joined the Atlantic Ocean. We returned to Montevideo, where we bought some interesting leather goods in a shop near the pier. Pat and I then went on our own to walk in the port near the docks and found a walking street with several art exhibits. We bought two watercolor paintings from local people on the small street. We also had lunch at a restaurant on that street in the outdoor portion, which had an extremely good seafood soup called Mariscos del Mar; Pat had excellent ravioli. The food was impressive, but the size of the portion was extremely large, as it had been all over South America. We then went back to the ship after an interesting tour in Montevideo, to journey up the extremely wide Platte River. It is named after Plata, which is silver in Spanish and is the widest river in the world—135 miles wide in some areas. We docked the next morning in Buenos Aires. We had an extra day on the ship in port, so we took a tour of a river suburb where summer homes are built on islands in the Platte River. We toured this whole area by boat and saw all of the different types of homes and restaurants on these multiple islands that are only reachable by boat. This was an interesting experience, but not a place that I would choose to have a summer home. The river has a tendency to rise suddenly and often the homes are inundated with water. Upon our return to the dock, we went back to the ship, where we spent our last night. Early the next morning we were herded off the ship, only to wait for our guides in Buenos Aires to pick us up; this part of the trip was the most unpleasant as we had to wait for an hour and a half before our guides were able to enter the port and pick us up with all of our luggage. We proceeded then in the rain through Buenos Aires, seeing the various interesting parts of the central city, but we were unable to get out and walk around because of the rain. We did experience a good sampling of the city with its historic buildings and multiple statues, including ones depicting the wagon trains of the gauchos going to settle the country in the 19th century.

We went to the Los Suitos Recoueta Hotel in the Boca section of the city, known for its restaurants and shops. It was well-located and we had a nice lunch in the hotel restaurant after settling into our rooms. That evening, we went to an exquisite Italian restaurant within walking distance of the hotel. That evening we were picked up by our guides and taken to a tango nightclub, where the historic originator of the tango had danced. We watched an entire tango show, which was quite fascinating with the athletic ability of the dancers, especially the women in their high heels flying around the stage with precision. The next day, we were taken by our guide Maria, an excellent English-speaking native of Buenos Aires to an Estancia, where we met a true gaucho, an older fellow who had the traditional dress. At this large farmhouse, we experienced the flavor of the Estancias and took a ride in a horse-drawn carriage followed by a barbequed lunch with steaks and sausages cooked by the hired ranch cook. The food was excellent, but Argentinean beef, although very flavorful, is very lean and not as tender as it is in the United States. I personally really enjoyed the flavor and style of the meat, but my friends did not appreciate it as much. Following lunch, we again looked around the Estancia and then went back to Buenos Aires where we had dinner that night in a Spanish restaurant with excellent steak. Following the excellent dinner, we packed our bags and the next day were taken to the Buenos Aires airport by Maria, who chaperoned us through all the difficult security checks right through to where we went into the VIP lounge prior to boarding the plane. Maria was one of the best guides that I think we ever had on our various trips. We traveled home without incident. The entire experience was good, with fairly good weather, albeit cold and windy in the extreme part of South America. I recommend this trip to anybody who is an experienced traveler. It is not a trip for people on their first cruise, because there were many days at sea, which I thoroughly enjoyed.

Digression #21

On the weekend of March 18-20, we attended the wedding of Pat's nephew, Bill Maurer and his wife Maya Fukii, whose parents lived in Evanston, Illinois, the home of Northwestern University, where her father is a microbiology professor. The Hotel Orrington was old, but redecorated and pleasant. The wedding was in a bright and cheerful non-denominational chapel, with gorgeous stained glass windows and a high ceiling. The reception at a local club was interesting, with causal food and drinks.

On April 2, I flew to Myrtle Beach to attend a golf reunion with my fraternity brothers from Bucknell. This was the fourth time I have joined the group, which has been meeting for about eight years. There were eight brothers attending, but only our perennial host Bud Pearson and I arrived Saturday. We had a nice dinner together, discussing the past and previous golf outings. The rest of the brothers arrived Sunday and Monday. Tuesday morning, seven golfers played the Legends course, similar to an English or Irish golf course. I was paired with Bob Beck, a lawyer from New Jersey whom I have known since 1953. On the first hole, he complained of his eyes burning. Mine weren't, which I thought was strange since I am so sensitive. On the next hole, he complained of ear pain but didn't consider it serious. On the third hole, after our second stroke, he stated he was tingling all over and I knew that was a dire sign. I ordered him into the cart and drove as fast as the cart would allow to the bag drop area. On the way in he got worse, with difficulty breathing so that I had to hold him in the cart. At the bag drop the starter called 911 and we waited 12 to 15 minutes for the ambulance to arrive. He was very pale with no pulse, but was breathing shallowly when they took him to a heart hospital in Myrtle Beach. Honk Schanley and Phil Cerveny were playing with us and when I left the third hole I told them to get car keys from the other group who had the two cars. The three of us went to the hospital and were asked to enter a consultation room where the doctor entered and told us Bob had died. We were devastated. Phil and I went to see him and I made sure his pupils were dilated and closed his eyes. Phil got his valuables to return to the family then we drove us back to our house on the beach. The others came back and together we mourned Bob's death. The group stayed together for the rest of the week, which is what we thought he would want us to do. I returned Saturday, April 9, the day he was buried. I'll never forget that horrendous experience and probably will be back on that golf cart heading to the bag drop for the rest of my life.

In May, Bob and Pat Hershock joined Pat and me at Cinnamon Beach and decided to buy a condo on the sixth floor of a building across from our building. We helped them furnish it and enjoyed five days introducing them to the Palm Coast area. We had come from a great Orbital Society meeting at a Hilton Beach Hotel complex in Dustin, Florida in the panhandle area. We brought fresh red snapper that I caught on a Gulf fishing trip after the meeting. The Dustin area is beautiful, but more crowded than Cinnamon Beach at this time.

On the way home, the four of us stopped to see Dick and Sue Estus in their fashionable home in Savannah, Georgia located on a beautiful marsh with boat access to the ocean. We toured Savannah, a quaint well-preserved historic southern city, where Dick is quite prominent in local affairs. We played golf at a beautiful private club on a property owned by the Henry Ford family. We also stopped in Hilton Head to see and play golf with the Posts, who had just moved to Sun City near Hilton Head. On our last night we dined with our old friends, the Hicks, the McCormicks, and the Posts. We then drove home, having used our new GPS (global positioning system), in Pat's new Jeep Wagoneer, to find our destinations throughout the trip. It worked so well we became addicted to it.

In June, we spent a long weekend in Dallas with my children and their families. The purpose of the visit was to see the new grandson, Matthew John, a delightful 6-month-old child. His brother, Michael Joseph, was almost 3 years old and was doing well. Nancy and her husband, Joe, were buying a new house in far suburban Dallas in a very nice self-contained community with good schools. Jeffrey has purchased a Mexican-style townhouse in another self-contained community with a pool and tennis courts. He hosts his children there on the weekends.

In July, Eric Happ, a recent graduate of the University of Pittsburgh joined Randy Beatty and me as a fellow in neuro-ophthalmology, orbital and ophthalmic plastic surgery. He was a former Naval flight surgeon, as was I, so we have something in common. He is married with three children and has quickly adapted to our practice. We said good-bye to Nick Schuitt and his wife, who moved to Minneapolis, Minnesota, his wife's home, where he joined another specialty practice with academic connection to the University of Minnesota.

The Italian Journey

On September 11, the Hershocks, Pat, and I headed for Rome, Italy. We arrived at the Hotel Splendid Royale, strategically located in central Rome with a great view of the city from its roof-top restaurant. Although tired, we had lunch outdoors at the roof-top restaurant, an exquisite light lunch which introduced us to the extremely high costs we would face in Italy.

We toured the Spanish steps and the Trevi Fountain. We had dinner at a great trattoria near the old city wall, which had great beef carpacio that was reasonably priced.

The next day we took a four-hour walking tour of ancient Rome, with a great guide from New Jersey who was studying archeology in Rome. We had supper at another trattoria where they brought whatever food they wanted you to have. It was a great restaurant with a jolly waiter. Of course, the wines were excellent. The next day we rented a small passenger Fiat van and drove to the Amalfi coast past Naples. The coast there is gorgeous, but the roads are extremely winding and narrow. We finally arrived at a resort on a cliff overlooking the Mediterranean

Sea called San Pietro near the town of Positano. The view from the resort, including from our room, was spectacular and the weather was excellent. The resort had an elevator down to the sea, so we relaxed there and I had a dip in the Mediterranean Sea. The water was cool, but refreshing and clear. We had a great lunch at the beach and dinner in the beautiful dining room overlooking the sea. The food was superb. On the second day, we went to Positano and toured the quaint town, did some shopping and had dinner at a great restaurant. The next day we rented a car and driver and went to Pompei, where we had a great tour with an elderly guide named Leno. The excavation sight and the story of the Vesuvius volcano eruption was very interesting. Our driver, Mario, was from Ravella, another picturesque town higher above the sea. We had lunch at a family-type restaurant with excellent pasta and wine. The view from Raovna Villa Hotel higher above Ravella was even more spectacular than from San Pietro. The next day we took the autopista north past Naples and Rome to Tuscany where we met the Cervenys at the railroad station. After a great lunch of linguine with seafood in the railroad station restaurant, we traveled to our rented villa near the town of Rodda, called Camposol. We were met at the villa by our maid, who showed us around this lovely villa surrounded by vineyards and olive orchards. It was spacious with plenty of bedrooms, each with its own shower, unusual in Italy. The villa had a great swimming pool and was within walking distance of the town, Rodda. We used the villa as our base and took daily trips to wineries, small towns and Florence. We took the train to Florence two days and had four-hour tours with an excellent guide to see the David sculpture, the wedding palace, and Renaissance paintings at the museum. We had lunch on the second trip at a great trattoria in the center of town with excellent stewed boar. We started having big lunches and dinners, but soon learned that was too much food and wine, so we settled on lunch out at great restaurants in the country or in one of the hill-top towns. Every meal was excellent and the people were friendly. One day we toured several wineries with our guide, Monica, whose family owned a neat wine bar in Rodda. We tasted some exceptional wine on that tour. One day we went to Sienna, a famous town that hosts a yearly horse race around the town square and bareback rides representing the various sections of Sienna. I was there on my first trip to Europe in 1977 and it certainly has changed, with a huge increase in the number of tourists and resultant loss of some of its charm. We had lunch in a great restaurant recommended by our cooking teacher, who came to the villa and gave us cooking lessons. The last long side trip was to Banfi winery in southern Tuscany, a very large American-owned winery with award-winning wines. We toured the facility with the New York distributor, Philipo, who was entertaining buyers. The lunch at the winery was an exquisite five-course meal with accompanying wines—a memorable experience. After two lovely weeks, we returned to Rome and flew home with great memories of a terrific trip.

The Tahiti Journey

On January 16, 2006, the Wuchers, Pat and I departed for Tahiti via Los Angeles, where we suffered a very long twelve-hour layover to arrive in Tahiti in the early morning. We were taken to the International Hotel, which is gorgeous with a beautiful lagoon on the ocean and where finally after several hours, we were taken to our tropical hut, which was situated over the water. The hut was rustic and had a deck, which had a gorgeous view of the lagoon and the reef as well as the island of Moorea across the water. Sunrise came from behind and illuminated Moorea and the sunset was behind her, both absolutely gorgeous. The hut was comfortable, but the air conditioner and toilet did not work, so we were transferred to a second hut where, fortunately, all of the equipment was in working order. Across the front of our hut, sea kayaks and canoes frequently passed. From our hut, we could see the resort behind us and another series of huts where the Sheimers were housed, having joined us in Tahiti. The first day we toured the city of Papeete, which is a typical tropical coastal town without much glamour. It was interesting that there were very few restaurants in the downtown area; all were in the suburban Papeete. The population of Tahiti is about 180,000 people with the population of the whole island group somewhere around 260,000 people. The second day, we took a tour on a minibus with our guide Bernie, a very large Hawaiian who has been living in Tahiti and Moorea for over twenty years, having married a native Polynesian. He was extremely knowledgeable and delightful as a guide, first taking us to the Tahitian museum, which depicts the history of the islands. His knowledge of that subject was enormous. We next traveled along the west coast with beautiful ocean views, to the restaurant associated with the Gaugin Museum. The restaurant doubled as a fish farm and was very interesting. It is owned by an Englishman who came to our table to greet us. The food was exceptional, with several native items on the menu including poi, which was sweetened, breadfruit, taro root and plantain. These are fairly starchy foods and somewhat tasteless unless mixed with other foods or sauces. The Tahitian beer has improved over time and was quite tasty. In the past, it had been fermented and bottled early and tended to cause diarrhea according to Bernie. During lunch, it was explained that Polynesia is a French protectorate and former French colony, managed and subsidized by the French as a trading post in the South Pacific. The present government is corrupt and there are more government jobs in Tahiti than in any other business. In Tahiti they still have a few cattle ranches and banana plantations, but their main business is tourism, which was adversely affected by 9/11 but has been gradually recovering. The climate is humid and because Tahiti is below the equator, January is a summer month. We did not realize that when we booked the trip, but it is not the rainy season, which we accepted gratefully after the cold December in Pittsburgh. The tour then traveled to the Gaugin Museum, which was somewhat of a disappointment because there are no original Gaugin paintings there; they are all distributed around the world, mostly in the United States—especially in the National Gallery of Art in Washington, D.C. The copies were there and the museum was on a beautiful point overlooking the water, but it was not air-conditioned and the displays were not very impressive.

We went to a beautiful waterfall near the highway with plants, which are even larger than the ones along the coast—particularly the flowers; for instance the ginger, and the birds of paradise were very large and beautiful. We were then taken to a seawater grotto near the coast on which seawater was washed in and out so it was self-cleaning. Near it was a freshwater pool fed by streams coming down from the mountains, enjoyed by the native Polynesians. As in most tropical islands, water is not a problem and there are many streams that pass down from the heights, which receive substantial rain creating a series of beautiful waterfalls. After the tour I decided to swim off the hut, which was very convenient, and swam across the lagoon to the second pool, which was near the Wuchers' room. I climbed over the rocks and wound up in their swimming pool, much to the shock and consternation of some of the people, especially Pat who did not appreciate my long-distance swimming effort. It was most enjoyable because the salt water is buoyant and clear. That evening, we enjoyed a barbecue with Polynesian native entertainment, which was quite interesting. It consisted of an entertainment group from the local Catholic school, French Polynesia being largely Catholic, and they were excellent in their hula dancing, both men and women. The food at the hotel was excellent, but the service was spotty as one finds in almost all tropical countries. The following morning, we packed our suitcases again, left the hut with some regret because it was such a beautiful location, and were taken to the Tahitian Princess cruise ship for boarding.

After boarding the ship, we had lunch and found our staterooms, which are decorated in a Victorian style, as is the entire ship. It is very unusual. I have never seen a ship decorated in an antique fashion such as this one. I think it was their idea of putting the passengers in the time of Gaugin in the late 1800s.

After the first night at sea, we arrived in Moorea, the island very close to Tahiti. Moorea is a beautiful island. Upon arrival, we went by tender into the small port and were immediately met by four-wheel drive vehicles, which were more like trucks. Six to eight people were placed in the back of the truck and in a convoy of four we were taken to the top of "Happy Mountain," which was featured in the film *South Pacific*. From the summit of that mountain, after a rough drive along dirt roads, we had a magnificent view of the harbors of Moorea. We were able to see Cook Harbor where our ship was moored, and also had a magnificent view around the rest of the island, which is marked by craggy peaks covered with foliage and slowly eroding because they are of soft material. The island is sinking at the rate of 4 millimeters a year and no large ranches are permitted because the foliage is necessary along the base of the mountains to discourage erosion. After returning from the peak of Happy Mountain, we toured a pineapple farm. Pineapples in Moorea are very sweet and grown only for local use. They also grow a green grapefruit, which is very sweet with a very thick skin.

From there, we traveled to a nursery/farm where several different plants were grown, including the hyacinth, ginger and bird of paradise. From there, we went to a juice factory where they make several different types of marmalade and juices from the local fruits such as grapefruit, papaya, lemon and lime. The next stop was an ancient temple, which consisted of some stones piled around a group of trees where apparently rituals took place such as marriage and various sacrifices of the ancient Indians. Then we were taken to a place called Belvedere, or beautiful view, with an exquisite view of the coastal areas of the islands and the reefs. Lastly, we were taken to a distillery where various types of liquor were made from local fruits and berries. The banana liquor was particularly good. We then returned to the ship, where we spent the afternoon at the pool. The food on ship was excellent in all aspects. The welcome aboard show featured Polynesian dancers and a singer/comedian. After the island of Moorea, we had two days at sea, the first passing the

Atolls where the French experimented with the atomic bomb. On the afternoon of the first day at sea, we went to an art auction and bought a painting of a Martini glass with some olives that were designed as golfers. I made the original bid and nobody else bid on the painting, so I got it for the base price.

The next day, we continued to cruise in the open sea and went to a wine tasting affair where the wines of California and Italy were demonstrated. It was an informal wine tasting and very pleasant.

The next morning we arrived at Nuku Hiva, a remote island and the largest of the Marquesa group. It is a volcano island with a deep and pretty harbor. The ship anchored in the harbor and we went onto the island with tenders where we were met with four-wheel drive vehicles. Ours was a Land Rover and piloted by a native Tahitian named Joel. His real job was as a waiter on a freighter/passenger ship. He drove us to various sites on the top of the island where we could photograph the bays and the craggy mountains from above. We then viewed a small church, which was simply designed with native materials. The church had multiple wooden carvings of Christian religious figures. We went to a beach where there was a craft shop and we purchased necklaces and a small mahogany statue. We returned to the bay of entry, where we visited another more elaborate Catholic church and another craft shop where Mary Ann bought a sarong-like skirt called a butterfly. We returned to the ship for lunch and some air conditioning. Following our return from Nuku Hiva, we had dinner at Sabitini's Italian Restaurant on the ship, which has a $20 cover charge. The food was exquisite, with a sampling of all of their Italian appetizers prior to serving the main course, which was baby lobster tails. After leaving the island of Nuku Hiva, we traveled overnight to an island called Hiva Oa. It is another island in the Marquesa group, which was supposed to be known for its native crafts. Unfortunately, the sea swells were too high so that the tenders could not get into the small shallow harbor from the open sea where the boat had to anchor, so we missed that island. We went on for two days at sea to the island of Rangiroa. During the two days at sea, we relaxed, played games, attended a second wine tasting of more expensive wines, which was quite impressive, and attended a cooking show where the head chef and the pastry chef demonstrated making two types of food, one a shrimp scampi-type dish and the other a mousse. After the chef demonstrated the shrimp scampi, I was called to make the same dish and Mary Ann and another girl were asked to sample the dishes blindfolded. The other woman's husband was at the other end making the same dish, although mine was more spicy; the women much preferred his less spicy version of the shrimp scampi. My dish was made by the head chef and was served at the evening meal. The next day, we arrived at Rangiroa, a very large atoll with a very flat island barely extending out of the surface of the ocean. It had a very large reef, which encircled a large quiet lagoon, the second largest atoll reef lagoon in the South Pacific. The boat anchored in quiet water and we were taken by tender to the dock, an old cement dock which looked like it had seen better days. There were several shops on the road to the dock, which had native jewelry and a Frenchman who painted with local sand of different colors on cotton. It was very impressive and I bought an unusual painting of a stingray. We then walked over rough terrain along the coast to a beach, which was also fairly rough—but off the beach there was snorkeling and scuba diving where small fish and small rays could be seen. The walk along the coast was difficult because the private property came right down to the water and one had to walk along the very edge, which was rough and uneven. We then returned to the ship to spend the afternoon playing games and relaxing, awaiting the overnight trip to Raiatea, one of the larger mountainous islands with fewer sights to see than most of the other islands. We arrived at Raiatea in the early morning and later went off the ship to the little town of Raiatea, adjacent to the dock. This was the only port in which we were able to dock the ship. They had many shops and souvenir stores near the ship and the shopping was very pleasant. I bought an outrigger canoe, which was designed and made in Raiatea. In the afternoon, we were taken by boat to the island of Tapaa, a nearby island where they took us to a vanilla farm and explained how the vanilla bean was discovered and developed. It is a complicated process resulting in a bean that is worth a considerable amount of money. It is interesting that you can make your own vanilla extract with about five vanilla beans placed in a bottle of cheap rum for about one month. They state that it makes vanilla extract as good as the type that is bought very expensively in the store. About eight vanilla beans cost fifteen dollars, so we declined to buy them. We were then taken by school buses to a black pearl farm. The interesting story of the black pearl was demonstrated to us. It is an expensive undertaking and it begins with black-lipped oysters brought from Japan and then matured for two years in sea water. Then a Japanese technician implants a bead of clam shell obtained from the Mississippi River into the sex organ of the oyster. After three more years, they open the oysters and see how many pearls they have. Approximately 40% are not developed or lost and of the 60% that are developed only 2% are considered to be close to a perfect pearl, which brings the highest price.

It is interesting that these pearls respond to the acid of the body's surface and need to be washed in distilled or salt water to preserve their health, as they are living things. If that is not done, they will finally become in time only the seed sphere of clam shell from the Mississippi River.

Early the next morning, we left Raiatea to arrive at Bora Bora a short time later. On our arrival at Bora Bora we boarded a tender and went into the island for a safari trip around the island in four-wheel drive vehicles, including climbing up very rough mountain roads to find significant views from the top of the island. The driver, Leona, a native from Moorea, whose father was from Bora Bora, was very strong and a very good driver. The roads were as rough as I have personally ever seen. The views from the top were magnificent. In the top of the mountain, several naval guns were placed during WWII to repel the Japanese, who never invaded the island. The island housed six thousand U.S. military personnel and was used a fueling stop for ships. We were then taken on a tour around the island's 17-mile perimeter. We stopped at another pearl factory, which was more advanced in terms of its total capacity to grow and manufacture pearls, as well as the jewelry associated with them. It was a magnificent display of the black pearls at this island pearl factory called "The Farm." After returning to the dock, Mary Ann Wucher and I took an ill-fated snorkeling tour which found us out over the lagoon snorkeling site in a driving rainstorm. We prevailed upon the two operators of the large comfortable launch to take us back to the dock because it was unsafe to snorkel in a driving rain with winds blowing up the waves so that the snorkel would fill with water if you were on the surface. Upon return to the ship, we completed our packing and spent the evening at the variety show. The following day, we returned to Tahiti, where we spent the day on the ship prior to leaving for the airport and home.

All in all, it was an interesting trip as the islands were beautiful, but considering the distance with the lengthy travel time, I'm not sure it is worth the effort and high cost of the trip.

Digression #22

In February 2006, the Hershocks, Pat and I took a train from Mt. Joy (near Lancaster, PA) through Philadelphia to New York, where we spent a long weekend enjoying the food and stage shows. We stayed at the Michelangelo Hotel, a recently renovated small hotel near the theater district. The rooms were comfortable and the service was excellent. We saw "Mama Mia" and "Dirty Rotten Scoundrels," both of which were very entertaining. We also saw a controversial series of exquisitely dissected anatomic specimens preserved in plastic called "The Body." We had dinner at PATSY'S, frequented by Frank Sinatra, and FELIDIA, the original Italian restaurant by Lidia, who owns a good restaurant we frequent in Pittsburgh, that carries her name Pat and I had not been in New York for several years and enjoyed it, including the train ride to and from the Big Apple.

In March, we learned that Tariq Bhatti, a previous fellow we recruited to take my place as a neuro-ophthalmologist/orbitologist in the department, decided not to join us from the University of Florida. We offered the job to our current fellow, Erik Happ, a Pittsburgh native and an excellent fellow, but he was already committed to a group in Paulsbo, west of Seattle in the state of Washington, to do neuro-ophthalmology and ophthalmic plastic surgery, so I was committed to another year of clinical practice.

The last week in March, with the Hershocks, we hosted four of our fraternity brothers and their wives at our condominiums in Cinnamon Beach. We had a great week of golf, both on our ocean Hamnock course, which they all liked, and at the King and The Bear Course at the Golf Hall of Fame above St. Augustine. The food at the various restaurants we attended was great, as was the fellowship together with the table games we played at night. The last day we learned that another brother, John Rotelli, had died after a long bout with renal cell carcinoma. The group of brothers had now shrunk by four.

On May 31, I closed the department optical shop, which had opened in 1988. Since 1992, Melodee Pebley had been our optician and had run the shop very successfully for several years. She is the best optician I have ever employed. We had very few complaints, but when we decided to take our optometrists off salary, they left the practice and were replaced by Paul and Kathy Freeman, independent contractors who didn't supply enough patients to keep the optical shop viable. It is regrettable because it diminishes the overall capability of the department. I owned it and neither the hospital nor my partners wanted to take over the responsibility. In 2006, optical competition has become fierce; I couldn't afford to risk losing money. I will miss Melodee as a person and will miss her skills as an optician.

At the end of June, Erik Happ, an excellent fellow, completed his year and went to the western coast of Washington near Seattle to join a group practice.

Kenya Gentle joined us as a fellow on July 5. She is from Chicago, but trained in ophthalmology in Down State Medical College in Brooklyn, New York.

The French and English Journeys

On August 29, 2006, the Hershocks and Pat and I traveled to Paris to the Louvre Hotel where we had stayed in 2000 at the Orbital Society meeting. The next day the Cervenys arrived and we were taken to the river barge LA CHOUETTE (which means owl) by the owners Bob and Bobbie Marsland. He was a former television producer and she was formerly in radio. They owned and operated the river barge with three staterooms with private baths and a nice living and dining area. On deck at mid ship was a large table with an awning, ideal for watching the sights while cruising. We hired the barge for six days, each day being taken by the owners on a trip following the path of Monet and other impressionist artists. Each day we had lunch or dinner off the barge at exquisite French country brasseries or restaurants. The food was spectacular and well presented. We ate at the inn where Van Gogh spent the last two months of his life and actually sat at his old table. Monet's home and garden where he did much of his painting was gorgeous and well-kept by a private foundation. The ruins of a castle built by Richard the Lionhearted to defend Normandy was interesting, with a great view of the Seine River from a rocky hill into which it was built. General Ronmel used it as his headquarters in WWII because of its stone bunker. Following the cruise on the Seine River from Paris to a small town with another old castle on a bluff over the river, we were taken to Rouen, where we rented a van to travel to Honfleur on the Normandy coast near the beaches used by the Allies in WWII. The hotel in Honfleur was very French and an old mansion with beautiful landscaping. A young family ran the hotel. From there, we went to the Normandy beaches and visited the museum depicting the invasion and were told how the allies built their own artificial harbor to bring in heavy equipment and tanks. It was a spectacular feat of engineering. We then went to the American cemetery where over 9000 GIs rest. It was an emotional experience, one I'll never forget. The cemetery is on U.S. soil and groomed exquisitely by an American company.

We took the fast ferry from Calais to Portsmouth across the English Channel on a beautiful day. In Portsmouth, we were met by a driver who took us to Salisbury to the Red Lion Hotel (the oldest in England) where the two-day Orbital Society meeting was held. It was a very interesting meeting and we toured Salisbury, including the Salisbury Cathedral. In an old mansion in Salisbury I saw the largest collection of English wine glasses of the 18th century. I collect old wine glasses, so it was of special interest to me. We saw many of our colleagues in the Orbital Society, including John Wright of London who had been retired for ten years.

After an extra day in Salisbury, we attended the Salisbury Museum with pictorial presentation of the history of Salisbury, including old Sarum, the ancient city built on a high bluff overlooking the area for defensive purposes.

We flew home from Gatwick Airport, travel being a real hassle with the terrorists trying to destroy people of all countries.

Digression #23

In early November 2006, Pat and I flew to Dallas, then traveled to McKinney, Texas where we stayed at the Country Charm, a Bed and Breakfast Inn, which is an old restored house with a garage, where we stayed in a large room with a full bath and independent access. We were there to see my children and grandchildren. McKinney is a quant little Dallas suburban town with a central square surrounded by several gift shops, restaurants, and two wine tasting rooms, both of which had excellent locally made wines

My daughter, Nancy and her husband, Joe Lawrence, bought a home in McKinney. There we visited my grandchildren, Michael Joseph and Matthew John, delightfully active and a joy to see. My son Jeff's daughter, Elena and her brother, Alan, older children, came to join us and we enjoyed being with them.

Pat and I spent part of the winter in Florida for the first time, enjoying the beach, the golf, and the company of our friends, Bob and Pat Hershock. We found several new restaurants and explored the area of our new winter home.

In February 2007 we lost our good friend, Reginald Pugh, a close friend and a superb oncologist, who spent several evenings with us at Hidden Valley. In March, Eric Happ our 2005-2006 fellow, decided to return to the department to take my place in the division of neuro-ophthalmology and orbital disease upon my retirement at the end of June, 2007. Garry Condon would take my place as chairman of the department. It was a relief to know that, together with my other part-ners, I was leaving the department in excellent condition.

In early May 2007, Pat and I attended the wedding of her niece, Elizabeth Maurer, in New Orleans. The city was recovering from the devastation of hurricane Katrina. The downtown, especially the French Quarter, had not suffered significant damage from the hurricane, so the tourists returned in force. We visited our favorite places, including the Acme Oyster House (best oysters in New Orleans), the Court of the Two Sisters (good food and great atmosphere), Pat O'Brien's (home of the dueling pianos), the Bon Ton Restaurant (best crayfish ettoufe lunch in town), and the Café Dumond (home of the famous Begnet). The wedding in the garden district, held at an old mansion, was non-traditional and very well done. The next day, we toured the part of the city that had been devastated by the hurricane with Bob Maurer, Pat's brother-in-law, who showed us the immense devastation. Large sections of low, moderate, and high-income homes were destroyed by the flood. At the time we were there, few people had returned to rebuild their devastated homes. We stayed at the Marriott Hotel on Canal Street, which had suffered little damage by the flood, and we had a pleasant stay there.

In early June 2007, Pat and I joined five fraternity brothers from the Phi Gamma Delta Class of 1957 for our fiftieth reunion at Bucknell University in Lewisburg, PA. We had a good time meeting old friends, including Bob Mitchell, a psychiatrist, who studied with me during our pre-med years. On a sad note, we have lost six brothers in the past three years. Of course, we drank a toast to each of them.

On June 30, 2007, I retired as chairman of the Department of Ophthalmology at Allegheny General Hospital. A very nice party was held for me, attended by family, friends, colleagues, and some of my fellows. A portrait of me was presented and later was hung in the department that I founded in 1985, a fitting culmination of my career.

Early retirement was difficult because I hadn't planned for it as I had most of my career. I enjoyed the summer of 2007 at Hidden Valley, where we were preparing our home for sale. Necessary maintenance and repairs were made, hoping for an offer, but none came that year, despite the purchase of the resort by a new developer who was renovating it.

The Russian Journey

In early October 2007, Pat and I arrived in Moscow, and were taken by bus, a slow trip due to the extreme traffic in Moscow, to the River Boat Lomonosov for a tour of Russia, including a Volga River cruise with the Viking Tour Group. Everyone in Russia has a car, even if they live in very modest quarters—hence the crowded roads. We toured Moscow with the group, including the enormous Red Square, surrounded by the Kremlin, the huge department store called the GUM (very expensive), St. Basil's Cathedral with its colorful roofs, and some museums. In front of the Kremlin is Lenin's Tomb, guarded by a lonely Russian soldier, as it is now largely ignored. The Kremlin allowed very limited access to the government buildings. One interesting site was a huge nineteenth century cannon, the largest ever built and only test fired once, which damaged it. The subway was clean and efficient, containing several copper statues of ordinary people, placed there by the communists, one of the few lasting things they ever did.

The Lomonosov took us through a series of canals to the Volga River. Our first stop was Uglich, home of the Church of the Blood, named for a son of Ivan the Terrible, who was supposedly killed there in 1155. The town was small and uncrowded and the church, full of Russian icons, was the main attraction. Yaroslavl, our next stop, a large commercial city on the Volga River, had many monuments and the Church of Elijah the Prophet, with its beautiful frescoes and many icons. We sailed onto Goritzy, home of the huge Krillo-Beluzersky Monastery, founded in 1397 by St. Cyril on Lake Siverskoye. It was destroyed by the Communists in the 20th century and the monks were killed or scattered. Now it is a historical site and tourist attraction with a museum and the ever-present icons. The Volga cruise was very tranquil, as thousands of white birch trees were displaying their yellow fall colors. On the cruise, we met Karl and Susan Roller from southern Colorado. He is a retired radiologist and she was a radiology technician. We spent most of the rest of the trip with them. We arrived at Lake Onega, the second largest lake in Europe and visited Kizhi Island, one of the most ancient inhabited sites in Russia. We toured the all-wooden Church of the Transfiguration, built without a single nail and with twenty-two onion domes. The old wooden buildings in the village were well-restored, housing several families, who live and work on the island in agriculture and fishing. Finally, we crossed Lake Ladoga, Europe's largest, and sailed up the Neva River to St. Petersburg. While on the cruise, we were entertained with a vodka and caviar tasting, a tea party where the tea was made with a samovar, and shows with the crew singing and dancing in Russian costumes.

St. Petersburg, Russia's most beautiful city, was also choked with traffic, but we managed to see the spectacular Hermitage Museum, the Winter Palace, and Catherine's Palace, done in the beautiful Russian baroque style. One day we went to the fantastic Peterhog Palace on the shore of the Baltic Sea, with its myriad of fountains and waterfalls. We toured Rasputin's house, where he was murdered by poison. The Peter and Paul Fortress was impressive, as was the entire city, my favorite in Russia.

We satisfied a curiosity to see Russia after the cold war. The people were friendly in a gruff way and we enjoyed the experience.

Digression #24

In late 2007, I joined SCORE (Service Corps of Retired Executives). Having worked in the jewelry business with my parents since I was very young and having managed the business aspects of the medical practices in which I was involved, I thought I could contribute to that group. I was the only physician in the group and after a training period, I became the counselor for medically-related businesses.

We spent the first two months of 2008 at our condo in Florida enjoying the beach and golf at our two golf courses with the Hershocks, who were building a house in Hammock Beach. We had to return to Pittsburgh in early March because we sold our house at Hidden Valley and had to move our personal things to our townhouse in Pittsburgh by the closing date, March 31. We were delighted to have sold our house in such a bad real-estate market. With the expert help of our own neighbors and friends, Rich and Nan Nichola and Tim and Reenie Pavlik, we managed to quickly remove the art work and dismantle the office room. With their help, and Rich's expert driving, all arrived safely to our Pittsburgh home. We did suffer seller's remorse because we loved that house and Hidden Valley.

The Northern China Journey

In June 2008, we went to China with Gerry and Lori Minetti, friends from Hidden Valley, two months before the Summer Olympics were to be held in Beijing. Gerry was a general in the Army and Lori had worked for the military. It was the first time any of us had been in northern China, and it was a perfect time. We were met at the Beijing Airport by our guide, Yang, who guided our group through the entire trip, starting with our ride to our four-star hotel through the crowded streets of the city. Next we toured the huge Tianeman Square, the only place we saw soldiers, who were there to dissuade any type of demonstration. The giant square was bordered by a large government building built by Mao Tse Tung, and the Forbidden Palace, which we toured. We were told that the picture of Mao in the square is replaced by a smaller one every year. The Forbidden Palace, reserved for royalty until the last dynasty ended in the early 20th century, was fantastic, with its many colorful buildings and rooms, done in red and yellow, the royal colors. That evening, after a splendid Peking duck dinner, we attended a Chinese Opera, with its colorful elaborate colorful costumes, strange sounding performers, and agile acrobats.

The next day we visited the Great Wall of China, a magnificent structure guarding the northern border of China along its entire length. On a relatively clear day we climbed some of its steep and uneven rampart to find spectacular views. Built over centuries to keep the Mongols out of China, it is truly one of the great wonders of the world. On the return trip, we toured the Sacred Way of the Ming Tombs bordered by large statues of various animals and deities.

The next day we visited the summer palace, with its beautiful pagodas and opulent buildings, built on the shore or a large lake. We saw a large marble boat, built by the last empress to honor the Navy after they lost a war to the Russian Navy. I think they would have preferred a more seaworthy fighting ship.

Leaving Beijing, we flew to Xian, and after enjoying a spectacular dinner show with terrific dancers and musicians, the next day we visited the home of the Terra Cotta Soldiers, another trip highlight. Built by Emperor Qin of the Qin Dynasty, the Terra Cotta Army was supposed to protect him in the after life about 2500 years ago. This historic treasure was found by a farmer while digging a well in 1973, and they are still uncovering and restoring this army of life-sized soldiers, horses and chariots. We were so impressed that Gerry and I each bought a five-foot replica of a terra cotta soldier and had them shipped home as a memento of this great trip. After a great lunch, we sampled some fortified wine that came in bottles that also contained snakes, turtles and other weird creatures that were supposed to be of medicinal value. It was an experience I won't forget and I won't repeat.

That afternoon, we flew to Chongqing on the Yangtze River, where we boarded our boat, the new Viking Century Sun, which was large and comfortable, with nice state rooms, good food, and great service. We sailed down river under a hazy sun to Fengdu, a resettlement town built halfway up a mountain so it would survive the marked rise of the Yangtze River brought about by the completion of the Three Gorges Dam down river. We were there when the river was only starting to rise, so we had to climb many cement steps that will be under water. The town was small, with a central market and several high rise apartment buildings in which the natives can relocate at minimal cost because the project is subsidized by the government.

Next we sailed through the lesser and greater Three Gorges, which displayed magnificent scenery with their high cliffs going straight up from the river. The following day, we visited the spectacular Three Gorges Dam, the largest in the world. It was an enormous project built to supply electricity and to prevent flooding in the delta, an important Chinese agricultural area. We explored various sites on the dam, crossing it by bus.

Along the river we visited several interesting places, including Donligh Lake with its Famous Yue Yang Tower, once visited by Mao, himself; the city of Wuhan with its famous museum displaying ancient replicas of the area, including a giant Gar fish the type of which used to roam the river; and Jingdezhen, home of a famous ceramic factory, where we watched the craftsmen make various ceramic pieces. We traveled by bus to the top of Mt. Jiuhua, where we saw the Buddhist Monks praying in their beautiful temples and experienced spectacular views from the top of the mountain.

The next day we reached Nanjing, where we disembarked and, on our way to Shanghai, we visited a famous silk factory in Suchow, where we saw the entire silk making process.

Arriving in Shanghai at night, we were treated to a spectacular view of the lighted city with its many skyscrapers, the New York of China. It had a definite business atmosphere, with a shrinking Old City, which was very interesting. The museum was very large, with many historic displays. We enjoyed a show with the playing of ancient bells, which were wonderful to see and hear.

Overall, we enjoyed the cultural and the historic areas of China. However, there are rapid changes occurring in all of China as they modernize and move toward capitalism. It was one of our most interesting and enjoyable trips.

Digression #25

In September 2008, we attended the Orbital Society meeting, followed by a two-day International Society meeting in New York hosted by my past fellow, Mike Kazim. Twenty-five members attended the private Orbital Society meeting, but over three hundred attended the international meeting, which was exciting in that only about twenty of us were interested in the orbit when I began to work in the orbit in 1972. This meeting, showing a growing interest in the diagnosis and treatment of orbital disease, is a fitting tribute to my career, as well as my colleagues who developed the treatment of orbital diseases.

In 2008 and in early 2009, I have begun efforts to return to ophthalmology by working to place eye examining lanes in established free medical clinics in Pittsburgh and in Bunnell, Florida, near my home in Palm Coast. The equipment and space has been obtained through volunteer efforts for which I am grateful. I have also arranged to work and teach at a young ophthalmology department at the University of Florida in Jacksonville, Florida on a part-time basis, to help them develop the department.

With exciting prospects and interesting travel ahead, I end this autobiography. I have had an interesting career and life and I am grateful to family, colleagues, teachers and friends who have traveled with me along the way.

An Abbreviated Male Kennerdell Family Tree

Dr. Edward Kennerdell
Born about 1755 in Wigan, England

Edward Kennerdell
Born 1788 in Wigen, England
Soldier and Weaver
Died 1869 in Kennerdell, Pennsylvania

John Kennerdell
Born in Bolton, England
Unknown Occupation
Died 1887 in Kittanning, Pennsylvania

Edward Kennerdell
Born in 1863 in Kittanning, Pennsylvania
Jeweler and Optician
Died 1939 in Tarentum, Pennsylvania

Frederick Kennerdell, O.D.
Born 1890 in Tarentum, Pennsylvania
Jeweler and Optometrist
Died 1971 in Natrona Heights, Pennsylvania

John S. Kennerdell, M.D.
Born 1935 in Natrona Heights, Pennsylvania
Neuro-Ophthalmologist and Orbital Surgeon

Jeffrey J. Kennerdell
Born 1964 in South Weymouth, Massachusetts
International Businessman

WA